Arctic Daughter

A Wilderness Journey

Jean Aspen

T0163876

ALASKA
NORTHWEST
BOOKS®

Arctic Daughter was originally published in 1988 by Bergamot Books, Minneapolis, Minnesota (ISBN 9780943127019), and a Delta Expedition trade paperback was published in 1993 by Dell Publishing, a division of Bantam, Doubleday Dell Publishing Group, Inc., with permission from Bergamot Books (ISBN 0-385-31400-0). A hardbound edition was published in 1993 by Menasha Ridge Press, Birmingham, Alabama (ISBN 9780897321211). "Arctic Journey," an excerpt from the book, appeared in the November 1993 issue of Reader's Digest (p. 189). An excerpt from Chapter 1 of Arctic Daughter was used with permission along with part of a chapter from Constance Helmerick's book Down the Wild River North in Making Connections: Mother-Daughter Travel Adventures, edited by Wendy Knight and published by Seal Press in 2003.

Aspen, Jean.
  Arctic daughter : a wilderness journey / by Jean Aspen.
    pages cm
  Originally published: Minneapolis, MN : Bergamot Books, 1988.
  ISBN 978-1-941821-16-9 (paperback)
  ISBN 978-1-941821-58-9 (e-book)
  ISBN 978-1-941821-76-3 (hardbound)
  1. Brooks Range (Alaska)—Biography. 2. Pioneers—Alaska—Brooks Range—Biography. 3. Alaska—Description and travel. 4. Frontier and pioneer life—Alaska—Brooks Range. I. Title.
  F912.B75A76 2015
  979.8'7—dc23
                    2014034764

Cover design: Jean Aspen and Vicki Knapton
Illustrations by Jean Aspen
Photographs by Jean Aspen, Phil Beisel, and Tom Irons
Map by Elizabeth Barnard

Published by Alaska Northwest Books®
An imprint of

GRAPHIC ARTS
BOOKS®

GraphicArtsBooks.com

Proudly distributed by Ingram Publisher Services.

For my mother, Constance Helmericks,

who taught me to dream.

Constance and Jeanie Helmericks, 1952.

Constance Helmericks, age twenty.

I love the summers in this land. But I also love the feel of winter winds against my cheek, when the snow squeals underfoot, and the ptarmigan, the white grouse, come whirling down from the Arrigetch Peaks once more—or any peaks in Alaska!—to talk along the valley by my house. I love the colors of the bleak wastelands where nobody goes. When the circling sun falls low, and the leaves hang and rattle in the wind, and cranberries turn to mahogany brown, and frosted blueberries taste of wine, then my cabin on the river will be snug and tight against the arctic gale. When wild grass has turned to hay and the wild geese wing their way once more over mountain and valley to the southern land below, the canoe is put away and the snowshoe will appear. But when the Arctic turns to green again and the geese return with the sun, I shall take my canoe from the tall cache, and I shall travel on the river to see some new place.

We Live in the Arctic
Constance Helmericks, 1947

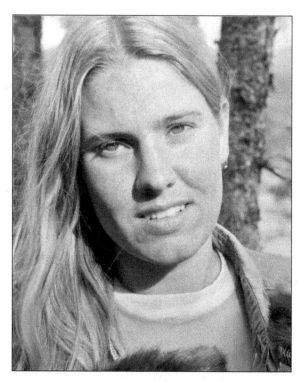

Jeanie, age twenty-five.

ACKNOWLEDGMENTS

I had just turned twenty-two and Phil was only a year older when we set forth into the arctic wilds. It was a time for testing ourselves and discovering our own strengths. In truth, I would never have envisioned such an undertaking nor had the tools to do it without my mother. There were, of course, others whose names I have forgotten that provided guidance and support along the way. I regret not paying closer attention, but at the time my need for independence blinded me to this greater community. With a few additions, I leave these acknowledgments as I wrote them in 1988.

Through their love and support, the following people helped create this book:

- My mother, Constance Helmericks, inspired and championed our adventure;
- Phil's parents, Cliff and Marion Beisel, stood behind us with love while knowing not the journey;
- Chris Olson, who died before I was born, and the generous Gwich'in people of Venetie helped us stay alive.
- My sister, Ann Helmericks, and her first husband, Steve Boice, retrieved us from Alaska and provided a home for me while I wrote the first drafts.
- Friends who encouraged me in writing and rewriting: Charlotte Cardon, Sue Clemans, Terrel Miedaner, Celia Weber, and my beloved aunt, Janet Cutler.
- Jennie Vemich and John Earl amended my creative spelling in days before spell-checkers.
- Donald Sayner taught me illustration and welcomed me into his studio as I created these drawings.
- Dr. Douglas Camfield guided my early prose and went to bat for me when I wanted to use this book as an honor's English thesis at the University of Arizona.

- My editor and first publisher, Barb Wieser, believed in me and worked to tighten my manuscript into a book.
- Doug Pfeiffer, Kathy Howard, Vicki Knapton, Angie Zbornik, and Michelle Blair helped revive the book for a new generation. Lindsay Wolter and writer Nan Leslie guided the process.
- My husband, Tom Irons, and our young son, Luke, stood unfailingly behind me, though the story wasn't theirs.
- And of course, Phil Beisel, my youthful sweetheart, without whom this adventure and all that followed would never have happened.

Phil and Jeanie Beisel, 1975.

ALASKA

Phil and Jeanie, our first winter, 1972.

PROLOGUE

More than four decades have elapsed since two naïve kids followed their dreams down the Yukon River and up into the mountains on a remarkable adventure. What for me began as a hiatus from college would ultimately become a lifetime centered on wilderness.

In updating my books for a new generation, I am grateful for this chance of amending some inadvertent slights and for the opportunity to add a note about sequence. In the original book I thought to honor the privacy of others by using pseudonyms, yet twenty years later when I again paddled out of the mountains with my husband, Tom, and our young son after another year in the wilderness, I was remembered in the little Indian village. "Why," people asked me, "did you change our names?" Referencing my early journals, I now wish to set that record straight.

In addition, because Phil and I lived in the Brooks Range for nearly four years, some events were included that compress those seasons. For example, the hike to the Arctic Continental Divide occurred in the summer of 1977, but to keep the book a reasonable length, I originally placed it in 1973, where it remains. In rereading this time capsule of my life, I was tempted to amend and polish my youthful voice, but have generally left it frozen in time. What right have I to direct that hopeful girl from my height of sixty-four years? Let her have her adventures and ideas, her untarnished enthusiasm. Any who wish to follow her wandering footprints into maturity can do so with my other books and documentary, going where she could not—across the mysterious expanse of my lifetime.

Wild Blessings,
Jeanie Aspen, October 2014

CHAPTER 1

My mother once said that I must have been imprinted very early on the Arctic for I spent the first three years of my life there. As a child I can remember people asking me, "Are you going to be an author and arctic explorer like your Mommy?"

"No," I would answer. "I'm going to be a doctor."

In my family the role of arctic explorer was occupied. Long before I was born my parents had spent years in Alaska's wilderness, living off the land, traveling by canoe and dogsled, and on foot. Later they pioneered in tiny planes across the vastness. Writing books and lecturing together had been their way of life until twelve years of companionship ended in an angry divorce about the time my memory begins.

I inherited the legacy. I grew up in Tucson, Arizona, listening to stories and leafing through the heavy family albums where across the pages of *Life* magazine little Jeanie toddles on her snowshoes. But she remained somehow out of my reach; a fairy child. Still I felt that undeniable pull, almost a memory. An eaglet hatched in a henhouse never really forgets. Across the dusty years it called, echoing between the sky and water of my restless soul—like a promise.

Yes, I was drawn to the Arctic, but not by the glamour of being an explorer. There was something more. Maybe the smell of autumn leaves or the stillness of a winter night; the faint song of running water heard even as I gazed upon the arid playground and waited out my childhood sentence in the public schools of Tucson. Perhaps it was the half-remembered family warmth of my first three years in a little cabin on Takahula Lake. Whatever drew me, it pulled me north as soon as I could fly—unerringly as the geese—to repeat another cycle. At the time, I denied any connection with my parents. Yet somehow I always knew that I would return.

My mother was also serving out her time in Tucson. She once said that she had lived her life by the first commandment, "Thou shalt have no other gods before me," for she saw God everywhere in the natural world, and her love of nature came first, even before her children. She was a wild spirit and she fretted being shackled, as she saw it, to the demands of two small children and poverty in the city heat, away from her beloved wilderness.

My earliest memories are of wild places, campfires, and trails along desert streams. "More walk, less talk," she would say, restricted even there by my short legs. As my legs grew, she began to dream of returning to the wilderness with her daughters. She managed to get her publisher, Little, Brown and Company, to advance the money for the three of us to canoe three thousand miles down the Mackenzie River system in northern Canada—a journey spanning two summers and resulting in her seventh book, *Down the Wild River North*. I was fourteen then and my sister, Annie, was twelve. Our mother was nearing fifty.

Before I turned twenty-two I put together my own expedition. Phil, my high school sweetheart and friend, was a year older. Looking at our pictures now I can see how very young we were, a couple of kids on an adventure. The year was 1972, a time when other kids our age were dying in the jungles of Vietnam. So perhaps not so young after all. I see myself with more clarity now than I did then, as if who I was to become was already in me. There I stand, a familiar stranger: a lovely blond girl of medium height, a bit chubby, with tanned skin and even white teeth. There is a sense of determination in the set of the jaw, confidence and excitement almost masking the questing in the blue-gray eyes.

Phil and I had prepared well for an extended journey into the wilderness: two years spent gleaning information from my mother, reading books, and pouring over maps. We would drift down the Yukon River, which flows westward across Alaska from Canada to empty into the Bering Sea, and then pull our canoe up a tributary north into the Brooks Range. There we planned to build a cabin and live alone for a year or more entirely off the land. The day after final exams of my junior year in college, we started north.

I have been asked why I would undertake such a journey. Why, I might counter, would any young person choose instead a mortgage and forty-hour-a-week job instead of freedom to explore a wild and beautiful land?

❖

At 2:00 A.M. the sun was just coming up as Phil's old pickup truck plowed through the last mudhole and into the tiny settlement of Circle, Alaska. End of the road. Three of us had driven north for ten days, Phil and I and a friend who had come along to take the truck back to Tucson. Gradually, we had left darkness behind as we neared the Arctic Circle, an imaginary line around the earth where the sun doesn't set for one day each summer and fails to rise one day each winter. Now at last, our rutted dirt track simply vanished into the biggest piece of river I had ever seen: the mighty, muddy Yukon. Like a moving lake, it reflected the early morning sun into our tired eyes.

Phil switched off the truck's engine and stretched. Silence rushed into the cab. We sat a moment, numb from the hours of jostling. Then I flipped up the door handle, enveloping us in the waiting mosquitoes. Within minutes we had our tents up beside the truck.

By 6:00 A.M. the sweltering heat of an early June day on the Yukon Flats drove us from sleep. We were camped on a sloping, grassy bank facing miles of open water and pale blue sky. The land spread flat and lush beneath the endless summer sun. Behind us a few tattered buildings were hidden from view in the dark spruce trees. Steam rising from the damp earth and foliage made the air heavy and hard to breath. Even the mosquitoes were hiding in the shade.

Feeling tired and cranky, I wandered down to the river and splashed muddy water over my face, drying it with the tail of my blue cotton work shirt. Then I brushed out my long hair, twisted it into a knot, and clipped it up with a large barrette.

Phil was already unloading our canoe and half a ton of equipment from the truck when I joined him. He looked up at my approach and paused to fold a red bandanna, slipping it over his chestnut hair as a sweatband. He was handsome in his way: heavy bones framing wide green eyes, square jaw beginning to disappear under a dark beard. The mouth was small for his face, overshadowed by a craggy nose—victim of high school sports. Phil was of average height, with a body well built and graceful, though his personal inclination was to bull his way through rather than use finesse. Perhaps his most striking feature was his eyebrows (or rather, eyebrow) for it spanned both eyes in a single, dramatic sweep.

It was hard for me to see his features objectively. Through the years of friendship, they had become as familiar as my own. We had been close since high school, hiking, rock climbing, dating. We met in the Southern Arizona Rescue Association when I was sixteen. Our friends had referred to us as "Phil-and-Jeanie" ever since, as if we had somehow joined to form a third organism. And to me, in a way we had. I wanted it to be that way. He had given me an engagement ring just before we started our journey, and the little diamond winked at me as I began unloading duffel.

We worked quietly together unpacking mounds of gear and piling it on the grass. The canoe and supplies that had crowded the front room of the little house we rented together that last semester in school now seemed to shrink before miles of open water.

My attention was interrupted as a shadow fell across me. I looked up at an older man in a dirty T-shirt and whiskers. Although his remaining hair was gray, the blistered, red face and cracked lips were those of a fair-haired person with too many seasons in the weather. From a flat, metal can he took a fresh chew of tobacco and tucked it thoughtfully under his lower lip.

"Whar ya goin'?" It came out more like a demand than a question.

I straightened slowly, wiping a sleeve over my forehead.

"Up into the Brooks Range."

"In that?" He spat toward the *Lady Grayling*, our nineteen-foot aluminum canoe, lying out of her element among the dandelions.

She did look small beside the Yukon.

"I fly up in that country sometimes in the winter and hunt wolves," he wheezed, watching me. "My neighbor, he gets lots of 'em buggers from the air, but I don't believe in it," he continued. "Mainly 'cause I ain't got no plane."

I glanced up in surprise, half expecting a grin. His face was impassive but for the slow rumination of the jaws and the shrewd china blue eyes. His self-assurance intimidated me: the solid way he planted his boots on the dandelions.

Go away, I thought. I bent over and went back to packing clothes. Choosing equipment and supplies had been no small task and this last day of organizing was important. There would be no one to help if we forgot something.

"They say we shouldn't poison these here bugs," he stated, still searching for something we could disagree upon. He shifted his weight, watching me work.

I nodded. "They're a big part of the food chain," I told him, fresh from my biology classes. Absently I scratched a welt-speckled arm.

He spit again, a stream of juice aimed expertly between stained teeth. "Shit." He studied me a moment. "I been pilotin' the River 'fore you was born, huntin' and trappin' this country."

I followed his gaze northward over the glittering water.

"'Course I ain't trapped now in years—not that I couldn't still do it." He seemed to have forgotten me, his eyes lingering on the river. "Jest ain't the game thar was. Wolves is mostly to blame. Wolves and Indians. I could teach you young pups a thing or two about trappin'." His attention came back to me defiantly.

"I imagine you could," I answered in a gentler note. Then I retreated into myself until he had gone.

Soon another man appeared, slowly treading the beach with a cane. He looked to be over seventy, a tiny prune of an Indian, dark and wrinkled. He was dressed in dark cotton clothing of indeterminate color, short rubber overshoes, and a purple baseball cap.

"You want whitefish? I give you big whitefish." His voice was soft and difficult to catch. He glanced up at me and then politely away.

He came only to my shoulder as I ambled beside him along the beach, asking questions about the river we hoped to ascend, a tributary of the Yukon that I had chosen from a map. The only maps available were four miles to the inch with two-hundred-foot contour intervals. The river appeared to have no major waterfalls, be fairly well timbered, and to cut deeply into an uninhabited area of the Brooks Range—a mass of seven mountain ranges that extend east to west across the entire northern third of Alaska. No one we knew had ever heard of this river; few even knew of the Brooks Range. The old man beside me knew this land, but he understood very little English and merely bobbed and smiled at most of what I said.

"I catch too many fish. Only me and my wife and no dogs anymore. Every day I come ask white people if they want fish. But they say no," he grinned, showing worn teeth. "That there my wife." He pointed toward a tiny, fat prune just disappearing into a small cabin of unpeeled logs. "I build that one her own house. Fifty-two year we married now. Church married! But I can't live with her."

He shook his head stubbornly. We halted beside his leaning cache and he reached into a slimy pail to hand me a fish. Then he stooped and wiped his hands in the grass. I thanked him and returned to the beach to clean the fish.

As I scraped the large scales, my eyes were drawn back to the Yukon. I had calculated that we had perhaps a 75 percent chance of surviving, green as we were. Neither of us had even hunted big game before. I wondered if I had misjudged the odds.

By late afternoon I was dizzy with fatigue. I crawled into the truck cab and curled up on the seat to nap, rolling the windows tight against the mosquitoes. Phil was still loading and reloading the canoe, a job he wished to do alone. He was inexperienced with canoes, but had a natural ability with equipment and a tendency to take charge.

When Phil woke me it was nearly midnight and the sun was setting into the Yukon. He looked very tired. I shivered slightly in the big breath of the river, rubbing the seat print from my cheek. Time to go. We would find our own place to camp away from the curious eyes of the village. I checked around the pickup a last time for overlooked items and sleepily headed down the bank to the canoe.

"It looks awfully full . . ." I protested.

Phil nodded toward the grassy bank where, even at this hour, the total population of ten had come down to watch us sink. "Pretend you know what you're doing," he intoned under his breath.

Together we shoved the grounded craft and I felt the heavy gauge aluminum give under my weight before she slid free into the water. The little ship wallowed deeply but remained afloat. Gingerly I climbed into the bow. My initial alarm increased when I turned to see Phil settling into the stern. We were inches from the river.

"We're crazy, Phil," I declared. "We're dangerously overloaded and we're just going to have to get rid of some of this junk!" I had forgotten the spectators and started to get out.

But we were already underway. Quickly the current snatched our little tub and spun it from shore, sweeping us into the orange and purple sunset. As the truck dwindled into the evening, we waved good-bye. Pursued by a cloud of mosquitoes, we set forth upon the Yukon.

I glanced back at the sound when Phil started our little outboard motor. The canoe gave a sluggish lurch. As he cut back on the power with a gentle curse, we watched a wave ride easily up and over the stern. *Lady Grayling* settled deeper while Phil motored quietly with one hand and bailed with the other.

"Got to watch that," he said shakily, staring in fascination at the two inches of freeboard that separated us from the river. The glossy, orange water betrayed no hint of its depth. Our little engine purred as we wove through the sky-dappled river for the fringe of faraway shore, that finely drawn ribbon of black reality that divided our world from the clouds and gave it order. The mosquitoes were reluctant to give up the chase, but one by one they stowed away or were left behind.

"We're off at last!" I called back cheerfully. I smiled, feeling the thrill of an irrevocable choice.

Phil had finished bailing and was peering toward that phantom shore. Absently he swatted at a lingering bug.

"I just knocked my glasses overboard."

"You're kidding," I said, knowing that he wasn't. "Your new ones?"
"Yes."
I studied the flawless surface that had swallowed Phil's new glasses.
"Let's camp at the first spot."
He nodded wearily.
Very soon the sun was gone, sliding into the spruce forest, and a diffused pink glow of boundless sky softened the summer. The shore we finally reached shelved gently from a willow bar into a quiet stretch of river. There we beached the canoe, making her fast to a sunken log. We snapped a fitted nylon tarp over the load and pitched our camp among the supple bushes. Without bothering with dinner, we crawled into our small, orange tent and zipped it tight against the bugs. Soon I had drifted into a sound sleep, lulled by the lap of wavelets against the canoe and the shrill cries of arctic terns as they darted for insects in the cool dawn sky.

Early day burned bright and hot when we deserted the stuffy tent for the smell of open water. I knelt in the sand, feeding sticks to a young fire and enjoying the stir of wind on my face. A gossamer mist of mosquitoes swirled in the eddy of my body, attracted by the warm animal smell.

The beach was a story of river moods, gathered from countless other shores. Along it wavered a series of parallel lines marking recent water levels in trails of twigs. Small plants were forcing their first two leaves upward through the mud. Because the Arctic receives most of its sunlight in an intense burst, plants and animals grow rapidly during the brief summer. However, environments with low productivity, such as deserts and the Arctic, are delicate, each niche being filled with a single species.

Here one could see the progression of life. Hardy, young willows formed a living net of fluttering green that locked down the sand with tough, red roots. Behind these stood older willows and the fast-growing balsam poplar, and sheltered by the poplar from the careless river, a two-foot forest of young spruce pushed through to claim the future.

I leaned contentedly back on my ankles and buttoned the throat of my denim shirt against the bugs. We were finally underway. This trip had started in my head, and we had taken one step after another to find ourselves here. That is what it takes, I thought: imagination and tenacity.

Phil dropped an armload of firewood and grinned down at me. It was the first smile I'd seen in days. "I want to repack the canoe after breakfast," he said. "It's poorly balanced. I think less weight in the stern would help." He had found his spare glasses—climbing goggles with dark prescription lenses. To save space, he had a set of clear lenses that could be inserted. Phil often forgot to wear glasses, as his driving record attested.

"I'll make us some breakfast, if you want to get started," I offered.

All our bulk staples—like cornmeal, flour, and sugar—were packed in square, five-gallon cans. We had designed a grub box, already dubbed "Wonderbox," with racks of plastic bottles to be refilled at intervals for easy access in camp. Freeze-dried camper foods were just coming onto the market and were far too expensive for our budget. I had also reasoned that we could pack more actual food as bulk staples. We hoped to supplement our supplies with rabbits and fish during the summer, and would of course need big game before winter. My mother had told me that an active person consumes his weight in prepared food each month, but a canoe's capacity is small—even ours with its eleven-hundred-pound limit.

Into a bucket of boiling water I dumped a handful of dried and salted horse meat, an animal we had bought and butchered for the trip. At forty-seven dollars it was protein we could afford and had furnished our first butchering experience. We had oven-dried the meat with much salt and then broken it into chips, which I planned to use in cooking until we found game. I was inexperienced in cooking with staples, and Phil was useless. To the boiling horse meat I added flour, lard, salt, and pepper to make a kind of horse-chip gravy. I stirred the pot and bedded it in the coals to simmer. Then I stripped off my clothes and dashed for the river. Phil was still repacking.

"Come and have a bath," I called, safely submerged. "You'll feel much better."

"When I'm done," came the voice from the duffel.

I upended with a splash, driving the mosquitoes from my scalp. "Come on, you'll enjoy it." I could imagine the specter of my disembodied head floating on a swirling sea of cocoa amid its own little, black cloud.

Reluctantly Phil undressed in the smoke of the fire (mosquitoes avoid smoke) and proffered one toe to the river. "It's cold!" he accused me. He wasn't big on water under any circumstances.

"Just rush in and get it over," I advised him. The cloud of bugs was settling contentedly onto his naked skin. With a grimace, he splashed through the water to join me.

Later I stood beside the driftwood fire as Phil brushed out my long hair. Over us, a cruising gull dipped sharply, head pivoting in keen interest, white on blue. The sudden hiss of the pot shifting startled me and I shoved a stick under the bail, lifting it to rake out more coals.

Thoughtfully my eyes trailed over the muddy beach where the tools and supplies that were to see us through a year alone were heaped in the sunlight. Every item had been chosen with care, from the folding sheet-metal Yukon stove for the cabin, to down clothing and rifles. We had discussed our possible needs at length, each of us making decisions in the areas we were most familiar.

Phil was arranging the load in layers. On the bottom were the watertight five-gallon cans of food and winter clothes as well as the gas tanks he had built to fit the canoe contours. Items like axes, wire, saw blades, one hundred feet of half-inch polypropylene rope, snowshoes, and a few traps were stuffed down beside these. Many kits, such as sewing, photography, medical, maps, journal, and personal items were packed in a middle layer. On top would be everyday items: tent and sleeping bags tucked into a canvas duffel sack, jackets, and a large Ensolite pad for the tent floor, rolled and tied. All the cookware nested into a seven-gallon kettle we called "Mightypot." To ensure that equipment would not be washed overboard in case of capsize, everything was lashed in.

This was our future. There were wicks for the tallow candles that we hoped would light our winter and a few special books. We needed fuel for the secondhand outboard motor and rope for pulling the canoe during the later stages of our journey. We had winter clothing, backpacks, and canoe patching materials. There were knives and whetstones, files, matches embedded in wax, an auger, tin snips, nails, hinges, bullets, panes of Plexiglas for cabin windows, measuring tape, and nylon twine. We had a fish net, binoculars, rivets, a plastic tarp to waterproof the sod roof, window putty, four small bottles of military mosquito repellent (the strongest available), film, and a small gas lantern: in short, everything we could conceive of needing and fit in a canoe.

Like many partners, we tended to specialize. Phil was physically stronger than me and good at building things. I, with my knowledge of the North and my dream, was the momentum behind our trip. And somewhere, unseen, was my mother with her stories and advice.

When repacking was completed and cargo again towered over the little craft, we turned to enjoying our breakfast. It was terrible. The jerky was the texture of cardboard and so salty as to be nearly inedible. Above us, arctic terns

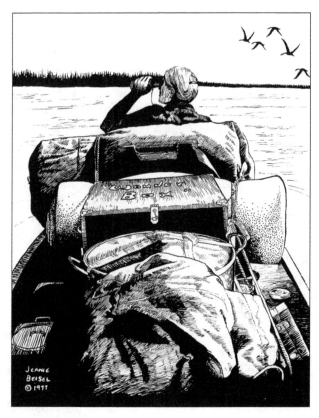

hovered and wheeled—dazzling flashes of life engrossed in their great summer task, a job of such importance they had flown from the Antarctic, a round-trip of thirty-six-thousand miles, for these few weeks of sun and insects to perform it. In all the world, only terns can make more terns.

It was afternoon before we got underway. As camp swept behind on a sea of dancing sun diamonds, we discovered that we were not yet across the river. In fact, with the kaleidoscope of wandering channels, big islands, merging backwaters, and sloughs, being "on shore" was a matter of definition. From the air, this area of the Yukon Flats resembles a plate of spaghetti, but we were comfortably ignorant of this for the map that might have helped had somehow been forgotten in the truck, a mistake that could well have proved fatal. God looks after fools, they say. But not always, I have come to find out.

As we slowly motored, we searched for that elusive other shore and our next landmark, the small town of Fort Yukon, some days travel away. When we stopped the engine far from land and drifted, we found ourselves on a smooth lake of sunlit water melting into flat, blue sky where magic islands seemed to float. Only the uneasy boils on the smooth surface and hypnotic hiss of silt against the hull told of our travel.

Night had already settled upon the lands to the south while our tireless sun circled the sky, dipping northward as evening descended. From shore came the first sigh of cool dampness as the earth awoke from its afternoon doze. We spun past high cutbanks anchored in shadow and guarded by fallen trees, "sweepers" thrashing in the current. It was no place to practice our beaching techniques. Here, close to land, we were suddenly reminded of the speed and power of the water. The dark shore seemed ominous after the inno-cent dazzle of the river. I squinted and rubbed my salt-crusted eyes, searching the shadows where soon we must land. I ought to have a hat, I thought irritably. Uncertainly, I chewed my lower lip where the skin was already peeling. A few more days of this and I'll be fried. I had forgotten the Arctic could be so hot.

A riffle broke the surface ahead and the cutbank suddenly dropped to meet it. A cutbank is where the river is eating into the shore, leaving a raw drop. "There!" I called, pointing.

Phil turned the canoe sharply upstream before nosing in to shore. Our motor conked out in the thick silt and in slow motion we slid to a stop in shal-low water. It was the end of the day and we both had dry feet. We glanced at one another and shrugged.

The medium through which our canoe would not pass was far from solid. I climbed stiffly overboard and felt the penetrating stab of boots filling with cold water. Last bubbles of air hiccuped free as together we dragged our load further aground.

"Bugs!" I had forgotten them.

"I can unpack. You start a smudge fire," Phil urged, then choked on a mosquito.

Waving my arms futilely, I snapped off twigs from the lower trunks of spruce trees for a fire. The bank was a snarl of dense trees, matted with the wreckage of spring breakup and still slippery with mud. Yet already plants were shooting up, pushing aside their dead in the wild summer urge to grow. I cleared a space in the underbrush and soon had a fire billowing smoke from a pile of waterlogged wood. The mosquitoes were thinning when I skidded down the short cutbank to help Phil.

"Empty the cooking things out by the fire and fetch a bucket of water," he called back as he lugged duffel up the bank, churning through dark mud. "I'll get the rest."

I noticed he had secured the canoe in three separate places, apprehensive that it might get away during the night.

"Think I'll try to find us a rabbit while you start supper," Phil said. I was staking down the tent floor in a thicket of wild roses. He joined me on his knees, pulling his pliers from their holster to nip off the thorny bushes. I could see that he was eager to be off.

"Yes, you go ahead. I can finish pitching camp." I felt somehow disappointed to be left with the camp chores while he went off hunting. I didn't plan this trip to be left out, I thought resentfully.

I watched him pick up my old .22 rifle, holding it comfortably in one hand. It was the same gun that my mother, little sister, and I had carried to the Arctic Ocean in our canoe.

"Phil, please don't lose sight of the river. A person could really get lost in this jungle. There just aren't any landmarks." The dank forest crowded thickly to the water's edge.

"Doesn't look much like rabbit country either, does it?" He squatted by the fire to dig through the journal box and paused to hold up his compass. Then he repacked the box and levered the lid shut. In a moment he had disappeared.

Soon I finished pitching camp. I stirred dinner, a horse chip-and-rice dish, before moving it onto coals away from the main fire. Then I got out the tackle box. It would be fun, I thought as I rigged my pole, if I caught a fish while he was gone.

Away from the smoke, I was again immersed in a sea of mosquitoes. Carefully, I traversed the broken bank seeking a spot to fish. None seemed promising. My first cast sank through shallow, muddy water and hooked into a submerged log. I wallowed out to retrieve my lure. After a few tries I retreated to the fire.

Time dragged. I glanced at my watch. Where was Phil? I wondered, awash with irritation and concern. Positioning another log on the blaze, I wagged to keep my body in the smoke and face free as I sifted the forest noises. Evening cool was definitely upon us now, and a damp breeze from the darkening woods crept out over the gold expanse of moving water. I watched the current, caught in its timeless song. Rivers are important to me. At night I often dream of drifting down rivers, the adventure of each bend unfolding before me. I have since childhood. They are the living blood of the earth. More than just moving water, there is something grand in their presence.

I sniffed the night, listening uneasily for Phil. Surely he had sense enough to stay near the water . . . ?

My mind wandered to my fourteenth summer and canoeing the Slave River in Canada. Or was it the Mackenzie the following year? I know it wasn't the Peace. The country had this same wild look—a summertime rain forest, flooded in breakup, strangled in vegetation. The sky had been rich blue that day, piled with cotton clouds. I had wanted to hunt rabbits (I never got one that year, but I looked) and I recall my mother saying:

"Jean," (she always called me that) "don't lose sight of the river or you may never find it again."

"Okay, sure," I had answered, impatient to be gone.

"I mean it now," she insisted, peering wisely over her reading glasses and laying aside her journal and pen. "You don't know everything yet." She remained sitting cross-legged in the moss by the smudge fire looking up at me—a plump, middle-aged woman with red hair. It is curious how our relationship reversed that summer, my aging mother suddenly depending on my strength and judgment.

Shooting her a look of annoyance I had taken that .22 (old even then) and started downstream. Over the river, thunderheads were building. The going was rough along the high cutbank and soon I met massive driftwood barricades, which forced me inland.

The forest had been gloomy in the hush of oppressively wet air. I followed the debris until I discovered a place to crawl over it. Here I turned back toward the river only to be checked once more. I found myself bashing through ever denser thickets. Finally I decided I would have to turn around.

Still I didn't emerge on shore. A gnawing fear whispered inside me, growing with the wind that rocked the spruce tops way above my head. I was suddenly aware of the rapidly changing sky. Lightning flashed and the first big drops splattered between the trees. Could I be mixed up? I glanced about, really frightened for the first time, listening for the river. Now the wind spoke and every tree complained darkly under the burden of it. The mosquitoes had vanished. Nearby something cracked explosively before the singing air. Tears streaked my scratched cheeks as confusion gave way to terror. Slowly I rotated and each direction looked identical.

I don't recall how long I wandered or if I prayed. Time means very little in such moments. I only remember my first glint of open sky. Heedless of the grasping branches I scrambled forward and burst into the face of the storm. The river! Despite my backtracking, I felt certain that I was still below camp. I scurried upstream along the bank, pelted by hail and spray. But no camp came into view.

"Mother!" I bawled into the wind, pivoting in frightened indecision. "Moth . . . ther!"

As if in answer, I heard the tiny "Pop!" of a rifle out of the gray ahead. I scrambled over the last few obstacles and found myself in camp.

I hugged my mother, feeling safe and foolish.

"Come on, let's get out of the storm," she had said warmly, ignoring my tears and drenched clothes. She put her arm about me and started for the tent. "I fired the .30-06 hoping you could hear it over the thunder."

I never forgot it. But now where was Phil?

The fire glowed red in the midnight dusk. Uneasily I rose for another bundle of sticks. I listened: nothing but the faraway call of geese, the hum of insects, and the muted crackle of fire sluggishly pushing smoke into the calm air. *What if he doesn't come back?* At last the thought surfaced in a black wave. What would I do? I could never find this place again if I went for help, and what good would it do anyway? I would wait here all summer if need be, but oh, please God, bring him safely back!

I was digging out my mother's .30-06 when Phil appeared in camp, heralded by clouds of fresh mosquitoes. He took a breath and plunged into the smoke.

"What happened?" I asked as he propped the .22 against a log. His dirty face was scratched and his hair was matted with twigs. Gently I drew my arms about his waist and he stroked my hair. For a long moment we stood there, holding to the security of each other's warmth.

"Come sit down," I said at last, taking his hand.

"I'm sure glad I took the compass," he admitted sheepishly. "There was a time when I was certain that the compass was wrong, but it seemed unwise to argue with it."

"Dinner is ready." I placed the cooking pot between his feet and pried up the lid. Steam enveloped him, fogging his spare glasses a moment. I seated myself across from him and smiled mischievously. "Let me tell you a story," I said.

As the days slid by under that constant sun, we fell into a rhythm with the river: a watchful harmony, an unequal truce. On a horizon of determined water we floated timelessly toward the sea, past hundreds of sunbaked islands,

Jeanie
Beisel
© 1977

dense forest, hidden channels, eddies and submerged logs, crumbling cut-banks, and sandbars. The earth and sun stood still amid vast plains of water-sky where giant islands rode slowly up to meet us, then dwindled behind into yesterday. And above the silence we could feel a careless song of power.

That song was with us always, even as we slept, one ear tuned for the canoe. We heard it by day as we drifted beneath cutbanks where muddy water sucked at the earth and trees held desperately to one last season, their boughs weighted with cones the dying offer. A wall of earth would suddenly collapse, rending the thin carpet of roots, sending spray upward as the earth slid into the river. We felt small, a speck of flotsam adrift in time and space. The river's song was with us, too, far from land in the whisper of silt against the canoe and the gentle swirl of the current.

From shore came the smells of a breathing forest under a midday sun, of balsam poplar, spruce, and something akin to fresh, hot caramel candy. A solemn train of dark spruce trees slid past, interspersed with the bright green flurries of new sandbars covered with willows. A venturesome yellow butter-fly lilted toward us, alighting as a splash of living butter on our silver bow.

Drowsiness would steal upon us in the warm, still air; a trust in this big, friendly river. Then from nowhere a tremor would slam through the canoe, swinging our stern crazily sideways, shipping water as we collided with an unseen bar. In panic we would fight the current, leaping overboard into the soft, invisible sand, shocked at our speed. I would brace against the straining craft while Phil changed another shear pin. Our old outboard didn't have a clutch, so the propeller turned as long as the engine was running. The "shear pin" was designed to break whenever the screw hit something. Once the pin was replaced, we would lead *Lady Grayling* into deeper water and climb aboard, gushing water from our boots, and be off again, not a visible speck of land for a mile on either side.

One evening we camped on the head of a sandbar that had recently emerged from spring flood. Bars are new land, a gift from the river. Bedraggled willows in full leaf were knitting over the scars of breakup, healing the ice-furrowed ground in shimmering layers of green. How resilient they seemed! We sat before a driftwood fire enjoying the breeze that kept away the mosqui-toes. The island clove the current, brushing aside the Yukon. This combined with the breeze to give an illusion of motion, as if the island itself were travel-ing upstream through the water.

"But our civilization cuts us off from nature," I was arguing, "and from one another. Compare your relationship with other drivers to your interaction with people walking."

Phil leaned contentedly against a bleached and battered stump, digging his bare toes into the warm sand. His feet, broad and flat, turned decidedly inward.

"You can't just throw it out," he answered. "After all, you've never plowed with a stick . . ."

"Even our play is organized," I broke in. "There is no spontaneity. What price do we pay for our physical comfort? What is 'quality of life'? Primitive people were able to spend more time together. They had a sense of community that we've lost. I'm not certain our toys are worth what we pay for them."

Phil was looking his old self as I watched him through the hot blaze of our fire. He was very brown, the light eyes striking in his tanned, bearded face, and looking slightly owlish behind spare glasses. His dark hair was already frosted red-gold by the sun. Mine was nearly white on top.

I pulled off my soggy boots, summer "shoepacs" with leather uppers, rubber bottoms, and felt insoles. Thoughtfully I wiped the lint from between my toes. Good feet, they have given me faithful service and often been hard used. It felt good to let them dry and air after days of wet boots.

Tasting my tea (saccharin-sweetened to conserve sugar), I settled the white enamel mug beside me in the sand. A few feet away, *Lady Grayling* rested, belly in the mud, while bright ripples of late afternoon sky and water reflected over her sides. Already a waterline two inches below the gunwale marked our loaded freeboard. Nearby, a distraught sandpiper teetered along the shoal, piping her discomfort at our presence.

"Each generation must examine its world and choose," I said, flashing Phil a glance. I do interrupt too much, I thought. Now he'll give me the silent treatment. "Coyotes may adapt to the L.A. freeways, but we build them."

Phil was studiously pruning his ragged cuticles with a pocketknife. His nails were still grease-stained, and I wondered idly how he managed to maintain this trace of his old life as a mechanic.

"We throw away our power as individuals for a feeling of security," I continued. "We have somehow lost our sense of communion with the planet and with each other."

I stared moodily into the flames, watching sticks disintegrate under their almost invisible touch. Water had leached the driftwood, leaving it porous and brittle.

At length he snapped his knife shut. "Finished?"

"Yes." I kept my eyes on the fire. A frantic colony of ants boiled from one end of a log, driven out by heat and smoke. Taking a twig, I helped the survivors to safety, knowing that an ant without its colony is dead. They are not individuals in the same way we are.

"You cannot separate yourself from your culture," he told me. "It's sophomoric to propose simple solutions. What you're talking about isn't just a matter of technology."

"Maybe," I conceded, "but I've had it with the artificial culture we have built. I've had it with forms to fill out in triplicate and rules. I would rather risk being killed than have a government restrict me for my own good."

"It's more complicated than that," he insisted. "Regulations are meant to protect others from you as well."

I snorted in exasperation. "I know there are good reasons behind most laws, but the result is a bleak world devoid of creativity and personal responsibility. Kids might fall out of trees and parents might sue—so down come the trees. School yards look like prison camps."

"Parents do sue . . ."

"Bleak." I interrupted again. "Who wants to grow up, no matter how safely, in a bleak and joyless world?"

I took a deep breath and let my eyes rest on the beach. It was so quietly itself, undisturbed by my arguments. "Phil, I need to know what being an animal means before I can understand what it is to be human. I want to be like these willows, sinking my roots into the earth and knowing the direction of the sun. I can't do that in the city." I studied him, this stranger that I wanted to spend a lifetime with, wondering if we can ever know anyone.

Whatever Phil was thinking, he only said, "I'd like to try to photograph the geese before dinner. I didn't hear them leave."

He pulled on his wet socks and boots and set off across the twenty-acre bar, camera and lenses slung around his neck, leaving large, pigeon-toed tracks in the sand. I smiled at his retreating back, thinking of the wise, old honkers I have chased.

There were sociable congregations of Canada geese on the Yukon, and nearly every sandspit boasted a wary clan. My mother had called them "bachelor birds," for they were not nesting. The breeding pairs were already established on ponds inland. Geese see everything and soon I heard the excited bark of many voices followed by the flip-flap of weighty bodies becoming airborne. With every wingbeat their beaks opened, warning other geese up and down the river. The cry was taken up on neighboring islands where black stalks of agitated necks bristled, before they too burst into flight.

Theirs is a world of sky and water. I marveled at the *V* of poetry staining the late afternoon where parting notes still lingered. I focused on them, drawing my mind to a point. Perhaps it is a question of vision, I decided. Some people find more inspiration in their backyards than others do in the Himalayas. Still, wouldn't it be easier here? The wild geese of my school years were the silver *V*s of fighters blasting out from Davis-Monthan Air Force Base.

Smoke curled with the steam from our unmistakable horse-chip dinner as I sat in stillness beneath a hemisphere of sunset and birds. When you live under it, the sky makes up half your life. Down the beach I could see the silhouette of Phil returning, looking small yet somehow complete, at home here as much as I. He greeted me with a soft smile and a handful of wildflowers and then joined me at the fire to recount the things he had seen.

I finished eating and handed the blackened pot and spoon to Phil where he sat tracing circles in the cooling sand with a polished stick. Across the channel an elevated cutbank stood sharply defined by the sinking sun. I could see that it had been the site of a burn in recent years. It was clothed in vigorous new bushes, wildflowers, and the carcasses of trees that had once lived there. A time for everything, I thought. Some life thrives only on old burns.

"I wonder if seagulls are good to eat or legal to shoot," I said, breaking the stillness.

"Probably not much there but feathers," Phil replied, roused from his own contemplations.

"I bet they taste fishy. At least it would be fresh meat." I had been raised believing that milk, eggs, and meat were the only proteins and hadn't known to pack more whole grains and beans. We had fallen into the habit of two meals of horse chips a day. It seemed a bother to stop for lunch, and we were also conscious of conserving food.

"We do need some fresh food soon," he agreed, "to improve our outlook as well as our diet." We had yet to catch a single snowshoe hare or fish—not a promising omen for people who intended to live off the land.

"Why don't we try to camp in a slough tomorrow and set out the fish net," I suggested. "There'll be LOTS of bugs, but we won't catch anything here. At least not without fresh bait. The current would carry our net away or shred it, and it's too muddy for fish to see a lure."

"Okay," Phil nodded in agreement.

I rose from the chilly ground and dusted off my trousers. My clothes were sooty and stained from life on the ground, but it didn't seem important. A lone duck flapped overhead, going somewhere. He veered sharply off to the north when he spotted us, members of a species universally shunned. I watched him, thinking that ducks were never meant to fly. But they do.

CHAPTER 2

Before I was born, my parents had wintered in a small cabin on the Alatna River in the Brooks Range, much as Phil and I intended. The following year they dismantled their homemade canoe and hitched a ride in a plane across the Continental Divide. They floated down the Colville River to the Arctic Ocean where they met a truly wild people, Eskimos living much as their ancestors had for hundreds of years. Life on the tundra is very different from the forest. These people were nomadic, following the seasonal migrations of game, and wise to the land. Without their help, my parents would never have survived the winter.

My mother told me stories of the Eskimos she knew. There was an old man who had never owned a rifle. He caught seals in a handmade net under the ice. He was eaten by a polar bear. Another old man had only an ancient single-shot .22 rifle to hunt grizzly. He would lie on his stomach on the tundra in the path of the browsing bear and move his hands to imitate ground squirrels. He once told my mother that he had seen "many babies left in the snow." These were good people who loved their children, but they were realists too. They knew that in a bad year the entire family would starve if there were too many of them.

Alaskan Indians were different from the Eskimos in many ways, but they shared a common heritage of recent primitive existence in this wild, northern land. Life close to nature can be a tough teacher.

Phil and I arrived in Fort Yukon early one bright morning. We nosed our canoe between a group of tethered flat-bottomed boats, and I jumped ashore with a line to stand ankle deep in mud, holding our bow.

"Is it okay to leave our outfit here?" Phil called to a small figure leaning against the general store and watching a fish wheel revolve in the current.

He was an older Indian, dressed in dark and dusty street clothes and beaded moose-hide moccasins. The visor of his blue baseball cap was flipped back to reveal a stubble of salt-and-pepper hair and obliquely observant eyes creased between wrinkles.

The man's mouth twitched in what may have been a smile as he shook his head. "They steal everything here."

The sun was already hot, reflecting off the string of Jon boats that rocked in a backwater of floating debris. The smell of the river mingled with a fishy odor. Not a hint of breeze stirred the muggy air. Behind us, the featureless blue sky was separated from its reflection by a ragged thread of green islands.

I tied the bow painter fast to the covey of boats and lumbered up the bank, pulling each foot free with an audible "sssssluck." Running a self-conscious hand over my wispy braids, I grinned at the quiet little man.

"Is this your fish wheel?" I asked him. "Are you catching any? Could we buy some?" A fish wheel is a wonder of simple technology. Turned by the current, it scoops the migrating salmon into a basket.

He smiled down at his feet saying in a low voice, "No good for fish here."

Why put a fish wheel where there were no fish? I wondered. From atop the bank I could see a clutter of wooden buildings and log cabins, some leaning at unusual angles.

"I think you'd better stay with the canoe while I try to buy a few things," Phil said, coming up behind me.

I settled onto the grassy bank a few feet above the canoe just as a skiff loaded with shouting Indians zoomed past a hundred feet offshore. Mesmerized by their speed, I watched them skim over a bar, noting how they could raise their outboard vertically on a lift to avoid hitting ground. The square bow and shallow draft of the flat-bottomed boat formed a practical combination for river travel. I felt a twinge of envy, followed by alarm as their waves struck our canoe, causing it to wallow deeply in the heaving, muddy water.

"Where you going?" came the soft voice behind me. I turned in surprise and saw the old man watching the bucking canoe, his face carefully neutral. I hadn't expected him to speak.

I explained our plans to him, feeling foolish. It was obvious, even to me, that we didn't really know what we were doing. At length the old gentleman ventured tactfully, "It's a very fast river. Many rocks."

"How will we find it?" I asked, eager to meet someone who had actually been there. We had imagined ourselves drifting downstream until we spotted the tributary entering from the north, but were beginning to realize the complexity of the Yukon.

"That side," he motioned with the flat of his hand. "You stay always that side."

The boat shot by again and I stared at the rocking canoe in hypnotic fascination, afraid it would sink before the town.

"Abraham Christian," he answered when I asked his name. He lived in a Native village in the mountains, and had come down the river to visit friends in Fort Yukon. Could we buy gas there? Yes.

"How far is it to your village?"

He shrugged. "One drum of gas."

Fifty-five gallons. How could we have forgotten that map? I chided myself. The one we had began in the mountains.

The Indians returned, swinging recklessly into the tethered boats that shied and bucked in ringing confusion. Abraham turned contemptuously to stare at the fish wheel as it creaked through endless cycles.

"Why do they keep a fish wheel here?" I inquired of his austere back, my mind still on food. "If this isn't a good place?"

He glanced at me in amusement, then dropped his gaze. "Tourists."

Before long Phil returned, surprising me with an expensive cola and a drooping chocolate bar. Then he took my seat on the grass while I set off to explore.

Fort Yukon was a shantytown of variety: sagging cabins, oil drums, and new pickup trucks—even though there were only a few miles of road. A horse-drawn road grader rusted beside the pieces of a modern one. A discarded bicycle lay in a heap of cans and bottles. Racks of moose antlers were nailed over doorways. And everywhere were playing children and chained dogs.

A flavor of leisure wafted from the dusty roads. It seemed an easy integration of life styles and cultures. There were a few modern government buildings including a Native Center where people could wash clothes or see a movie, but the rest of the town lacked indoor plumbing. The town's electric generator supplied power to homes, however water was delivered by truck to white and Native alike.

Thoughtfully I circled back to Phil, the canoe, and the shimmering plain of river.

"You look as melted as the chocolate," I said, coming up behind him.

"All done?" he asked, getting to his feet and brushing off his trousers.

"Get some pictures?"

I nodded.

"Let's get going."

The Indians were still cavorting in the skittish boats. Standing there, I was inspired to sneak a photo of them. "Go ahead," I heard my mother's voice from somewhere in my past, "get the picture. You'll never see these people again." Covertly I aimed my telephoto in their direction only to confront a dark face scowling back up the lens at me. Unsteadily the men boiled from the boat and surged up the bank. A pockmarked face pushed close, raging, "God-damn, smart-ass tourists!"

The man was short and heavy with a mop of black hair overhanging muddy eyes, bleary with drink. I caught a look of helpless anger as his face withdrew.

This was our introduction to Albert and Jessie Williams of Venetie. My mother was wrong about not seeing them again. I was to find that you never really leave your past behind.

The following morning I lay quietly under damp folds of down listening to the soft music of rain on the tent fly and ignoring the demands of my bladder. Light coming through the nylon of our orange pup tent was subdued by a low overcast. With his back to me, Phil was propped on one elbow, leafing through our bird book.

"Well, it's ten o'clock," I said. "I suppose we ought to get up."

We were clothed in the night things we would wear all summer—I in light pajamas, he in a T-shirt and underpants. The cramped tent was humid from our breathing; the waterproof floor, cold and slippery where it protruded from under the Ensolite pad. Phil stretched and slid his book into the journal box (an army ammunition case) and snapped the lid shut. Then he wriggled deep into our zipped-together sleeping bags and ran his cold hands up my back.

"Well, what do you want to do? Get wet or starve?" I asked.

He cocked his head and listened. "I really don't think it's raining that hard."

"Maybe. But just think of the soggy bushes out there." I rolled over and snuggled my behind into the curve of his stomach and legs. My back ached from lying down. "What say you volunteer to dig out the wool shirts?"

The day before we had entered a small slough that slithered for miles into the forest. Here we decided to try our gill net. After pitching camp, we chose a spot and (for want of a better idea) cut a pole, looped the net over it, and pushed it out from shore.

"Come on. Here's your shirt," Phil said as he slid back into the bags and plastered his wet feet on my calves. "Water's up since yesterday. Don't you want to see if we caught any fish? Maybe the net's solid with them."

The scratchy wool felt good as I dressed in the confined tent while Phil curled out of the way. I reached outside for my boots, which were upended under a corner of the rainfly, and crawled out of the tent. I emerged into a gray and scented world of bugs, where bird calls echoed between black-trunked trees. Clouds clung to the ground in tenuous trails, hiding even the direction of the sun. I sniffed deeply of dripping forest and poplar smoke as I knelt on the bit of sloping mudbank to start a fire. It was a good day to lie low, for out in the channel small whitecaps crowded before a blustering wind.

There were indeed fish that morning: three scaly suckers. Flavorless, mushy creatures with numerous forked ribs, they nevertheless bolstered our spirits, for they were our first catch. Soon the rain returned, splattering cold drops into our tin plates. We ate and returned to bed. Lying fitfully within the sticky bags, we read aloud until nearly midnight.

The next day was not favorable for travel either. A high overcast chilled the drab sky from which a cold western wind descended to kick up waves. Still, we regretted every lost day. After another fishy breakfast we packed our outfit and set off.

Even on the slough, water slopped more than occasionally over the gunwale as we crept along. Although we had eaten some of our supplies, we were still riding dangerously low. When we reentered the main Yukon we motored quietly a few feet from shore. The sullen, rushing river, as faceless as the gray sky, now seemed malevolent as big waves built up over miles of open water. The river was peppered with large islands, some distinguishable from shoreline only at close range, where narrow channels were sucked off between trees. Here the relentless current smashed, piling up debris on the headlands in a deadly trap.

Again the shore opened ahead. Beset with indecision, we watched the crisis approaching. Which way? Should we risk a small channel that could meander for miles, perhaps losing itself in thickets and logjams, or stick with the main channel and chance missing our chosen river? We had almost decided to avoid this little offshoot when Phil spotted geese. By the time he had photographed the departing birds, we found ourselves dragged sideways into the channel.

Thus two accidents, a stiff breeze and a flock of geese, charted our course. The river we sought collides with the Yukon in a confusion of arms, most of which would have added greatly to our journey (had we found them at all). But nature had provided a way, a wandering, secret way, to enter miles above that tangle—and somehow we found it.

Our path snaked swiftly inland through fields of waving willows, green and gray in the shimmering wind. The mud strand was carpeted with the rich velvet of joint grass and the elaborate print of bird tracks. At our approach, startled ducks flung themselves into the air from hidden reed beds. We caught sliding glimpses of open areas, ponds and marshes, through the shifting trees. Within the cozy safety of the slough we began to relax.

We stopped for dinner at a confluence of waterways and built a fire atop a grassy cutbank. Nearby, stood three or four deserted cabins. Below us the chocolate channel plowed into a small river. It had a friendly look, this river, not unlike the slough, but where the two swept together, a slight color change persisted. My heart lightened at this brave promise from snowy peaks hundreds of miles away. Our river! We had picked it from the map and now here it was: a real wilderness river! My gaze lingered on it affectionately.

We were waiting for the wind to drop, as it generally did at night, before trying our hand at upstream travel. Eventually we would need to "line" the canoe upstream, pulling it on foot, but hoped to put that off awhile. This was the beginning of a hard and often discouraging chapter in our new existence. Our days of floating were over.

"Someone's coming," I said, cocking one ear into the wind. I emptied my plate of fish bones into the fire and lumbered to my feet.

Behind us a boat suddenly materialized with Albert and Jessie Williams, two of my brief photographic acquaintances. With them was a proud and well-muscled young man, beaded headband holding back his shoulder-length, black hair. They sighted us and swung toward shore, almost swamping *Lady Grayling*. I clambered down the five-foot cutbank, which was flaking into the river, and jumped onto soggy tussocks of grass rooted in melting mud.

"Would you like some tea?" I called in greeting as I reached for their bowline.

"No, no. We gotta get back to Venetie tonight," Jessie said. "We just stop to see are you okay." She was a well-padded woman with short, dark hair, a round face, and intelligent eyes.

"Oh, we're fine!" I answered enthusiastically. "Sure you won't stop for some tea?"

Jessie shook her head resolutely. "No, we gotta get back to the village tonight." She studied our overloaded canoe in open skepticism. "You like, we can take something for you. We got lotta room. Wouldn't be no bother."

Albert seemed to be looking past me. He said nothing.

Phil scanned our outfit with indecision. "Thanks for the offer," he replied politely, "but we'll do okay." We were beginning to tire of skeptical looks.

"You got plenty of food?" Jessie inquired with the same directness. We nodded. Albert pulled the starter rope and the young man shoved off with the butt of his rifle. I watched, intrigued as his new .30-30 sank into the ooze. Then the big engine caught with a rumble and the boat shot upstream and was gone.

That first evening was deceptively easy. By midnight the wind stilled and we set out north, our five-horse outboard opening the wide bends before us. The water turned milky gray where our small bow wave broke the lavender reflection of sky and dark trees, beginning to take on the look of a healthy river.

Sitting in the front seat, I gazed at it with a new sense of excitement. There was promise in the early morning air and purpose in the smooth bends when, for the first time, we caught sight of mountains clear and small ahead.

Cold dawn was upon us when we stopped on a sandbar to build a large driftwood fire. In the arctic summer, the splendor of sunset-sunrise may take several hours—day bleeding back into day. This river wasn't so bad after all, we concurred as we sipped steaming mugs of spice tea and watched the brilliant morning fade into sunrise. We had come quite a way and seen the mountains: the great Brooks Range! Mudbanks of the Yukon had given way to sand and gravel. We pitched our tent in that picture-book camp and headed for bed full of the happy miles we would make on the morrow.

A few hours later we woke to flapping nylon and blasting grit. Cold sheets of wind-borne sand thundered down the beach, obscuring the far shore and forming dunes. The stinging particles sifted into everything, filling our eyes, ears, and sleeping bags. The tent billowed and strained at its moorings, frequently ripping free. Driven forth at last by hunger, we ate a gritty oatmeal breakfast, eyes squinted against the blast, and went back to bed.

When we emerged into the still amber of evening, our calm beach had returned.

For the next few days we traveled by night to avoid the wind. Every mile became tougher until each yard was a battle with the quickening river. We discontinued use of the motor except for occasional quieter stretches, and even then used it only at the loss of many shear pins, much gas, and the edges of our propeller. Our progress shrank to less than five miles a day as, on foot now, we hauled our stubborn canoe and her half ton of dreams up the rapids.

We became discouraged as plans of starting our cabin early withered and the elusive mountains slipped ever backward at our plodding. The longest day of the year came and went, marking the annual descent back into winter, and we weren't even to the village! "We have to get back tonight," they had said. "Very fast river." The memories lilted through my brain.

But there were good signs too, as we never tired of pointing out to one another. The Yukon jungle lay behind us now, mud and all. This country had an open, healthy feel. The living water was inlaid in bars of tawny sand and colored stones. Although we saw no game, the shore was often marked with tracks of bear, beaver, wolf, and moose. Trees were smaller here and spaced with patches of wildflowers: lupine, wild pea, fireweed, prickly rose, and gentle gifts for which I had no names.

By now it was late June and the steadily dropping water was becoming clearer every day. New sandbars surfaced, growing up through the swift, shallow river like young plants. We feared that the canoe might escape while we slept, so each night she was firmly grounded out of the current and well shackled. And every morning found her high and dry. It always took consider-able effort to badger her back in, but the peace of mind was worth it. This was big empty country. Phil now wore the .22 Magnum pistol, not for protection, but as a hedge against starvation should we ever lose the canoe, and we both carried matches in waterproof containers, mosquito repellent, and our pocketknives.

Energy, I was thinking. So that's what it's all about. Living in a land of bulldozers, I had never realized how fragile yet tenacious our little selves are. Think of what it means to own a mule! To travel downstream instead of up! All the work of life must be done by something: the hauling of wood and water, the building, the growing of food, the travel from place to place. And mostly it was done like this, by human muscles. No wonder people wanted to take the load off their backs and put it on machines, I thought, looking upstream. But then, I admitted, glancing back the way we had come, progress certainly means more to you this way.

Early one morning found me immersed in icy water and chill dawn breeze, tired and discouraged. Minutes before we had broken a shear pin and, paddling furiously, found a foothold near the base of a crumbling gravel cutbank.

"What's taking you so long?" I snapped. I was holding to a sweeper with one hand and the canoe with the other. Beneath my numb feet, the relentless current sucked away the sand as I fought for balance, water to my waist.

"I dropped the blasted shear pin!" Phil wailed. He disappeared from view and groped about blindly under water.

I shifted my grip, fighting the restless canoe. "Let's just camp. Maybe we can walk it over to that island." We scanned the whorls of morning-streaked river, oblivious to the song of sleepless arctic summer. "I think we need to eat better," I said dully. "A person can't work like a mule on a handful of oatmeal." Yet we had caught no more fish and seen no rabbits.

We made camp on a flower-decked cutbank under shifting clouds. It was a young bank, composed of fine, brown sand. Clumps of Eskimo potato ladened with pink blossoms grew between pioneer balsam poplar and the tiny spruce trees that would eventually reforest the land. When the first hardy plants invade a new sandbar, they transform it into a place where insects, small animals, and slower growing trees can get a foothold. Now the capricious river wanted it back. That is what cutbank means.

We had finished our starchy meal when we caught the distinct buzz of an outboard. Very soon a river boat leapt into view, spinning down current. They spotted us and careened rashly shoreward, cutting the motor at the last instant. To my astonishment, the big boat settled gently beside our canoe.

"Difference between planing and displacement hulls," Phil answered my surprise. "Besides, he's not loaded."

It was Albert and Jessie out for an evening ride. They were bundled against the wind of travel, and they toiled stiffly up the bank while their handsome young friend fastened the boat. He was introduced to us as John "Sonny" Erick Jr. His long hair was tied back this time with a pink silk scarf. He grinned shyly as I handed him a cup of mint tea.

"We was a bit worried about you," Jessie stated, holding her chapped hands out to the blaze of our fire. "Our chief, even, Abraham Christian, he come lookin' for you last night."

"Oh, it takes us awhile." I smiled sheepishly. "Uh . . . how far is it from here?"

"I think maybe fifteen miles?" she turned to Sonny and he nodded.

Fifteen miles! That would take us days! I lifted our little blackened tea kettle from the fire and squatted near the cups, steam drifting back over my hand as I poured. I was embarrassed by our apparent helplessness. "Sugar?" I asked, handing Jessie a scalding mug.

She spooned it in. "I always like lotta sugar in my tea," she grinned. "You?" she handed me the bottle.

"I prefer mine plain," I lied, thinking about our diminishing supplies.

The clouds were again closing in. A fine spray of mist prickled my face and soon big drops were dancing in the dust around the fire.

"We can give you a ride," Jessie offered, setting her empty cup on the lid of the grub box. "We got lotta room and we just put everything in, your little boat and all."

This time we accepted with gratitude and relief. Adding three-quarters of a ton slowed their progress, but we sailed right over riffles and rapids at what seemed an incredible rate to me. I shouted a happy conversation with Jessie above the roar of the engine. Already I had quite forgotten the river. It slipped by with such ease that I was surprised I had ever taken it seriously.

❊

Morning song of Venetie, the discordant howl of two hundred chained dogs, woke us in our graveyard camp overlooking the Gwich'in Indian village. Beginning like a distant wind, it swept upon us until all was drowned in a rush of voices.

Phil and I poked among the old grave markers for something to burn as the first guests began arriving, their trudge up the steep hill heralded by renewed howls. We had been assured that it was okay to camp here, for the actual cemetery had been moved because of the encroaching river. Still, there were nervous titters from our visitors about ghosts.

Our first adult visitor was the ancient patriarch of the prolific Frank family. Slowly he topped the bluff, leaning on a walking stick. He had dressed to greet us in a rumpled, white shirt, black tie, and shiny black suit. He wore glasses and smoked a pipe. Atop his head was a quilted cap with a visor.

"Hi. I'm Jeanie and this is Phil," I said. I stuck out my hand and grinned. He touched it politely, smiled, and glanced away.

"I'm Johnny Frank," announced the bandy-legged little man. He pointed to the cabin where he lived with his wife, Sarah. Accepting the cup of sugary tea, he sat cross-legged in the dust by our fire. In broken English, Johnny Frank answered questions and told us stories while children shrilled and giggled in waves about us. He said that few in the village had been far up the river, saying, "Nobody walk no more."

"Tell us about the river," I persisted.

"Many year now I have not go there." He brushed mosquitoes from his leathery neck with a small, dark hand and smiled winningly. His worn suit seemed in keeping with his personal dignity as he sat amicably in the dirt by our breakfast fire. "Too many rock, I tell you. Too fast that river." He shook his wrinkled head at some memory. "You can't take no boat there, I tell you that. Why you want to go?"

"We like the woods," I answered.

He nodded eagerly in agreement. "Trapline. Lotta fur sometime. Sometime no good. That lynx, you catch him, maybe he plenty good sometime. Two year ago, rabbit everywhere," he extended his small arms to encompass the village. "Oh, plenty lynx that time," he beamed. "But nobody trap too much now. They just wait for Native checks. No good, them people now days," he declared, clamping his jaw shut. "Drink, all the time drink! This a dry village. You know what that mean? Nobody supposed to drink here. But they go down to Fort Yukon and bring it back, then everybody drink. Drink and fight! Drink and fight. No good. God as my witness, I never drink, not one time, and now I ninety-one years old. I work when I was young and I know what my life was for. What they live for? To drink and then shoot each other!"

"Gran'pa present," a child tugged at his sleeve. Old Johnny Frank smiled angelically. "All my gran'kids love me and my great-gran'kids," he proclaimed. From his pocket he fished out a crisp dollar. A rush ensued, and soon the kids were off down the hill to buy candy and tobacco at the village store. "My gran'son, you know him? He get lotta moose last winter with the snow-go. In the village, everybody eats lotta moose then. In Fort Yukon, they got freezers so they just keep their own moose, just hide it, put it away."

❖

By our third day in the village we knew almost every adult on sight and a good many by name. There were perhaps 120 people and they were friendly and curious about us. We met Jessie returning from the airstrip and the daily mail plane. Phil was carrying boxes of welfare food for one of the larger Frank families. There were no vehicles, or even roads, in town. Followed by skipping children, we dropped off the groceries and trailed after Jessie back to her cabin, each chewing on an apple.

As we passed the last cabin, an ancient woman, bent double and nearly blind with the seasons, hailed us from her yard. "You want come in for whitefish? I just got good whitefish." Her cabin was large and well-tended with wood stacked before her door by neighbors. The small village retained its sense of community: sometimes petty and gossipy perhaps, like any group of people living together, but still a unit that cared about its members. Remarkably, we were included and had been given food and support, though we had little to offer in return.

"No thank you, Grandmother," I called to her. "I will come visit you this evening."

The path wound among broken and discarded equipment and the inevitable skinny dogs. Here was a culture that for years had been supported by the government. People who once lived happily with few possessions had discovered the toys of civilization. It seemed to me that by comparing themselves with others, they had also discovered poverty. I knew that it was not a simple problem. The land, which once supported migratory bands of Indians who starved when game was scarce, could not sustain a growing population. They couldn't go back, any more than we could return to the days of covered wagons, yet moving to cities meant giving up village support and their way of life.

My eyes lingered covetously on the Jon boats tied along shore. How would we make it into the mountains before winter? We had offered to buy the needed fifty-five gallons of gas for anyone who would transport us upstream to the abandoned gold town beyond the first fork of the river, but no one stepped forward and daily the river level dropped, making upstream travel more difficult.

Jessie and Albert's cabin was constructed of unpeeled, green-cut logs and papered inside with stained cardboard and pictures cut from magazines. Because Jessie held the dual positions of village health aid and post mistress, the cabin was a hub of activity throughout the day. The main room was divided by a high, linoleum-topped counter. Behind the counter were a propane stove, cupboard, dish drainer, various pans, and an open five-gallon slop bucket for dog feed. Across the room stood an oil heater, a sofa, several chairs, and a gas-powered wringer washer. Over the heater, rows of wires were strung for drying socks and mittens. Only the village school had electricity, and the people hauled water from the river in buckets.

While Phil and I chatted with Jessie around the counter, Albert brooded in a corner of the dark cabin. Like most of the villagers, his days seemed a tedium of inactivity. For hours he would sit beside his cache, staring at the ground. He seemed a sad and lonely man and in poor health. I found the silences between us too great to span, but in truth I never tried. Albert Williams, I thought, watching him covertly while I talked with Jessie, the early missionaries were wrong. A man should keep his own name. I wondered what else had been taken from him.

"You want some fish?" Jessie asked, turning from the propane stove with a skillet of fried grayling. She had been generous, often feeding us meals or snacks of dried caribou, pilot bread, and jam. Although they seemed at a loss to understand us, the whole village treated us with kindness. The three of us ate in silence, each wondering what to say. Although her English was good, our backgrounds were so different that we often misunderstood one another.

"We caught some fish too," I boasted, "only they were suckers."

"Oh, we don't eat those," she told me seriously. "Too many bones."

My attention was drawn to something bubbling mysteriously on the back burner.

"Whitefish guts," Jessie said, following my gaze. "Very good." She seemed defensive. "You try some?" So far she had fed us muskrats (boiled in their skins) and boiled geese, heads and all.

"Sure. . . ." I forked out a bit and gingerly tasted them. The guts were much like oysters.

"Is there anyone else we could ask to take us upriver?" I finally asked.

"Maybe Robert Frank takes you when he get back from drinkin' in Fort Yukon," Jessie replied irritably. "I worry about you," she said after a minute. "Maybe you get into lotta trouble. Two years back, this white man, he went and live by himself. We never see him again until the Trooper, he go back there in the wintertime, lookin' for him. That man, he builded himself a little house, so small he couldn't even stand up and with no real door, just canvas. And he didn't have no food. He eat up everything and then he shoot himself."

She got up and placed tea before us on the counter. "Even good Native boys, sometime they get killed. Last winter a Native boy (he know what he was doing too!) die when his snow-go break down not too far from the village either." Jessie watched us, chin in hand, from her stool on the other side of the counter.

I guessed that others were wondering too as they studied our little canoe or talked quietly with us. Some of the young men had borrowed *Lady Grayling* for a frolic near the shore, for none had ever been in a canoe before. "We'll be okay," I smiled reassuringly. "Next spring we'll be fat as beavers. Just call us the upstream Indians."

She looked uncomfortable for a minute and then declared, "You aren't Indians."

The door of the cabin stood open and drugged mosquitoes drifted in and out of the punk smoke. The smell of the slowly burning insecticide coil tinged my thoughts, reminding me of the Mackenzie River and other people who had entered my life briefly along those faraway banks. Outside in the hot sunlight, flies buzzed about the dogs. Often sadly neglected, they were kept as status symbols, a cultural hangover from the days before snowmobiles. I remembered Great Slave Lake in Canada where the dogs were abandoned on small islands to survive the summer or die. In the fall, they would be gathered and fattened for winter work.

A dog was probably the last thing we needed, but watching them from Jessie's cabin, I decided I wanted one. Phil and I both loved dogs, and I missed that relationship. Seeing the ratio of dogs to humans, I assumed we were in the ideal location to acquire a pet. We set off, following one lead after another around the village. People were friendly and proud, bragging about their dogs—which were all shapes, colors, and sizes—but no one wished to part with a single animal.

It was evening when our quest brought us to young Sonny Eric Jr.'s place.

"Just woke up," he said, swinging open the door of the small cabin reputed by old Johnny Frank to be a haunt of the undesirable.

"We're trying to buy a puppy," I began. "One to take up the river with us. Somebody told us you had some."

Reluctantly, he led us around the corner of the cabin to a makeshift wire pen enclosing a dozen colorful balls of fur. "I had to put 'em in jail." He pointed to the tumbling puppies. "They broke into Abraham Christian's cache and ate up all his dry salmon. And he wanted that fish for himself."

I laughed and Sonny looked up in surprise from tying on a blue head-band. I suddenly was aware that humor takes more than a common language: it takes shared assumptions.

"I'm gonna race these dogs," he finally stated, obviously embarrassed at the request. The spring intervillage dog races were a big social occasion. "I don't want to sell none of 'em."

That evening Robert Frank returned from Fort Yukon, his boat ladened with a cow moose he had shot along the river. After we spoke with him, he agreed to take us up to the old abandoned gold town, which was probably as far as his boat could go in the rapid-strewn river.

It was sprinkling fitfully the next morning as Phil and I trudged up and down the hill behind town, lugging gasoline on the footpath from the airstrip. As we broke camp, Sonny Eric Jr. appeared unexpectedly with the runty mon-grel I liked. He told us that he had dreamed he would be killed in a boat acci-dent. To prevent this, he said, we should take the puppy.

So for five dollars we acquired a bundle of problems that we named Net-Chet-Siil, or "Little Girl" in the Gwich'in dialect of Athabascan. She was a pretty little thing, just weaned—all honey and cream with strawberry tongue and licorice-drop nose. Her coat was thick and soft, her tummy bald and freckled, fuzzy ears flopped over her puppy-blue eyes, and her voice carried for miles.

As we loaded our outfit aboard the Jon boat everyone in the village came down to see us off. With a wave of farewell we shoved into the current.

Go! Go! Go! Pleeeease! I pleaded silently as we crept up the tumbling river.

Robert Frank seemed surprised by our sluggish pace. He shouted a conversation with Phil above the roar of the outboard, and I caught the words, "One time I got four moose in this boat! I chartered a plane on floats and just fly around and look for 'em!"

He was a handsome, cheerful man of medium stature, about thirty and already head of a large family. Like many of his generation, tawny eyes, bronze skin, and big bones spoke of better nutrition and perhaps a mixing of genetics. He motioned to Ken, a slender youth of seventeen, and turned the motor over to him. Then settling his back to the wind, Robert Frank cupped his hands about a cigarette and opened a can of soda. Ken drove the powerful engine, standing proudly in the stern, young legs apart, eyes scanning the water, and long hair streaming.

I held our new puppy in my arms. Net-Chet-Siil burrowed under my red woolen coat, soft and wriggly next to my body, as I craned forward, urging the boat. We plowed toward the foothills as rainbows and showers played over a landscape bathed in nameless shades of velvet green. I saw Robert shake his head as Ken again swung the motor up to avoid sudden shelves of gravel.

"I think I go back to the village and get more gas tonight," Robert shouted to Phil, flipping the empty soda can overboard. "We sure use it up this way." Phil reached into his pocket and drew out our remaining cash, handing it to him. It was the last money we had in the world. Finally, I crawled under the overturned canoe to get out of the cold drizzle.

Then we were stopping. I stuck my head out as Phil ran nimbly forward and leapt ashore with the bowline. A pair of tiny old men greeted us cheerfully as we climbed the bank to arrange ourselves about their smoldering fire. Like other places we had noticed along the river, this was a well-used camping spot for the Indians. It was situated on a small cutbank in the protection of mature spruce trees, many of which had been stripped of bark. The bark, which comes away easily in large sheets in the spring, was used like plywood to cover lean-tos.

After a brief conference in their own language, one of the old men, Ambrose Williams, turned to Phil with a big smile and said, "This my lucky day! I see moose over there. I shoot 'em and he swim across and die on this side. I didn't have no boat. I was just gonna eat those little fishes and I don't like 'em." He pointed to a can of sardines.

The three young men unloaded the boat and set off to retrieve the skinned and disjointed carcass of a yearling bull. This they heaved onto a bed of willows in the shade near camp. No one seemed concerned about the flies, which will lay their eggs on meat, converting it to maggots in a short while. The two old men stood quietly by as the quarters were hefted ashore. I thought of the skill that lay in those small, veiny hands. Butchering a moose is no small chore.

We ringed their smudge fire, sipping coffee while the Indians exchanged news. Finally Robert turned to us in English saying, "Jim Christian, Abraham is his brother. He don't speak English good. His gran'son, Jimmy Christian, he was supposed to take 'em up the East Fork to their cabin, but he run out of gas and went down to Fort Yukon to drink and just leave 'em here."

Old Jim Christian grinned and nodded, perhaps not understanding a word. There was something gentle about him. Like his companion, he was of slight build, coming only to my shoulder, dark and weathered. His almost beardless face was carved by history, as were his small, gnarled hands. In the near blindness of age he wore thick glasses. He was dressed in baggy slacks, red-checked flannel shirt, and beaded moose-hide moccasins. His short-brim cap secured a flutter of gauzy material to protect his neck from bugs.

Ambrose Williams offered us the interesting animal matter that was gurgling in a thick, green soup over the fire. The others were already at work with their pocketknives stabbing long strings out of a five-gallon can.

"Moose guts," Robert said, glancing over his knife as he chewed. "The old people, they really like this stuff. They eat it when they was young." Ambrose nodded and smiled.

Phil and I looked timidly at one another and dug out our knives. When in Rome, I thought. Phil leaned over and whispered, "They still have the shit in them!" I nodded and smiled. Rubbery, but not bad.

Next came boiled tenderloin. The backbone was severed with a knife at each vertebra and plunked into our large kettle. Most Native cooking seems designed to reduce preparation of the food, not a bad idea for people living outdoors. We finished the meal with the usual sugar-laced tea and the budding antlers of the young bull. Jim Christian singed the velvety skin by roasting them in the fire.

We camped with them that night. After breakfast of boiled moose the next morning, I squatted on the bank, scraping impervious moose tallow from Mightypot with sand. Ambrose had a tape recorder playing Native chants sewn together with his fiddling. I listened, feeling across the cultural chasm that separated my world of science from this ancient heritage. I was intrigued and would have stayed to listen, but Robert, who had taken most of the moose to the village and returned during the night with extra gasoline, considered the old folk dull company and was impatient to be off. I hurriedly packed up our camp gear and loaded the riverboat while the recorder fiddled on and Ambrose danced.

"You know," I said to Phil as we shoved off and the waving old men dwindled into arctic vastness, "in our culture we'd lock those two up someplace safe where they couldn't hurt themselves. Did you hear that old Ambrose spends every winter alone up on the Wind River? As blind as he is too. I suppose someday he'll die out there and people will wonder why somebody didn't stop him. But he's alive now."

We hadn't been long underway when a major fork veered off taking most of the water with it. Because of the shallows, I and half of the gear remained at the junction while Phil and the other half continued on up the diminished river.

As the noise of the engine melted into the river, I looked around. We were now in hilly country, able to glimpse mountains through breaks in the green. Underfoot was a springy, six-inch carpet of multicolored sphagnum moss, lacy white reindeer lichen, and dainty sprigs of lingonberry, also known as lowbush or mountain cranberry. This was woven with minute flowers and inconspicuous plants of many varieties. The scattered trees, spindly and often draped in threads of pale green moss, contrasted somberly with the bright ground cover. The land seemed brilliant and fresh after the dank Yukon Flats and the dusty village.

This new country pleased me, evoking some forgotten childhood memory. Its very openness should enhance our ability to see animals, I decided. As if to prove me right, I caught the cautious hippity-hop of a feeding snowshoe hare, brown now in its summer attire. I unsheathed my old .22 rifle and soon was cleaning the luckless rabbit—our first game. A flash drew my attention to a hole in a tree where a pair of yellow flickers tended a brood of demanding young. Everybody is busy this time of year. I rinsed the hare, very unimpressive now, and was saddened that it was a nursing mother. Guiltily, I tasted the milk on my bloody fingers, then washed the fluids from my hands in the river.

When the boat returned to shuttle me upstream, I was ready. Phil had set up camp by the time we arrived, and a short while later I was preparing rabbit and dumplings. The Indians seemed tired of our slow travel and we did our best to make them comfortable. As we sat gnawing diminutive bones and glancing at one another, Robert announced that he could take his boat no further. Tomorrow they would leave us and head happily downstream hunting.

As for us, we would be left entirely to our own strength and imagination. These were the last people we would see in almost a year.

CHAPTER 3

Beautiful as the wilderness is, I don't recall enjoying it that first summer. Somehow we had expected the sweetness of an extended hike and were unprepared for the continual stress that faced us. We found ourselves in the position of wild animals, dependent upon the land, but unlike them we were neither highly adapted nor specifically trained for this role.

I heard the Indians leave early, the guttural growl of their big engine hushing the woods. The sound faded as they slipped down current and was lost in the song of the river. It was the first of July.

It felt good to be alone. I lay still, listening to Phil's deep breathing. The ceaseless babble of water soothed me, tempting me back into the fairyland of sleep, where I had been doing . . . what? I couldn't quite remember. Closing my eyes, I shut out the day ahead and listened. The river sounded like people all talking at once, the pitch seeming to rise and fall. Sunlight dappled my face, teasing me. I rolled onto my elbows. The screen door of the tent was dotted with mosquitoes and I shook it before zipping down one corner to let Net-Chet-Siil out.

The Arctic was no longer in bloom. The succulent green of deep summer was swollen with mature plants coming to fruition. Many had burst from hidden roots, rocketing into the brief summer on energy stored the year before. I call this country "Arctic" because it is north of the Arctic Circle, but the ecosystem is better referred to as taiga. Unlike the tundra of high Arctic, lower vegetation here is mostly boreal forest of spindly white and black spruce.

We were camped on a thinly spruced cutbank. I lay on my stomach and studied the bright ground cover a few inches from my face. Each curl of moss was perfect to its kind. An earthy smell rose from the warm carpet to mingle with the spice of Labrador tea and the rich vanilla scent of spruce bark. The river had changed too. Semitransparent like fine jade, it tumbled over large stones. Close green hills descended to gravel bars, obscuring the mountains beyond.

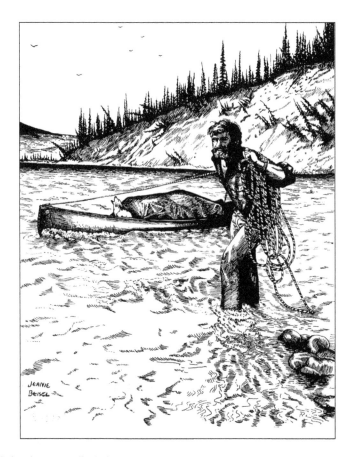

"They've gone?" Phil asked.

"Uh-huh." I dropped my gaze to his upturned face and kissed him on the lumpy bridge of his nose. "I was just contemplating getting up."

Even from the tent I could see that the flies were busy with our half-dried moose meat, tasting it with their feet for moist crevices in which to deposit eggs. A parting gift from Ambrose, we had cut the meat into strips to hang near the fire the evening before.

Glancing back at Phil, I could see that he was already repacking in his mind. Net-Chet bounced forward at the sound of our voices, demanding to be readmitted.

"No!" I snapped, unhooking her sharp claws from the frail mosquito netting. "Now go on!"

"Looks like a nice day," Phil announced, sitting up and reaching for his red-checked wool shirt. The faded blue T-shirt he slept in looked dingy. He stretched and glanced at his watch. Then he shook his wrist and listened a moment. "It's dead."

He looked at me and we both shrugged. "Who cares what time it is," I answered.

"Isn't it good to be here?" he grinned.

"I wish I knew where here was. When do we get on the map?"

"We'll just have to keep comparing the map with the country until we get them matched. Our map starts on this side of the old gold town, so if we find it, we'll know exactly where we are."

"Robert said it isn't really on the river anymore," I reminded him. I was pulling on my jeans and I lay back to tug up and zip them. "We could miss it."

Phil opened the tent door and crawled out on hands and knees. "I'm going to start loading the canoe," he said over his shoulder.

"I want to do some laundry before we start."

Had we known that we were scarcely halfway from the village to the old ghost town, perhaps things would have seemed different, but that morning we were full of hope.

Two hard days and five miles later, we stood panting in the shallows, leaning heavily against the tug of the canoe while white water boiled around our knees. We almost didn't make that one, I thought, staring back down the foaming trough.

The principle of lining a canoe upstream is simple. The craft is worked on a long rope—one end fastened to the bow, the other to the rear thwart. When the stern is pulled in, the canoe ferries out from shore on its keel. A shifting balance of tension is maintained as conditions change. Lining works well with a moderate current and an even bottom. In rapids, however, we needed direct contact with the craft to hold her and it often took all of our combined strength.

I caught Phil's glance and shook my head. "Not yet." My arms felt weak and my legs shook with fatigue. Overhead an afternoon thunderstorm growled darkly into the cobalt sky, mounting as we watched. The weather seemed to have changed as we neared the mountains, or perhaps it was only the advancing summer. A warning gust of wind swept upon us, kicking up spray and turning the river a flat, metallic gray as the sun blinked under.

"Well, here it comes," Phil stated as the first drops hit. He took a firmer grip on the bow decking. "I can handle it from here. Why don't you go on up to those spruce trees and get a fire started? Here, take the tea things."

I gave in too easily, and tucking Net-Chet under one arm, ran wobble-kneed over the rocks for the distant forest. My feet were numb from the cold water and my pants clung to my legs. Scattered sheets of blowing rain raked the willows that crowded the nearby bar and flattened the few pioneer plants that poked between stones down on the beach. Ahead loomed the dark, thrashing trees.

I entered the woods abruptly. Humming and swaying, the trees wrapped about me, dense and secret. I cleared a space in the thick moss and kicked into the duff. Beneath the green feathers of sphagnum moss, the years had layered a deep bed of peat interlaced with twigs and punky logs. The flames took easily to the twigs, burrowing into the dry duff with alarming speed.

It was raining hard now. From the relative safety of the forest I could see a little figure out on the river struggling through the driving sheets. A mist rose from the rocks where the rain exploded on impact. Phil became a shadow, a small toiling wraith in a world of gray. Stinging hail joined the deluge, and Net-Chet began to whine as a fine patter sifted through the needles of our shelter. By crouching against the trunk of a tree I managed to avoid most of the rain.

"Quiet, Net-Chet!" I turned on her. Phil was trying to beach the canoe, dragging it onto a rocky spit in search of a place to tie it. I dared not leave the fire to help him. At last he was running up the beach, blindly, head down into the rain. Poor guy, couldn't get much wetter, I thought.

Phil entered the forest and I seated him on a carpeted hummock of roots, close to the bole of an old spruce. He was soaked and shivering. I poured scalding water over the tea grounds in his stained enamel mug and crawled under the branches with him. His hair was plastered down and streaks of dirt drained into his beard, joining the trapped mosquitoes. Net-Chet was curled up on my only summer coat, so I squatted over the blaze warming my fingers.

"Have some almost jerky," I offered from a cloth sack. The mist sifting through the trees was becoming a drizzle punctuated with big drops. Lightning scared the gray world beyond the trees. "It tastes pretty good if you don't look too close. Hey, you know your shirt is running?" I fingered a red stain around his cold, dripping wrist where the dye had leached.

We crouched together, feeling the comfort of wet warmth pass between us, chewing raw, rubbery moose while the storm raged. "Here's another batch," Phil said, excising the wriggly pearl of a maggot with the point of his pocketknife.

"Just don't tell me about it. I'm not looking," I replied in disgust.

"More protein," he teased.

I shot him a sour glance. "The cycle is amazing when you think of it. Moose to maggot to fish food in a few weeks." I closed the cloth game bag and slid it behind us to keep dry. I had made it by sewing two large kerchiefs together. It allowed air circulation while keeping out flies.

The storm rode northward on an expanding evening sky as we gathered up our tea things and carried our squirming puppy back to the canoe. The clean land was tinted tangerine by a low sun. The air felt clammy on our cooled bodies, and cold water spilled into my boots as we pushed the craft back into the current. Within fifty yards we hit a rapid that swamped her. Fighting for every foot of progress, we towed her ashore and unloaded everything, spreading our belongings on the stones to dry.

It was Phil's twenty-fourth birthday. I baked him a cake in late evening sunlight, using our treasured flour and sugar, baking it before the fire with our folding reflector oven.

One drizzling afternoon a few days later we rounded a bend and stood before the mountains. For the first time, no foothills blocked our view. We grounded the canoe and dropped onto the wet rocks to study the map.

"Where do you suppose the ghost town is?" I asked Phil. "We've got to be getting close. Do you think we could have missed it?" We glanced from map to mountains attempting to fit it together. Somewhere nearby was the abandoned gold town. Ahead were dusky blue peaks, jagged and almost naked of trees. Behind us the shaggy, meandering shoreline was lost in a lush belt of foothills, dividing us from the past.

"About four miles to the inch . . ." he shook his head. "It's hard to tell. The creek we saw yesterday could be this one . . . or maybe this . . ." he traced a muddy finger along the map. "Hope it wasn't this one or we've missed it."

"Well, I'm not going back." It had started to rain again and Phil bent over the map, shielding it with his body. From her nest in the canoe, Net-Chet was complaining ever more insistently. The bugs were vicious on the bar, stinging as they bit into my wet face. They seemed to prefer rainy days as long as there was no wind. Irritably, I shoved *Lady Grayling*, stern first, into the current, playing the rope through my chapped hands to adjust the pitch.

"I'll take it awhile," I said, glad for a chance to warm up. I threw my weight into the rope, running it over my right shoulder and using my left hand to control the angle. Water piled into the side of the canoe, forcing it out. The river was shallow and pebbly, hooking slowly into another broad curve. I relaxed, placing each foot with care and feeling the thigh muscles tighten rhythmically, dependably. Step, splash. Step, splash. Slowly the bottom deteriorated into slippery rocks and rushing water. Step, jerk, stumble, tug. The canoe fought back, hanging up, yanking. Progress.

I peered ahead. Did a creek join at the bend? The Indians had told us that the abandoned town was difficult to find. Built near the water in the 1890s, it had been left inland when the river changed course, willows reclaiming the old channel. They said a sternwheeler had come up on the spring flood in those days.

"It's a stream," Phil called from the shore a little distance ahead. "Let's camp and see if we can locate the town in the morning."

"Got a place picked out?" I asked. My eyes searched the shore for a safe harbor.

"This looks about as good as any."

Together we heaved the bow firmly aground. I reached into the front seat and pulled up my coat, setting the squalling pup ashore. Phil tied the painters to a large drift log embedded in gravel and fastened the cable around a boulder.

Minutes later I had the tent set up and sleeping bags spread out. Phil unloaded camp gear and lashed the fitted tarp back over the craft. Crawling inside just as the clouds opened, we stripped off our wet clothes and piled them under Net-Chet. From bed I stroked her delicate head and listened to the storm. We lay reading aloud while the rain drummed on the tent fly and fog built up inside the tent.

I tucked my hands between my legs to warm them and tried to forget my hunger. Concentrating on Phil's voice as he read, I gradually slipped into a dream. I was swimming after a drowning infant. I dove beneath a muddy current and pulled up the lifeless child. As I kicked for shore, I breathed into her lungs, perhaps too hard, for by the time I climbed the beach she had degenerated into two transparent balloons.

I woke in the stillness of gray, midnight overcast. The tent was empty. I lay motionless in the silence listening for Phil's presence. I could feel the uneven press of stones against my spine and hear the distant murmur of the river to my right. To my left, a soft twittering of sleepy birds delineated the edge of the forest. Then a slight shift in the air brought the scent of wood smoke and I relaxed.

I sat up and reached for the shirt I had used as a pillow. Shaking the dog's mud from my wet trousers, I forced my legs into them and hunched my way out of the tent. The Arctic had a somber look that evening, chill and drab. Across the rocks I could see the canoe, dark against the mottled water. Nearby, a small fire added the only touch of color, the slight movement of a dark figure squatting over it the only sign of life.

Phil looked up at my approach and smiled. "I chopped up the last of the old moose ribs and boiled them," he said. Giving the pot a stir and replacing the lid, he ran a spoon under the bail and carefully lifted the blackened little pot from the coals. "See what you think of it. I put in some dried veggies and flour for thickening. Watch out for bone splinters."

He seated me on a log he had hauled near the fire. I could see the uneven drag marks trailing up the beach.

"Have you fed the dog?" I asked, placing the pot between my feet. I pried up the lid and a sour, meaty smell assailed me in a billow of steam. Phil poured us each a cup of tea and squatted on his haunches across from me.

"I gave her some of the soup." He hesitated a moment and then said, "I know we decided not to shoot the little tree squirrels, but we have to feed her something..."

"Okay," I answered, not looking up. The thick, grayish soup tasted good. "I guess bringing her was a mistake, wasn't it?"

He didn't answer. He dipped a twig into his tea and fished about. "The trouble with finding a mosquito leg in your tea," he said, changing the subject, "is you wonder where the rest of it went."

"Only one?" I smiled.

The next morning was sunny and warm. We discovered a dozen grayling living where the small creek emptied into our river. Grayling are silver fish, twelve to fifteen inches long, with big iridescent dorsal fins of turquoise. They live in clear water and are fun to catch, for you can see them. You often find several living together in some glass-clear "hole." Like children, Phil and I played along the bank, catching fish and cooking them over the fire in the sunshine.

It was late afternoon before we set out to look for the ghost town and evening was upon us when we discovered it slumbering among the fireweed. The rotting cabins stood quietly, a part of the woods from which they had been fashioned, and yet so different. Washed by three-quarters of a century, there lingered still that strange ugliness that clings to abandoned dwellings. Where once there had been voices, only the song of a white-crowned sparrow, the tired creak of spruce tree, and the gentle quiver of wind in the tall weeds spoke. Through the seasons it had remained, this old cluster of log piles that had been the homes of men.

The cabins, their dirt floors covered with wildflowers, seemed small and dank—mere holes to crawl into out of the snow. Trees sprouted in the narrow doorways and on the warped sod roofs. Rotten wooden barrels that had contained flour or nails, treasures in a wild land, lay scattered in the blooming fireweed. Fallen doghouses built in rows had once confined the hard but necessary lives of slave dogs, long dead.

Many of the cabins were no longer standing. Most were rooflessly tumbling back into the earth. Perhaps thirty people had lived here. A red tree squirrel raced along a naked ridgepole, vibrating at our intrusion, his tail flicking in agitated jerks with each "Chit! Chit! Chit!" I listened for the whisper of dreams from the dark walls and seemed to catch a sigh of loneliness. What becomes of men, I wondered, who strive for the pot of gold and perhaps miss the rainbow? But was I too quick to judge? Perhaps here, too, was someone's grand adventure.

We rummaged through quaint old garbage: patent medicines, faded newspapers, tools of another era. These tools had made life possible in this land, and the land hasn't changed. After a long time in the dirty, dim interior of a cabin that still boasted a roof, I stepped into the lavender twilight and came face to face with a wolf. He didn't look startled or even impressed. He was tan in color with a black face. Standing perhaps three feet at the shoulder, he coolly returned my gaze a long moment before turning with indifference and trotting out of the clearing on long, silent legs. Net-Chet was engaged in searching for a vole and was blissfully ignorant of her close call.

Finding the old gold town put us at last on the map, and we carefully marked each day's travel with little penciled lines. It was encouraging to see the daily change in the landscape that now marked our upstream progress. The river no longer rambled freely, but was often bounded on one side or the other by a two-hundred-foot cutbank, confining it to a broad glacial cut where it swung from side to side as if seeking escape.

I tried to imagine what the land had looked like ten thousand years ago when a massive ice field capped the Brooks Range and a river of ice had carved this valley. A people very much like ourselves had hunted moose and bear in the Yukon flats, and fished the rivers washing out of the glaciers. In the fall, they picked cranberries and blueberries with their children, and in the spring they saw the ice go out and watched the birds return. They nursed their babies and cared for their old people and told stories around the night fires.

One day the river swung abruptly, butting into the bare bones of a mountain mass. For some time it had paralleled the range as if undecided, then turned resolutely northward, wedging open a wide valley into its secret heart. Soon we were leaving our familiar gray crags behind for another set of landmarks.

As the river began its climb in earnest, we developed a different method for surmounting rapids. These were now strewn with large boulders, "boat eaters" we called them, interspersed with deep holes. Water gushed over slippery rocks the size of basketballs and crumbling bluffs often dropped steeply into the river at a bend, affording no beach. In the past, we had grabbed the bow and muscled the canoe up the watery stairs together. Now one of us braced against a boulder, holding the craft in the turbulence of its wake, while the other worked the rope upstream. Finding secure footing, the one with the rope would haul the canoe (and the person guiding it) hand-over-hand up the racing chute. Already behind us lay nearly a thousand feet of elevation.

We were approaching another fork in the river when we pitched camp on a sandy, white beach late one afternoon. It was a clear, still day and the low-hanging sun gave the country that peculiar golden quality that outlines every detail in color. A few yards upstream a sandspit protruded into the current in graduating shades of blue, sheltering the canoe from the main stream.

There were few mosquitoes on the bar. Their numbers naturally diminish by midsummer. We stripped off our clothes and hung them on small willow bushes to dry. A slight breeze tickled the naked hairs on my back and legs as I worked, but did nothing to deter several bloodsucking flies. They were as long as a finger joint with iridescent, rainbow eyes and sharp, triangular mouths.

I staked down the tent floor as Net-Chet circled my legs, whining. She was never happy until home was established. Pushing in the last peg, I tightened the nylon guy lines. Phil had plucked a small seagull and was heating water to cook it when I plopped down in the warm sand by the fire. A large spider danced away, lugging her egg sack.

"We need to refill Wonderbox," I said.

"Again?" Phil was squatting near the blaze, positioning the teapot.

"Well, we're out of pancake mix, oatmeal, sugar, and powdered eggs."

He looked helplessly at me. "We've eaten a third of our supplies."

"I know, but we have to eat something. And so does Net-Chet, and she eats almost as much as we do. If there were more small game or fish . . ." I trailed off. We both knew the problem. In the far north small animal populations are cyclic. We had seen only four arctic hares all summer and no spruce grouse. Our attempts to fish on the main river had been fruitless. We now ate the tiny tree squirrels.

"Well, we may be hunting big game before too long," he stated.

"I haven't seen any of that either," I said. We stared at one another in silence.

Phil poured boiling water into two mugs and added sand from a plastic bottle. I grinned at him. The day before I had spilled some sugar and he had saved it, dirt and all.

"To my golden retriever," he smiled, handing me a cup. "The way you jumped into the rapids after that gull I shot."

"A Bonaparte's gull. Honestly, Phil. Next it'll be chickadees," I teased him. "Here's mud in your tea." We sipped in silence. "We might be better off if we ate more. As it is we are dull-witted and weak. Very ineffective."

"Any way you look at it, it's a gamble. Use up all our supplies and keep strong to find more, or ration food and starve longer," he answered.

A vague hunger had come to live with us, an uneasy craving that even a full belly could not quench. We had planned to depend on small game for protein, but instead found ourselves living on diminished servings of starch. A listless apathy haunted our movements and we found ourselves inclined to sleep away long hours, even entire days.

"I feel like I could eat a whole moose myself," Phil told me seriously. "Waiter! Bring me a moose, medium rare, and a bushel of apples." Phil was a big fan of apples. His mother would buy them by the box, for he ate eight or ten a day.

"If we do shoot a moose we'll sit and eat for a week." I grinned at the thought.

"Can you imagine drying a moose in the summer? Out here?"

He had a point. Curing the horse had been hard work, even with a table, oven, and refrigerator. "I'd like a bacon, lettuce, and tomato sandwich," I said suddenly.

He leaned forward with a wicked grin. "Well, I'd like a chocolate cream pie with a tender, flaky crust and mounds of real whipped cream."

He had me there.

Net-Chet rose from her place on my coat and nosed into my lap. She really was a lovely animal, I thought, stroking her silky ears. Similar to a golden collie in color, she had a white diamond on her forehead and snowy ruff and legs. Her tail had the curl of a husky, but her fine bones seemed to promise a smaller dog.

Cool air settled over the beach, creeping up from the singing river and out of the forest. Our empty clothing danced on the bushes in the evening breeze. We three drew closer to the fire and to one another as blue silence filled our thoughts. I looked across the river and let in the presence of wilderness. I could imagine viewing us from directly overhead and then pulling back until we disappeared into the landscape, further and further until even these mountains were lost in the Arctic. For a moment, I let go of my worries about tomorrow and sought to encompass the vast, interlocking beauty of this living country.

As if part of my thoughts, a cow and a well-grown calf moose materialized from the willows on the far bank. Transfixed, we watched this apparition. Often we had seen tracks, tangible evidence of the unseen denizens of this land, but they were the tracks of ghosts. The big, timid animals emerged specter-like from the shadows, ears and noses questing the uncertainties of the bar. People who think that moose look awkward and clumsy have not watched them in their world or tried to follow them through thickets. Moose are giant deer.

For a long moment they poised in frozen silence, their dark forms as motionless as the mountains. Perhaps these secret creatures sensed something amiss or maybe a whiff of smoke betrayed us. As if in slow motion, they shied and dissolved into the trees, leaving the land empty.

To celebrate the sighting, we ate our last two squares of chocolate.

In mid-July we hit a spell of rain and wind that smelled unsettlingly of autumn. Through days of icy clothes we trudged on as the river became a muddy, swollen torrent. The rain and the increased snowmelt in high mountains turned the water into a frigid slurry that numbed our legs and sucked warmth from our bodies.

As August neared, the urge to nest began to tug at us in earnest. We watched the country now with new intensity. The desire to be settled into a little cabin of our own, warm and well-fed, arose in me almost as a physical ache. No longer adventurous, I felt like a child who is tired from play and seeks safety and rest. Like denning animals we studied the riverbanks, testing, sniffing, searching for the right combination. Not here, not this—but soon. The presence of the Arctic was always with us now, like a giant third person, tireless, patient, uncaring. We could feel the inescapable flood of winter already creeping down from the Pole. Soon it would become a white torrent, surging southward to reclaim the land it rightfully owns. At night our fire had a cozy, red glow in the waning daylight.

We had originally planned to journey far upriver and be free at last of the pressure of humanity that had defined our previous lives—to be on our own. I had even chosen a possible cabin site on the map that now looked depressingly far away in this world. The futility of our goal was becoming ever more apparent, but still we struggled toward it, the weight of its distance heavy upon us.

What difference did it make? I began to wonder. It took time for our isolation to penetrate: we were so accustomed to the signs of man. No trails, no tracks in the sand, no telephone wires. At first we didn't notice. Not a beer can, not a cigarette butt, not a gum wrapper. Our senses were slow to appreciate their absence.

One day we decided that our outboard motor was of no further use, and built a cache for it and the gas tanks. Because of the rapids we hadn't used it for some time and wanted to reduce the load. We were in the mountains proper now. No foothills were these bald and silent observers of our nightly camps and small daily battles. It felt comforting to be in the mountains. True, over that peak lay another and still another, all wild and without the track of man, but there was security in being able to see the horizons of our world. This was our valley, our future home.

❧

After a discouraging day and the usual fruitless hunt for food, we were sitting quietly by our fire, sharing a pot of cornmeal mush. We had given up plates, having neither the detergent nor energy to waste on them. There was only a quart of powdered detergent for the entire year for clothes and dishes. We spoke less these days, our voices low as we enjoyed little jokes that no one else would think funny.

Our camp was perched on a slender strip of mud that separated the roaring, brown current from the dark forest. A few feet away, the dirty and battered canoe was snugged up in a shoal, rocking slightly to the backwash of waves. Pools of rainwater sagged in the blue nylon tarp lashed over her load. Water dripped from the end of my nose into the pot as I took my turn eating. There would have been little point in wearing rain apparel even if we had it, for much of our day was spent in the river. Our possessions were few, and because we had no way to dry clothing, changing was useless. Like the moose, we got wet when it rained, and in truth, were rarely dry.

I breathed in the cool, night smells and rocked forward on my sitting log to push a charred branch further into the fire. Across from me, Phil squatted flat-footed on a rock like some great, hungry bird. He was comfortable in that position, although I have met few adults who are, and I secretly suspected some defect. Nearby, Net-Chet was finishing off a tree squirrel, head, hide, guts, bones, and all. Oblivious to the drizzle, she chomped, holding the gory remains with her front paws. I watched her work down the hindquarters, shearing the bones with a rhythmic crunch. She finished and sniffed about for missed tidbits.

Through a clean stillness, sounds dropped like pebbles: bird songs, the drip of overhanging alders, the intimate crackle of fire, and the torpid drone of a few chilled mosquitoes. I noticed the rain was slackening. A breath of wind touched the saturated earth, and far beyond the clouds, the sun sloped northward into the summer night. As it reached the rim of mountains it seemed to gather strength. A small spot in the cloud cover began to fade, brightening at first to a light gray and then a pale yellow. There it smoldered as it slid along the peaks, fanned at last to an almost unbearable orange. Then for a moment it burned through, catching the ragged clouds afire before they closed back in.

I handed Phil the pot and spoon and got stiffly to my feet. I was still hungry. Steam drifted from my wet jeans as I presented my behind to the blaze. Slowly I rotated before the fire, roasting my cold limbs. The skin heated, yet the deep chill of my bones remained.

"The rain has almost stopped." I sniffed, staring up at the expressionless sky. "Perhaps tomorrow will be good."

I lifted the can of tea from Wonderbox and dropped the lid again. Then I squatted near the fire to pour hot water into our cups. When Phil leaned forward for his mug, I popped a vitamin into his mouth. My parents had lived for years at a time on nothing but meat, but it seemed that the small expense and weight of vitamins was worthwhile insurance. Phil's jaws opened with such innocence that I had to laugh.

"You're so trusting," I grinned. "Maybe someday I'll slip you a spider."

"Nope," he replied. "You're afraid to pick them up."

"Dig up any more birch bark recipes?" I kidded.

He made a face. We had spent a day collecting "edible" plants that Phil had read about, and nearly ruined our stomachs on such delicacies as powdered lichen "flour extender" and birch bark "spaghetti." The book said the lichen had a "slightly nauseous taste," something I can affirm. Most of the recipes called for using a wild plant to spice some main dish. If I had the main dish, I thought, I wouldn't need herbs. The Arctic is a poor place to be a vegetarian. The number of species is limited, and except for berries in the fall there are few plants fit for the human digestive tract—especially in the quantity necessary for survival.

Methodically Phil scraped the pot, then rinsed it and drank the water. I watched him, wishing I had some special surprise up my sleeve. Of late he had been increasingly plagued with stomach cramps and it worried me.

Finally I broached the subject that had been on both our minds. "Phil, we've got to talk about the dog."

He looked uncomfortable, but said nothing.

"What's wrong with us?"

Still nothing.

"I've been thinking about this," I persevered. "We take everything she does as a personal threat."

"There's just no place out here for a spoiled pet," he answered defensively.

"That's what I had been thinking, that she's too demanding. But is that the real problem? Think about it—is she really that bad?"

He avoided my eyes and reached for his cup. "No," he said at length, his voice very quiet. "She's okay, I guess." He turned to face me a moment. "Is there something wrong with me?" He looked pained. "I'm not a dog beater! Dogs are my favorite people. I speak dog, remember?"

"What about me? I almost drowned her today!"

I had encouraged Phil to hunt while I handled the canoe alone. It seemed a quiet stretch of river, but I soon found myself bucking sweepers in a fast, deep current. Gradually, the bottom had dropped from beneath me. I worked my way along the cutbank, hanging on to the roots and thrashing branches with one hand, the canoe line with the other. It was raining and I felt half drowned, frightened, and scratched as I fought the river. Through it all Net-Chet never ceased her piercing screech from the safety of the front seat. I thought she might be happier ashore so I worked the boat in and tossed her up on the broken bank. But no! In a fury I turned on her. Freeing one hand, I flung her into the water.

All my anger vanished in that instant. I watched in horror as her little head disappeared under the flood. She bobbed up almost at once, shrunken and scared, swimming wildly for shore. Then she hit the canoe, struggled a moment, and was sucked under. Panic welled up in me and stunned remorse, but there was nothing I could do! A long time later she popped up at the stern and resumed her furious paddling. I had pulled the canoe up into the sweepers and tied it, then gone after Net-Chet. Phil found us both soaked and crying when he returned.

"Phil," I continued insistently. "I'm not going to drop this. What does she do that's so terrible? She buries her food. Okay, to us that's a threat, but to a dog it's normal. Yesterday she refused to stay in the canoe, which she hates, and you became impatient. Then she got scared and hid, which made you angry. So when you found her, you beat her. Yes, it is ugly. Look at her. We are all she has in the world and she's afraid of us."

"I know." He was close to tears, head hanging. "I've never had an animal fear me before."

I leaned sideways and put my arm about his shoulders, smelling the wet wool smell of him. "Don't you see? I've never even seen you mad before. Why, you get angry at the canoe lately! The canoe! An inanimate object!"

"The main thing that drives me crazy is her constant whining," he confessed. "If she would just SHUT UP!"

"Don't I know it!" Net-Chet had tremendous control. She could pitch a whine so that it was scarcely audible, like a single mosquito in the bedroom at night, yet in the canoe her shrieks of loneliness carried above the loudest rapid, like a train whistle. "We can't beat it out of her. She'd rather be punished than ignored. Now look: here she is, alone in a wilderness, no home, no other dogs, no way to survive without us. She hates travel. She has nothing but the two of us, and we have nothing left over for her."

"I know," he said unhappily. "Sometimes I really love the little nuisance. Other times I almost hate her. How can we even hunt with that racket?"

"It was a mistake to bring her," I confessed. I looked at Net-Chet. She was sprawled on my coat, her freckled tummy skyward in the trusting security of sleep. "But she doesn't deserve this. If we can't accept her for the puppy she is and cope somehow, we had better destroy her. Anything else would be unkind." I let the thought hang between us like a cloud. At least I brought it up, I thought, stirring the coals idly with a charred stick.

I stopped and glanced about. Across the river two wolves appeared. They had come down to drink and it was some moments before they too looked up in the watchful habit of wild things. They studied us awhile, a mated pair perhaps, black and white together. Our minds, like theirs, were intent on food, but our rifles lay in the canoe a few yards away. The two turned and vanished into the spruce trees.

"If we're going to hunt we should keep the rifles with us," Phil said.

"What do you think they find to eat out here?" I wondered aloud.

"Same as us."

"I just don't see how they can catch enough to keep alive day by day. I know they're supposed to eat mostly rodents this time of year. Still, it must be a full-time job."

For three days a storm raged and we remained on the bar. During brief lulls we emerged like damp ground squirrels to sniff the weather. Water crept into camp, crowding us higher as the river became an angry sluice. The wind hurled into our frail tent, while clouds crashed blackly over us. We lay in our small, buffeted refuge and read aloud from a novel. Why, I wondered, do people write about imaginary, earthshaking deeds? The real heroes are everywhere: people dieting, crippled children, old folks taking care of one another, middle-aged women going back to school, fathers holding down two jobs, single parents. Life is full of unsung heroes.

On the third morning we returned to the river and spent an entire day making less than a mile in the icy torrent. The river was one continuous rapids—a foaming sea of mud and tireless wind. Yet even above the wind and water we were tormented by piercing wails from the front seat where Net-Chet rode on my red wool coat.

We woke the following morning to a gusting rain, rolled over in tandem, and went back to sleep. We could sleep much of the twenty-four hours and still feel tired.

"Oh, Phil, how I hate to face it," I admitted about noon. Gazing out upon the endless boil of brown water through the tent screen, I felt drugged, stuporous. Our mud-splattered *Lady Grayling* waited patiently for the day's struggle. A cold breeze fingered the spruce trees, shaking off a patter of morning's rain. It hit the tent fly in a rattle of drops.

It was afternoon when we finally crawled into a clearing day of liquid skies and soap-bubble clouds. We decided to scout the country instead of breaking camp, and with the sun to our backs set off together, unconsciously turning upstream into the future. Chet stayed with the tent, happy for a day in camp.

As we hiked, water wheezed out holes in our summer shoepacs—boots that were never meant for eternal soaking. The rich blue of my checkered wool shirt had faded to gray across the shoulders; Phil's red one was patched in several places, as were our ragged jeans. We had lost perhaps twenty pounds apiece. My pants were held up at the waist with a hank of rope.

We followed the curve of river where the sandbar deteriorated into a shoreline of large stones. At the river bend we climbed a raw cutbank ten feet above the water. Softly we walked between spruce trees searching for rabbits. Each of us carried a rifle, prepared for large or small game. Amid the woodland paths, distinct in the slow-growing lichens, we wandered through tunnels of sunlight. At one point I heard a rustle and handed Phil the .22 rifle. I sat on the lip of the bank, the .30-06 resting easily between my knees, and watched the far shore where the trees were brushed with brilliance in the low sunlight.

I was daydreaming again, pretending that caribou were silhouetted on that bank. Caribou were about the right size, around three hundred pounds, and legal to shoot throughout the year. I had rehearsed the shot many times: just behind the elbow, a few inches up from the belly line, as my mother had taught me. I was like Kipling's mongoose, Rikki-tikki-tavi, who had never met a live cobra before, though his mother had fed him dead ones. I had already downed several hundred animals in this fashion, from every imaginable angle, using even the .22 and my pocketknife.

I heard the crunch of gravel as Phil rejoined me, squatting in his customary vulture position. We traded rifles and then sat watching the far shore in comfortable silence. It was a wide bend, the bank obliquely across from us perhaps a hundred yards away. A rocky bar gave way abruptly to a forest of stunted black spruce and muskeg—a swampy broken terrain peculiar to the Arctic. My gaze flowed up the shore and scaled the luminous peaks beyond. Snow yet lingered among the high, barren rocks and I watched the white patches intently to see if any were sheep. Then I dropped my eyes to the shoreline again.

"Phil! A moose!" My hand reached out to touch his leg.

On the beach across from us a dark shape was just entering the bushes. It hesitated with its rump to us, half screened by foliage. Phil dropped to a sitting position and pumped a shell into the .30-06 chamber, looping his elbow through the leather sling to stabilize the rifle. But he could see no place to shoot, the moose half screened by willows. We held our breaths. Come down on the beach! Please come down on the beach! I intoned silently, as if I could move the animal with my will.

It was then I saw the other animal. Small and brown, it flitted into the trees in front of the moose.

"It's a cow and calf!" I whispered, urgently. "We don't want to shoot a cow with a calf!"

At that moment we spotted the wolf, gray and white, maneuvering out behind the moose. I was startled by the thunder of the rifle. The wolf leapt sideways and vanished. Phil rammed another shell in.

"Damn! Missed him!"

The moose hadn't moved. Now it backed out of the willows and moved onto the beach. To the water it glided, shoulders rippling smoothly under the glossy, dark hide. It stood a moment broadside in the mellow sunlight. Big, velvety antlers sprayed back over the high shoulders as he poised at the water's edge.

"It's a bull! It's a bull!" I couldn't believe my eyes.

Phil sighted through his scope. The moose flinched as the bullet struck. I had a sinking feeling. We could not kill this forest spirit with a tiny flake of metal. He would dissolve away wounded into the bushes, leaving his tracks to fill with the river and melt into faceless sand.

"Shoot him again!" I urged.

Phil shot. The moose shivered and turned to disappear into the brush. Holding our rifles aloft, we plunged down the bank and into the muddy river. We gripped our free hands tightly to steady one another as, kicking against the broken bottom, we were swept toward the rapids below. Gradually the water became shallower and soon we were able to wade. The tension was unbearable as we walked back upstream toward the beach. Wet mud told the story in deep footprints. We skirted them, looking.

"Blood!" Phil whispered in relief, stooping to touch dark splashes on the rocks.

Then through the trees we saw him. He was lying in the moss, fuzzy antlers turning gracefully as he looked about. Phil fired a final shot from where we stood into the back of his splendid head. We took our time approaching the fallen specter, giving him privacy to die in peace. My mother used to say that the animal should never know what hit him.

Studying the tracks, we pieced the story together. When the moose first hit the beach, both wolves were behind him. Then the one I had mistaken for a calf moved to the front while the gray one crept close to his heels. At the first shot, the wolves dispersed and the moose turned for the safety of the river.

I have since seen moose do this many times. They are excellent swimmers and can often leave their natural predators behind. Healthy adult moose may stand their ground against wolves, and it is generally the old, young, and sick that fall prey.

"Give me a hand," Phil called. "Let's see if we can turn him on his back. My word but he's solid! Maybe a thousand pounds. Ought to last us awhile."

The moose was very deep through the chest and had long slender legs. While I balanced him on the ridge of his spine, Phil twisted the heavy neck backward, planting the spread of antlers in the moss. His coat was short and sleek with summer, a rich chocolate brown with cool, blond legs and a warm, gray belly. Like his upper legs and chest, his throat was black, and from it dangled a shiny black "bell." The split hooves were small and neat for his size, deer feet of polished black with matching dew claws. The tail was tiny.

It was his remarkable face that held my attention. The nose was unusually long and slender, delicate almost. His long lips were sensuously soft; the nostrils elongated into slits that could be closed when underwater. Big ears were placed near the top of his head and below these, a ridge of bone extended across his forehead. From either side of this grew the trunks of fuzzy, new antlers. Beneath the antlers were large and gentle brown eyes, clear as glass and open in the vacant gaze of death.

I left Phil and his pocketknife to their task and started a fire of driftwood down on the rocky shoreline before heading back to camp for the canoe. It was already chilly, the sun gone, and a purple twilight blanketed the fading land.

I laughed as I splashed into the river and I emerged laughing on the far shore. Carelessly I skipped over the rocks in my squishy boots, oblivious to the unnecessary noise. How beautiful and gentle was the Arctic that evening! I arrived back at camp still laughing after my mile run.

By the time I returned to the moose towing the empty canoe with Net-Chet aboard, midnight dusk lay deep over the ground. The land seemed strangely quiet and empty. When Phil appeared out of the trees and came down to greet us, Chet sniffed him suspiciously. Feeling chilled and stiff, I sat down with a groan on the bare rocks to rebuild the dead fire. Phil hadn't taken a break since I left him, and only a few scattered coals remained. He knelt and began to blow softly on the embers.

"Did you check where your bullets went?" I asked.

"They were within three inches of each other, so my shooting isn't off. It's the scope. They were both in the paunch. He could have lived for days. Now I'm sure I missed the wolf."

"Wolf? You shot at the wolf? Why?"

"I couldn't have killed the moose at that angle," he reasoned. "Besides, we agreed not to shoot a mamma, but we had to get something."

"You look tired." I said. He didn't respond. "How about some dinner?"

Phil returned to the moose while I set a bucket of saltless, muddy water on the fire to boil and dropped in pieces of meat and fat from the quarter he had hauled down to the beach. Then I climbed the twilit bank. Phil looked up from the steaming carcass. Knee-high piles of guts surrounded him and the ground was saturated with blood. A strong smell of hot meat and viscera hung in the chill air.

"How do you suppose we'll ever dry it all before the flies get it?" I asked.

"It'll be a job," he smiled wearily. "But it's worth it! Look!" He spread his arms. "No more worry about food." I looked instead at his gaunt face. "Glut yourself! No more wasting all day hunting for squirrels and gulls."

"Ours, all ours!" I gloated with him, still not believing it.

"Until the flies wake up," he replied soberly.

After a meal of tough, boiled meat and tea we finished cutting up the moose and together lugged the pieces down to the canoe. Mist curled off the painted water and early morning dampness hung in the air as we heaved the slippery pieces aboard, one at a time. In went a five-gallon bucket of organs and fat I had stripped from the intestines. In went the liver. Even the emptied stomach found a place in our load.

When we had finished, we sat wearily by the dying coals a last minute, enjoying the warmth on our stiff, damp bodies. Chet lay nearby, groaning loudly from the pain in her distended belly. I felt like kicking her.

"He's pretty lean. Not compared to the horse perhaps, but lean anyway," Phil commented.

"I noticed that." My mother had told us that a person could starve to death on lean meat. The Eskimos call it "rabbit starvation," she had said. In civilization we never see truly lean meat, for domestic stock is bred to "marble" fat into the muscle. At best, moose meat has less than half the calories of lean beef.

"Well, hopefully they will be fatter by fall." I stretched my stiff legs out. "It'll be good to dry our clothes out tonight," I said, pulling at the blood-caked fabric of my pants.

"This morning," he corrected. Behind him a washed turquoise sky crept northward beyond the luminous, yellow clouds, heralding a new day. I could see the lines of fatigue on his face by the growing light. Phil had always seemed so strong and dependable. I looked at him now, small and fallible, just like me. I had thought of him as older and stronger. I suddenly realized that he needed me as much as I did him if we were going to survive.

CHAPTER 4

I was pulled from two hours of dreamless sleep into a rosy dawn by the cries of birds. A family of gray jays descended from the woods—dark forms gliding across the tinted river. A pair of charcoal-plumed juveniles floated behind their grizzled parents, all of them stashing meat and fat in the trees. Eagerly they ripped off chunks and filled their craws, then departed to disgorge into secret niches and return for more. Food is precious and it belongs to the one who eats it. These persistent thieves can carry off an entire moose given the opportunity.

I shut my eyes, and sank into the sleeping bags seeking unconsciousness in the soothing whispers of the river. But the birds were stealing our meat. I had to get up.

Jays were not our only guests. I crawled from the tent and pulled on my cold, stiff trousers. Three ravens extended their wings for balance as they tore into the moose. Even a mew gull had joined the banquet. I stretched and shut my eyes. My head throbbed with fatigue and the eyelids felt like sandpaper. I pushed my contact lenses into place. Sleeping with them at the corners of my eyes was a trick I had learned years before on the Mackenzie River. It worked when there was no clean way to handle them, and I hadn't taken them out all summer. When I opened my eyes, the moose and birds were still there. Already the flies were waking up.

Pulling on my mildewed socks and boots, I left the laces to flop and began gathering driftwood. The lower beach was swept clean, but the higher willows were matted with sticks. Further inland stood a spruce forest, and from this came the sound of chopping. A sturdy frame of poles, perhaps eight feet high and ten on a side, was taking shape down near the canoe: a rack to dry meat on. Toward this I turned with my arms full of wood.

At my approach the ravens skipped back a pace, watching me with impatience. The disjointed carcass lay on a bed of cut willows, long legs arrayed to enhance air circulation. On the windward side I kindled a fire to discourage the flies, then squatted in the sand and began to skin the big, furry head.

Resting on its own velvety stand of antlers, the head stared bleakly at the ground. Starting at the throat, I slit the thick hide down to the wiggly pad of his chin then slipped the skin back from the long jaw bones. Here the lips confronted me. Like the chin, they seemed integral with the hide, whiskers growing from deep within the spongy, cream-colored tissue. The lips were covered inside with gray and white cone-shaped bumps about a quarter of an inch long. The bottom front teeth, long and loose, meshed with a hard pallet of gray and white scales. There were no upper front teeth. The mouth was still warm, and white fly eggs crusted the gums. I shook the head and irritable buzzes echoed from inside the cavernous nostrils and sinuses.

The day was emerging, bleached and flat, without shadow or color. Haze from distant forest fires muffled the valley, erasing familiar marks from our mountains. Remote and aloof they seemed now in the bright, empty sky. The still air felt dense and sticky. Into the breathless heat of morning I worked skinning the head, adrift in the drone of countless flies.

Phil finished constructing the rack and lashed the poles together with wire, guying the structure with parachute cord. Over it he tied a big, plastic tarp. We had brought the tarp to waterproof under the sod roof of our cabin. Now we used it to hold smoke around the meat, protecting it from flies as well as rain. Phil raked coals from the fire and started two more. Then he sat nearby in the sand boning out the ribs.

"Where do they all come from?" I asked, shooing flies as I worked. "They must smell meat for miles." I had peeled the heavy hide down to the white sockets of the eyes and the base of the antlers. Kneeling next to the head, I tried to remove the jaw bones. I leaned back and wiped the sweat from my eyes. "I can't get the tongue out."

"Try cutting along the bottom of the jaw," Phil suggested, glancing up from his work. "Are you hungry?"

I nodded and paused to run the steel over my knife. A steel keeps a finished edge on the knife so that it doesn't need to be sharpened as often. Phil had taken a butchering course at the university our last semester and bought good cutlery.

The day was turning hot. There was a brooding feel to the sultry air. I set the steel on a pile of neck meat. The slender jaw bones extended about eighteen inches, gradually closing to join at the front teeth in a small arch of bone. I ran my pocketknife along the inside of each bone. Pulling the tongue out and back, I severed it near the neck, exposing the mouth cavity. The tongue, like the mouth, was a slate gray, its upper surface roughened while the bottom was smooth.

Phil was preparing breakfast, squatting by a cooking fire as he sliced meat on a piece of driftwood. I got stiffly to my feet and rinsed the tongue in the river. Filling a bucket with water I set the tongue on the fire to boil. Then I sat in the sand and accepted a cup of spice tea and a fork. The fork was crusted with grime and I wiped it on my pants, which were already stiff with gore from loading the great, slippery quarters into the canoe the night before.

"We can cook the meat off the head if you can figure some way to chop it up," I said. "I've cut all I can from the outside. The quarters should keep several days, but the head and organs are going fast." Large pieces of meat skin over in the air and remain good for some time if kept relatively cool.

"What do you want to do about the liver?" he asked. There was about twenty-five pounds of it.

"I thought we'd try drying it. Stomach too. If nothing else, we can use it for dog food. I want to save every morsel we can. We ought to render most of the fat down, but we can try drying some too. I don't know how well it'll dry. I suspect it'll turn rancid, but we can try. There really isn't much."

I forked a strip of fried tenderloin from the skillet and sat chewing. It was lean and dark. My gums were sore from poor diet, but I relaxed in contentment at the rich flavor. Phil was silent, also engrossed in chewing. Unless you have known hunger, you cannot know the simple joy of eating.

Behind him the rows of poles were already draped with thin strips of unsalted moose meat. The reason meat deteriorates is that it is good food for microorganisms and insects. One method of preserving it is to remove water. We could have used salt or sugar in this process, but it's unnecessary. The Indians felt the taste of "drymeat" is spoiled by these additives.

Phil and I worked together through the heat of the day and into evening, cutting and turning the strips as they crusted on one side. With the gradual descent of twilight, the birds and flies went to sleep, but we continued our labor, slicing meat and tending the fires in shifts throughout the long night hours.

❉

On the second day a wind began, and by the third we could hardly see through the blowing sand that scoured the beach. Nearly blinded by the tireless cold blast, we sat and sliced, determined to save our meat. Wind ripped away the tarp, shredding it, and sand drifted over the falling jerky. Our eyes became swollen from smoke and sand as we clung to the fires for warmth. Day and night we took turns, catching snatches of sleep as we worked.

We finished cutting the last quarter into strips on the fourth day, and began the process of breaking and boiling the long bones for their fat. The wind subsided and we started to take in dried meat, sorting and packing it away. Thicker pieces were sliced again and laid on a tarp. There were surprisingly few maggots, and apart from sand, we seemed to be getting things under control.

Then clouds drifted in, layer upon layer of dark ships, blotting out all hope. By evening of the fifth day it had started to drizzle. Perhaps we could have salvaged something, but our plastic tarp was in tatters and the job overwhelmed us. We were at the end of our endurance. Exhausted and defeated, we retreated into the tent. A quiet, drenching rain fell for twenty straight hours while we slept.

When the rain ceased we crawled out to survey the damage. Rows of foul-smelling rubbery jerky awaited us. Flies swarmed over the meat, depositing their ugly broods. We restarted the fires, determinedly picking up the cause after our long rest. I began by dragging the hide and bones back into the woods and washing down the beach with buckets of water. My liver-drying experiment had failed, and much of it too disappeared into the trees. The bed of willows had handfuls of fly eggs, and I gave it all to the fish. By afternoon a surprising amount of order had been restored.

Evening found me sitting cross-legged in the damp sand, munching raw kidney fat as I sliced the half-cured meat on my lap. Smoke swirled around me in the chill night air. Phil was sleeping the first shift in the nearby tent. With practiced ease I sorted the jerky, noting with satisfaction how rapidly it was redrying. My cold hands were tender from a dozen knife cuts. At intervals I would stretch them toward the flames. We should be seeing stars soon, I thought as a great, golden moon rose out of the smoky blue north. It was the first full moon we had seen all summer. In the Arctic, the moon is visible for two weeks and gone for two. One sees only the sliver phases during the summer and the fuller ones in winter.

August, the month the stars return, I thought. In more temperate climates, August is considered summer, but here the Northern Hemisphere was clearly past solstice, revolving back into cold and darkness. Time for us to be underway; to find a place of our own.

Distant trees stood etched clearly against the eastern sky where a band of yellow bled into blue-gray. Rocking forward I sucked in the chill smell of autumn and exhaled it as steam. I reached for a piece of wood and cracked it over my knee before feeding it into the fragrant blaze. Slowly the fire tasted it, sending yellow flames up from the coals.

Before me appeared a secret cabin, warm and candlelit. It had a cozy stove in the middle and maybe a fireplace at one end. How could I manage a fireplace? Would mud and rocks work? In my mind I gathered and placed rocks. An open fire is very cheerful, but chimneys draw warm air out too, I considered. There were Plexiglas windowpanes and I arranged them all on the south side for maximum sunlight during the arctic winter. If only I had some white paint to brighten the interior. I could peel the logs; that would help.

I sniffed the hushed air and listened before continuing my dreams. It had to have a floor. Rock perhaps, but that seemed as cold and unappealing as dirt. My parents had a dirt floor the year they wintered on the Alatna River. Most of the old cabins did. Moose hide stretched over poles maybe? If only we had a way to ripsaw lumber . . .

I glanced up again and scanned the dark bushes, feeling suddenly vulnerable. Something disquieting hung on the edge of my thoughts making my skin prickle. Outlines were uncertain and seemed to shift and fade, alien and remote. I'm just not accustomed to darkness, I assured myself, returning to the task. After a summer of constant light, the deepening twilight seemed to brood with unseen menace.

My little cabin failed to reappear. I could not shake the feeling that someone was watching me. A cold sensation crept up the back of my neck. To hell with it, I decided at last. It may be silly, but I'm going to bed. With a last look at the dark woods, I joined Phil in the tent, zipping the fragile screen door shut against the night.

While scouring the beach for wood the next morning, I found the grizzly tracks, big as dinner plates. He had come upon us in the dusk, a shadow among shadows, to linger at the forest edge. As in a half-remembered dream, I traced the silent footprints to the bone pile, sensing each track materialize before me in the sand. Appearing out of nothing, one by one, they drifted back into the trees and dissolved in the moss.

❀

Eleven days after we killed the moose, we were back on the river. We were stronger now and rested, ready to take up the journey again. I hopped over the stones with Net-Chet tucked under one arm until camp was left behind. She hadn't wanted to come. Out in the current, Phil strained with the canoe. The river had dropped and rocks now peppered the rapids. The canoe seats were ladened with two wooden crates and a duffel bag of dried meat—the moose reduced to perhaps 250 pounds of jerky, rendered tallow, and marrow cooked from leg bones.

The water pouring endlessly by our familiar shore had cleared to a deep green. It was evening, calm and cool, and a light sprinkle pattered occasionally over the wet stones, squeezed from an expanding sky. The day had been one of cleanup and repair. I had boiled our stale clothing while we bathed and played in the clean water. It had rained off and on all day as we sorted and packed the moose and our belongings.

When we reached the wide bend where the moose had been shot, we loaded the dog into the canoe, and straddling the boxes of meat, paddled hard for the far shore. I left Phil toiling slowly upriver with a disconsolate Net-Chet, and walked inland a few yards to check the kill site. The area had been a scene of great activity. Everything was gone. Even the ground was scraped bare and embossed with the teeth marks of wolves.

Taking a last look, I ran to catch up with the canoe, settling into an awkward trot over the stones. I could see Phil plodding into the distance, small in the gathering dusk. From atop the load intermittent screeches of loneliness drifted from Net-Chet's little backward-facing figure.

"We repaid the wolves," I said, slowing to a walk beside the canoe. "They returned with their pups—or a small army of foxes," I grinned and handed him the black tail feather of a raven. "Everyone was there, even our bear. He uprooted several small trees." We walked for a time in silence, me on shore, Phil a few yards out in the current. "Moose guts are what we need this fall to attract a bear," I decided. "Bears have fat on them. My mother said we need to get a bear for our winter fat."

Phil's patched boots made sucking sounds in the wet gravel. He looked older in his shaggy beard. His big, green eyes seemed strangely hawk-like, offset in a lean face by the jutting nose and predatory brows. His lips were chapped and weathered. The muscles in his neck and forearms knotted in cords as he threw his weight into the rope. If Phil were a tree, I decided, watching him, he would be a spruce: somber, slow to change, dependable, strong. I'd probably be a birch or aspen: spontaneous, sun-dappled in summer, full of life and color; withdrawn into my roots in winter. I wondered suddenly how I looked now.

❦

Three days of lining upriver passed and discouragement again settled upon us. Travel was as hard as ever. We were checking another river bend for possible cabin sites. Somewhere above me I could hear Phil traversing the scantily forested hillside. On the steep slope below, our evening camp punctuated the wilderness as a small splash of orange. Next to it, a singing rapids, white and emerald, caught the late evening sun. Already the gray shoreline sank into shade. Emerging sheer and dark from the waves stood a great stone monolith, perhaps a hundred feet high, splitting the bright current. It was a memorable and awesome sight, with lichen-colored cliffs dropping into the river and a top fringed in trees.

I knotted a strip of rope about my waist securing my pants, and tucked my handkerchief into a back pocket. We had only ten rolls of toilet paper to last a year and needed to use them sparingly. Early in the trip I had adopted this method, washing my special kerchief in the river frequently. It worked far better than sticks and moss. I also had a year's supply of tampons. My mother had washed old socks on her expeditions.

I scanned the hill restlessly. The cabin needed to be high enough to avoid flooding and on relatively level, firm ground. We wanted a southern exposure to catch the winter sun. There had to be enough dead-standing timber nearby for building and fuel. As we progressed north and climbed into the mountains, good trees were becoming scarce. We were now at fourteen hundred feet and tree line was around two thousand, but there was great variation in timber due to drainage and soil conditions. At best this country sported crooked flag poles and often only muskeg. From a distance, muskeg may look like firm ground— for it can be found on the side of a hill where one would not expect bog—but it is broken, wet, and fissured by frost.

Phil appeared above me, working his way down the uneven slope. He shook his head. "Nothing here."

On the sandbar below us the small, wailing figure of Net-Chet shrilly proclaimed her loneliness to the world.

Phil was studying the map. "Tomorrow, let's see if we can find the old trail that's supposed to cut from here over to the creek," he said pointing northward along the base of the mountains. "There should be an old cabin or two, and maybe we will find something useful." Ahead the river swung to the other side of the wide valley. There it traveled for some miles, snugged against foothills, before angling back at the junction of a creek. The valley between the bends looked swampy.

I nodded and Phil started down through the trees. Soon we were in deeply rutted muskeg. Under the thin mat of vegetation, melting pockets of ice—remnants of glaciation—left the ground in chaotic collapse. The riverbank itself was greatly undercut. As I lowered myself carefully over the tangle of mud and branches to the sandbar, I could see dirty ice beneath it, ice that was thousands of years old.

Net-Chet was overjoyed at our return, wagging and circling our legs in delight. While Phil set the teapot on, I lifted a bucket of boiled "drymeat," our standard meal, from the coals and sat down on a log.

"My jaws are sore," I grumbled, chewing monotonously. "You'd think it would soften some." My gums were tender too. Phil joined me, stabbing into the pot with his pocketknife for the dark, leathery strips.

"How about a treat?" I suggested. "We haven't had one in quite awhile."

"Treat?" He turned slowly toward me, opening his eyes wide.

I had to laugh at his little boy act. "Sure. Maybe some oatmeal." This was a thin gruel sweetened with saccharin. Sometimes I would add a handful of the ripening blueberries and call it "pudding."

Tonight I made pudding. We ate in silence for a time. I was lost in a dream of the cabin, still unable to construct a floor. I slipped from my sitting log onto the sand and began tracing the floor plan. Phil scooted around to watch.

"How big a structure do you have in mind?" he asked presently.

"Big," I answered. "Big enough to live in all winter."

"I had thought to put up a little cabin, say eight by ten and four and a half feet high, and at least have a home before snow falls," he suggested.

"That's what all these old places look like," I countered, already defensive. "Holes to crawl into out of the weather. I want a real home. I want bookshelves so we can look at our books whenever we want, and a kitchen table, and a high snug bed. Most of all I want a floor."

He just shook his head. We both knew the trees were too twisted to split and that we had no way to ripsaw boards. We are tuning in to one another,

I thought watching him study my drawing: relinquishing the snappy come-back to listen to each other.

"It's so difficult to get a foothold," I admitted. "So incredibly hard. Like drying the moose without even a table or a cutting board. Maybe what we need is to set up a shed roof first so we can at least stand up on rainy days. Just being able to keep dry would make such a difference."

"I like that idea," he answered. "I must admit I'm burned out on this upstream travel."

"What do you think we'll find at those old cabins?" I asked casually. I'd been daydreaming about a cast-iron skillet. It was a silly dream and embarrassed me. We would be lucky to salvage a few nails or old tin cans for scrap metal. "Maybe we'll find a new skillet," I hinted. Our cheap Teflon skillet was warped and ineffectual.

Phil looked sheepish. "How about a big can of strawberry jam?" he asked innocently. "That's the sort of thing that people leave behind, isn't it?"

I had to laugh. So he'd been dreaming too.

"Right! And some white paint for the walls. I want our home to be airy and light inside. And lumber."

"Crackers and canned milk."

"Your mind is on food," I teased. "What about a sled?"

"More tools . . ."

"A cast-iron stove with an oven. What I wouldn't give for a good stove. I know our little folding steel one will work, but wouldn't it be grand if we found a good one?" We had purchased a fifty-five gallon drum to make into a stove, but left it with the truck for lack of space. "Think we could carry it away if we found one?"

"If we find it, I'll carry it," he assured me.

Next morning we set out early and soon found the old trail. The path was rough and game-maintained but carried the decisive bent of human thought. Straight and intentional it ran, slicing above the two-mile loop of river and hugging the fringe of stunted spruce that separated the mountain from the lower muskeg. As we climbed, a wild land of lakes and nesting ducks spread below us, already yellowing with autumn. At times the trail formed a zigzag slot where our unseen feet groped and slid in black mire, through muskeg. Here wobbly tussocks of cotton grass protruded from an icy bog. These sprouted so thickly in spots that we could not see the "ground." Beneath the chocolate ooze was the slick hardness of ice.

Net-Chet had a grand time, burrowing along or leaping on the deceptive hummocks, her nose quivering with news of other animals. It was good to see her having fun. Into a tunnel she plunged to emerge crunching a rabbit's foot— leavings of some hunter. A young junco flitted unsteadily to a twig before her, little body bristling with half-grown feathers, but Chet was unaware, nose in the grass, furry bottom wagging at the sky.

The trail nestled into the mountain, becoming drier as we climbed. We found ourselves traversing splashes of birch between mature stands of spruce trees, their red-brown bark smelling of vanilla in the morning sunlight. Moss replaced the muskeg, and shiny, red cranberries popped underfoot as softly we trod the carpet. A crisp smell of fall washed down from nearby peaks, min- gling with the scent of Labrador tea and blueberries. Birch trees fluttered, shaking the light from their leaves. Birds that had been silent with the care of nestlings now called repeatedly to fledglings that darted clumsily before us.

As we curled into the mountain cleft, we came suddenly upon the rem- nants of an old garden. It was choked with alder, and its split-wood fence was returning to soil. Inside were a homemade wheelbarrow and a hoe. A few more steps brought us to the rotting abutments of a log bridge.

We hopped the creek on stones and spent some time scouting around for the cabin. Animals had confused the trails. Moose tracks stabbed deeply into the sod, and bear diggings obscured the old ruts. Then, through the trees I spied a gold and purple swath of fireweed, which always seems to grow where man has been.

We broke into the clearing and stood for a moment in silence. There was something secret about the place, a sheltered sense of care. Unlike the ghost town, this fragile bubble of history had been lost in the timeless wilderness and forgotten. No human voice had disturbed the memories here for forty years. No alien thought had violated the spell. Even as we stepped forward, time seeped into the glade, and a sigh whispered past us as the memories began to fade.

Before us were several structures in various stages of decay. Between them stood a sturdy little cache, untouched by decades of rain and snow. It was about eight feet square and firmly rooted on four-foot posts. The logs were peeled and neatly dovetailed at the joints. From its sod roof, half-grown trees sprouted. Still solid and snug, it was the work of a man who understood wood and enjoyed it.

We spent the day there forming a strange friendship with the past. It was indeed strawberry jam day. Here were the tools we had thought to do without.

Here too were ideas from one who had known and loved this land. We collected the scattered utensils, bottles, nails, and cans from about the clearing and carefully stashed them in the little cache. I watched anxiously while Phil wriggled under the wreckage of the main cabin to hand out other treasures.

"Hey, there's a wooden floor under here!" he exclaimed from beneath the rubble of twisted logs and sod.

"Do you think we can dig it out and salvage it? Be careful," I called as his feet disappeared into the rotting pile.

Gradually, we pieced together the life of Chris Olson—for this was his name, as we discovered from labels on crates. People reveal themselves through their possessions. Though long dead, Chris was to become a special friend to us, and much of our well-being we owe to that long-ago man.

Chris Olson enjoyed the North. There were other men in the woods then looking for ways to endure the Depression, yet Chris was different: he made this country home. It was evident in his garden and makeshift inventions.

Chris was a man who took care of his tools. He kept sled dogs, and when they died he buried them in little graves covered with rocks and surrounded by tiny fences. He ate moose and caribou. In winter he trapped, forging wide trails up and down the creek for his sled. He wore shovels and picks down to stubs, one swing at a time, looking for gold. I could almost see him there, digging, as I peered into the cavernous hole over which an outhouse teetered, the hand-made seat worn smooth by use. Whipsawed lumber, I thought, touching the ancient boards. If only we can find a place to build, I will have a floor!

Years later, I learned that Chris sank a shaft 190 feet only to be drowned out by the creek. He had grown old in this cabin, though he had been in the valley for years. He left a few white hairs caught inside the cache, metal rim spectacles by his bed, and medicine bottles. He lived alone, sleeping in a wooden frame filled with dried grass. He was a big man (or at least he had big feet). He shaved with a soap stick and straightedge razor. He didn't read much, maybe he couldn't, but he had a collection of 78 rpm records and a wind-up Victrola.

It was winter when Chris Olson died. He put his snowshoes by the door, his handmade skis in the cabin, and his tools down in the midst of daily living. On his sled a load of firewood remained, dissolving into moss. Perhaps he weakened slowly, using up supplies. Maybe death came upon him suddenly—a heart attack or an accident. His chained dogs starved in their houses, dwindling to piles of bones. Quiet settled over the clearing.

A friend came by in summer and buried Chris in the little fenced garden before his cabin door, covering the grave with stones from the creek. He took those things he needed and could carry back across the mountains. So the records stayed and the Victrola went and perhaps an ax or auger. For us, Chris Olson left wooden kegs for storing berries and clean tin cans. Here were axes, shovels, and picks. There was a mattock, a sledge, a vice, a maul, an anvil, hammers, planes, and a bucksaw. There was even a Yukon stove, larger and of better quality than ours, with a stovepipe oven and cake pans to fit. He had tools for working wood and metal. There were enamel dishes, silverware, cooking pots, a dishpan, a ceramic bean pot, a glass kerosene lantern, and a big teakettle.

To other eyes, these gifts might have seemed shabby. They were worn by use and weather, caked with mud, mildew, and rust, but in a land of trees and rocks, a nail—no matter how bent—is a nail. We laughed and grubbed, oblivious to the sinking sun, until twilight overtook us.

It was dusk when we left the clearing, descending the spine of a ridge that paralleled the stream. My arms were ladened with tools that I hoped soon to use: a shovel and a mattock—a heavy hoe with an ax on one side of the head. Somewhere during the afternoon, clouds had drifted in unnoticed, and a fine drizzle narrowed our darkening world. Net-Chet, now cold and weary, waddled gamely along, staying close to my legs. An old trail, wet and rutted with moose tracks, led down the ridge toward the river. This route, if it were passable, would take us some miles out of our way, but give us added knowledge of the country. We hesitated a moment at the fork, then committed ourselves to the strange course.

We made good time until the path topped a rocky knoll and disappeared. Below us, the creek dropped sharply and we could hear it cascading into the gloom several hundred feet down to our right. Ahead, the gray evening sky melted into the valley floor. Finding no trail in the eerie half-light, we cut for the river, cleaving off the crest into a thicket of aspen. As we descended with our tools, clanking and thrashing through branches, the night seemed to listen. Driven back by our stumbling, silence flowed in behind us, drawing up the shadows. I thought suddenly of bears. Hair prickled on my neck and I fought back the fear of being lost in this unfamiliar darkness.

We finally blundered from the steep hillside into a dense, black forest. Between the spruce trees we once more picked up a scanty path overhung by dripping foliage. Our feet sought out the faint trail that our eyes could not see, seeking the packed ground in the darkness. Our pants became soaked by bushes. At last the big trees opened and our path slid from the timber down to the foggy river.

"We've got no one to miss us," I stated, dropping my load of tools on the wet rocks by the river. "Let's take care of ourselves."

I was relieved to be in the open, away from the brooding trees. Soon a bright circle of warmth enclosed us, pushing back the night. Fog rose from the river into the chill air, wrapping eerily about us. We sat on the slick rocks chewing jerky, our first meal since breakfast. I held the tired, wet puppy on my lap, turning and fluffing her before the blaze until she stopped shivering.

Net-Chet slept in Phil's arms the last miles as we plodded through a strange land beside the familiar song of the river, adrift in a shifting world of darkness and mist. The ragged shoreline wavered in the cold fog. Morning was stealing upon us when our little pile of belongings appeared unharmed out of the gray wilderness ahead.

❀

Two days later we passed the confluence of Chris Olson's Creek with the river. The water was very shallow and swift now, gushing mint green over shelving gray slate. A chill north wind whipped sheets of sand toward us, blistering our faces and gritting teeth and eyeballs.

"Nothing," I said under my breath as I paused to study the shore for cabin sites. We had discussed building near Chris Olson's cabin, but decided against it on several points. It was nearly a mile from the river and the canoe, we felt there would better hunting along the open bars, and old cabins have too many memories. We wanted our own place.

By afternoon we were almost a mile above the creek junction. I tucked my numb fingers under my armpits and glanced at Phil, trying to keep the despair from my eyes. "Let's cross to the island."

Net-Chet plunged bravely through the current as we crossed the channel, her head pressed to my knees to keep from being swept down-stream. She seemed unhappy most of the time, poor little beast, whining even to herself.

The island had a good stand of mature spruce. "Lot of trees," I said hope-fully. I grabbed the bow and hauled *Lady Grayling* firmly aground on a sloping sandbar at the tail of the island. "At least it's solid."

Phil met my gaze a moment and then pointed to the driftwood lodged back in the trees.

"It can't be too bad or the trees wouldn't grow." Angry tears filled my eyes. "Next year isn't likely to be the fifty-year flood, is it?"

"If we're going to build a cabin, it may as well last," he insisted, always so damn patient.

We traversed the island, emerging from the woods on the far side. Another island rose nearby, as well forested as the first. We waded a narrow, swift channel and paced to its head and out onto a long gravel beach.

"Phil, we've gotta find someplace soon!" I blurted out, my eyes flooding with misery. I sank down onto the rocks and put my head in my hands. Net-Chet edged wetly into my lap, shivering. "The further we get from Chris's the harder it will be. We won't even get our floor!"

He sat quietly beside me and reached out to stroke my hair. "We'll find just the right place," he assured me. "You wait and see."

The river beyond was still and deep, an unusual sight. Here a string of five islands spread the river, damming it with a connecting ridge of submerged rock. This created a lake of quiet water that stretched away to the northeast reflecting the long sweep of hill and cliff, bounded perhaps a mile away by a white ribbon of rapids.

My attention was drawn to another island on which several ravens rested. Ravens are intelligent, long-lived birds, often associated with magic in Native folklore. They are larger than crows and can be surprisingly musical. These seemed to be involved in a ritual dance. I had never seen anything like it. They would draw together, raising their wings, then bounce upward to come fluttering down like leaves. We watched, transfixed by the odd ceremony.

"Come on," Phil roused me at last, "the west shore looks good from here. I think we can wade across along the rocks."

The reef led us diagonally upstream—rapids below, still pool above. As we came dripping ashore, a large white wolf flushed into the woods. From the gentle bank, a carpet of sphagnum moss and cranberries climbed smoothly between mature spruce trees up the knees of a hill. There was a safe boat landing and a broad southern exposure with a clear view of the islands and the mountains beyond. Twenty feet above the water, a narrow bench cut the slope, not actually level, but usable.

We crisscrossed the hill, calling out excitedly to one another as we explored it. Here at last was home, overlooking the five islands and quiet stretch of water. Abruptly our journey ended.

Satisfied and exalted, we retraced our steps for the canoe. After all the miles, at last we drew our load up snug against this shore and called it Home. Once these belongings had littered our living room floor in Tucson. Now they were here: down parkas, sugar, fishnet, gas lantern, snowshoes, books, flour, backpacks, underwear, rifles, traps, camera, toilet paper. How precious and small it all looked as we unloaded it onto the bank in the late afternoon sunlight.

That night I dreamed I was in a large school trying to find the right classroom. I was late and didn't know where to go. I ran down the hall, past rows of lockers. All the doors were closing and in desperation I chose one and entered. It was a calculus class and I sat in terror, unable to remember any calculus, knowing that soon I would be called upon.

For two days we worked with renewed vigor, axes flashing in the sun. We left the trees and ground cover alone as we cleared away thickets of alder and willow. While Phil started laying out the cabin foundation, I brushed a trail to the toilet hole and began to dig. We didn't build an outhouse. There was no need to screen ourselves from the view, and squatting by the hole was more comfortable in freezing weather than sitting. There were plenty of small trees to hold on to.

Nights were getting dark now, and cold. The second evening I startled a large black wolf behind camp. That night they started to sing, their wild spirits claiming the blackness. We could hear the older wolf voices, the parents, mingled with the young singsong of adolescents in the pride of their first fall. Net-Chet whimpered while I thought of cabin walls. It was a beautiful and haunting sound, deep and melodic. These were not my small desert coyotes, but powerful carnivores weighing as much as I and standing close to three feet at the shoulder. This was their valley. I knew that there were no documented cases of the North American wolf ever attacking humans, but under the night sky I felt very small and vulnerable.

By unspoken agreement, Phil cleared back the brush behind the tent the next morning.

The third night we spotted our first stars. Dusk came gliding into the clearing, stealing over the calm water and down out of the trees. I sat cross-legged on the cold ground, reading aloud by firelight. Near me, Phil looked worn but happy. His callused hands were carefully mending my frayed boots by the flickering light. Net-Chet rolled closer to the fire, whining irritably in her sleep as a faraway owl hooted.

Suddenly the shore seemed alive with wolves! The first we knew of them was Chet's startled "Woof!" They had not stumbled upon us, but circled down from three directions, pinning us against the river.

"Good heavens!" I whispered, grabbing the puppy. I leapt to my bare feet as Phil unzipped the tent for a rifle. It was too dark to see, but he fired a warning. A wolf just behind the tent moved nervously, and Net-Chet let fly, soaking my leg.

"They're all over the place!" I whispered, feeling conspicuous in the firelight. A powerful and ancient fear awoke in me. The hair rose along my neck as sleeping racial memories stirred. I was a child again facing the jaws of a Doberman. I was a primitive man in a world of big carnivores. I was barefooted. I was afraid.

The second shot slammed into a wolf a few feet away. The others circled further up the hill, retreating slowly with forlorn cries. Still we did not approach the fallen animal. It lay just beyond the firelight, ominous and black. Finally Phil handed me the rifle and cautiously moved toward the carcass.

It was a young male, a puppy of Chet's age. Although the size of an adult German shepherd, he still had his milk teeth. He was gray with a dark muzzle and very large paws. He had died suddenly, a big hole blown through his thin chest and a look of surprise in his golden eyes.

"Why, he's only a puppy, just hide and bone," Phil said, stroking the long, scanty fur. "I wonder what they were doing?" He took out his pocketknife and began to slip off the skin, bending low in the flickering light.

I watched the shadows uneasily, hoping nothing would appear. A last grieving call drifted down the hillside and floated out across the river.

Fear, like frost, melts in the morning sun. We awoke to a crisp August day. Buttermilk clouds printed the pale, blue sky. Net-Chet, however, had not forgotten. Perhaps she had never really believed in wolves, but the stories in the grass had come true. She screamed in horror whenever she was startled and refused to leave my side. For his part, Phil tanked up on tea and set about marking our boundaries, wolf-style.

I fried wolf liver for breakfast. Phil finished skinning the head and extracting the brains to use in tanning. The stomach was nearly empty, containing two mice and some blueberries, leaves and all. When food is scarce, wild animals eat what they can find. The meat was the light pink of a young animal. It had very little smell, but tasted much as you might expect wolf to taste, slightly musky. Net-Chet refused to touch it and went hungry.

Days passed in toil. Phil lined out the cabin using a plumb bob made from a .30-06 bullet. His level, known as "Phil's almost level," was a medicine bottle from Chris filled with water and tied to a stick. He cut and removed sods from the site, thankful for the heavy mattock and shovel. These we stacked out of the way to be planted later on the cabin roof. We dug into the hill, leveling the bare earth and setting large stones as a foundation. I made numerous cross-country trips to Chris Olson's cache for tools and worked on digging the toilet. At three feet I hit what I thought was slate rock, but a few days later it had thawed into mud and I realized that it was "permafrost," the permanently frozen ground of the Arctic.

Blueberries were ripe, and I spent much time collecting winter stores. Cranberries were more numerous and would withstand frost, so I left them for later. Chet often accompanied me, complaining of our slow progress: berry-picking bored her. On my frequent trips to the cache, I started cutting a trail, running it straight up the hill away from the river. Then it would run southwest to "Cranberry Hill," the ridge overlooking Olson Creek, where I could pick up Chris's old trail. The land between was rough and deceptive.

Then the autumn rains began. Somewhere we had lost the violent storms of summer. For days the soft, drenching rain fell until the thick ground was a sponge to the foot and every ring of the ax brought cascades of ice water out of the dark trees. Streams appeared everywhere, excess water on its way through our camp to the sullen, brown river. Day after day our little pile of belongings sat drearily in the soaking rain.

We spent the time lying in our damp little tent listening to the drum of rain on the tarp and reading aloud from Michener's *Hawaii*. All about us poplar trees were turning gold and the tannic acid smell of fallen leaves lingered on the riverbars. Nowhere but in the tent was there a nook for us. We had no warmth, no place to dry wet clothes except next to our skins inside those clammy sleeping bags. We felt panic at the slipping days, but gained nothing by exhausting our cold bodies in the rain. So we lay in the bags, often fully clothed except for boots, and read. Our breath condensed and ran down the walls forming puddles, while rain beat endlessly down. We didn't even rise to cook, for it was nearly impossible to start a fire, and we would only end up soaked. We drank cold, muddy water from a bottle in the tent and chewed damp jerky, and dreamed about Hawaii.

We were grateful not to be on the river. Where once it had been a sunny stream, now it was cold and bleak. Even camped it was difficult to keep anything dry. Phil had almost finished tanning the wolf hide for winter mittens, but in the steamy dampness it began to mildew and became laced with maggots. The jerky turned sour and slimy, and we were plagued with diarrhea. It could have been caused by "rabbit starvation," the lack of fat in a protein diet, but at the time we thought it was the spoiled meat. Phil's stomach bothered him constantly, waking him in the night with pain.

I put away the book in the dim light and hunched further into the smelly down, tucking my cold hands between my legs. "It's too dark," I said. "I can't see the words." My body was sore from lying inert and the thought of another endless night made me irritable. "We should move the tent to give our backs a new set of lumps."

The monotonous patter of rain had lost its music. An odor of wet feathers and wool saturated the tent. Phil sat munching crumbs of jerky and lint from the cloth bag, his bearded head touching the roof while frigid air seeped into the bags. He looked thin in his dirty T-shirt. I ought to dig out our long-handled underwear, I thought. Everything seemed too much effort.

It was evident that we would consume the entire moose in less than six weeks. How many moose would we need to kill to see us through the winter? And where were they?

Phil stashed the jerky sack and slid back under the covers.

"Did you ever think how much we take food for granted?" I asked. "I have memories of supermarket aisles—food everywhere. Do you realize there is NOTHING you could do right now to get an apple?"

He groaned.

I was thinking that the "starving people of India" were always such a long way off. Unreal. What was it like to watch your child starve?

We were silent awhile. "I have really enjoyed my dreams lately," I told him suddenly. I smiled and rolled close, wrapping myself about his bony body, smelling the familiar unwashed whiskers. "Lately it's great gooey pastries, chocolate éclairs, donuts, apple turnovers, and strawberry shortcake with mountains of whipped cream. It's as if my brain is escaping the only way it can."

Net-Chet shifted in her sleep, pushing in the tent wall. She was preparing for winter with a downy set of underwear about an inch long. We hoped the guard hairs would come in later. She was dry under the tent fly, but insecure and unhappy to be out of the tent. Perhaps some ancient memory told her of the coming winter.

"That was some dream you had last night," Phil reminded me. He flopped onto his side, pounded his moist clothes into a pillow, and grinned, waiting for me to remember. His haggard face was strangely foreign in the gloom.

I frowned. "Yes . . . I was being attacked by wolves. One leaped at me and I shoved him onto his back. He was struggling and I could only hold his head back, my hands around his great furry throat . . ."

"My great furry throat!"

"That's right! That's right! Well what about the night you woke up chewing on my bra while dreaming about the world's toughest jerky?"

"Oh, I dreamed I conquered the Arctic in my chewed up bra!" he sang out into the evening. His thin voice was swallowed up in the great, dripping land.

Chet curled more tightly, whining in her sleep, her little body almost collapsing the tent wall. Outside I heard the rain stop and a soft wind begin. My intestines suddenly called and I bolted from bed. Grabbing the shovel (for I had yet to finish the toilet hole) I set rapidly off up the beach. My pink and white pajamas were now a uniform gray, worn through at the bunny feet and knees. I shivered in the wet sedges over my hastily constructed hole as a shower of drops spattered from an overhanging tree.

Across the river the leaves were gold and the grass was streaked yellow. Over the dusky water the sky was clearing. A single star shimmered in that deep patch of faraway blue. I covered the hole and started back. Phil met me going out in his bare feet, T-shirt, and ragged underwear. Silently I handed him the shovel.

The next morning we woke early to an icy south wind that smelled of snow. The sky was clear. Phil decided to use my new trail to cut logs at a place we called the "Cathedral Grove." It was a lovely group of trees up on the hill, almost parklike, with mature spruce trees and open spaces where we had already removed many of the dead snags.

It is dangerous to fell timber in a wind, but every day was precious. Taking his double bit ax comfortably in one hand, he draped the hauling slings over his shoulder and called Net-Chet. She had grown over the summer and was now a fifteen-pound beauty with a soft, showy coat. She had large, perky ears and a curly tail. She was beginning to lose her baby teeth and her baby shape. Cavorting on long, slender legs, she danced after him.

I finished digging thawed mud out of the toilet hole and spreading it on the trail. Taking my ax and berry pail, I grabbed a pocket full of jerky and set out for the day. Picking lint and sand from the drymeat, I ate as I climbed the hill. Already the voles were depleting the berries, leaving little piles of husks. I fell to grazing near the path, cranberries springing up under my fingers. The lacy leaves were fresh with dew, and a rich earth smell enveloped me as the ground began to warm.

I picked contentedly beneath the shifting flutter of yellow birch leaves. From the hill I could see a shifting vista of turquoise river adrift in autumn colors. The naked high country had turned to burgundy where arctic birch, bearberries, and blueberry bushes were brushed by frost. On the peaks a dusting of new snow touched the liquid sky.

Time is somehow different here, I thought, gazing over the valley. To say it is nine o'clock is meaningless. With the passing days, the jumble and trivia were fading from my mind. At first it was replaced by memory flashes, trite and forgotten episodes from that other world, exercises of an idle brain. Then fantasies appeared. Thoughts became as real as spoken words. Often Phil and I would work all day in near silence, each within his own world.

I was dreaming of moose meat and Thanksgiving. If only I could get two spruce chickens and hide them away, I would plan a grand surprise. Cotton clouds rolled past in the Indian summer sky. A squirrel was busy drying mush-

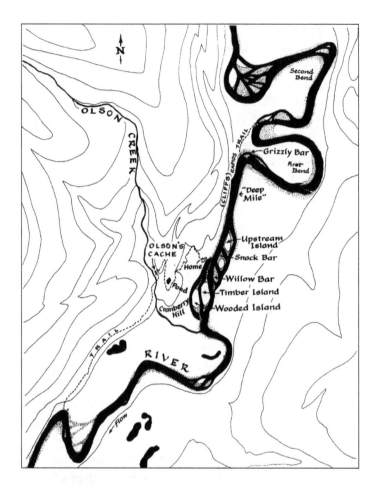

rooms for winter, hanging them in a nearby tree. Now what could I use for stuffing? Oatmeal, of course! And powdered onions, eggs, and sage. Yes, I would really prepare a feast, if only I could find those grouse.

I could hear Phil at work below me, the rhythmic knock of his ax carried distantly on the breeze, mingled with an occasional loud complaint from Chet. About noon I heard a prolonged shriek. It continued for some time and I concluded it must be a bird. Cranberry sauce, I thought. I would make cranberry sauce. I listened again, strangely uneasy.

I filled my berry bucket and left it by the trail as I continued on with Chris Olson's ax. I was learning not to fear a double bit and had become quite proficient with it. In work I discover my strength, listening to the repetitive swing of my body. By evening my trail extended half way up the hill, a hard-won ribbon of space, gliding through the trees behind me. Aldo Leopold wrote that each man kills the thing he loves. Perhaps it is true. I had debated over every twig cut.

It was too dark to swing an ax when I started homeward over my trail. How beautiful it looked in the twilight, that smooth snaking path; how differently it organized the hill. A flurry of startled white erupted before me, a wolf. I broke into the Cathedral Grove and saw that Phil had been hard at work, felling and hauling. From there to the river a little trough was gouged in the trail telling of the hours of lugging, sometimes with pulleys. How frail our efforts, but how tenacious. The real triumph of life is persistence.

I entered camp to find Phil in tears.

"We have a problem," he said miserably. Net-Chet took one step toward me and fell to screaming.

"I didn't mean to do it!" he sobbed. "She wouldn't stay put when I was dropping a tree and I just gave her a toss. Nothing, just tossed her. . . ."

I hugged him until he could talk.

"I tried to examine her," he told me, "but she's just in too much pain. I gave her one of those codeine capsules and then another later, but it didn't help."

I sat in the damp moss and carefully lifted the trembling puppy. She convulsed in pain and terror, lolling stupefied in the urine that soaked my lap. I began to cry too.

A great gray owl swooped low out of the trees to survey us and glide on, noiseless wings pumping the heavy body out over the water. Every predator within miles would come to the sound of a wounded animal. It was cold in the gathering dusk as we sat helplessly with our little bundle of misery.

"Maybe we should shoot her," Phil suggested in desperation. New tears filled his eyes. We both had grown to love her. "She hasn't had much of a life so far, has she?"

"No," I said, taking charge. "First bring me my medical kit."

Phil set to work on the splint I ordered, glad for something to do. I filled a syringe with Novocain and injected it into the left hind leg until the muscles relaxed. Gently I examined the leg. I could feel the slender bone ends grate together as the foot moved. Only one of the two parallel bones was broken and we could use its neighbor to help stabilize it. When Phil finished whittling the splint, we stretched her leg out and tied it down. Unfortunately we had no plaster, and a dog's foot isn't built for traction.

For three days we struggled, trying to keep Chet quiet and her leg immobile, but the traumatized muscles contracted relentlessly, pulling the poor little foot up and out. Her body was wracked with tremors and chills. Our bedding became soaked with urine. We even tried a modified sprained ankle bandage around her hock, but the pressure necessary for traction soon cut off circulation and the foot began to swell. Our hours were filled with the sounds of her misery, compounding our own.

As a last effort, we taped the hock, laying a strip of nylon cloth under the adhesive. This was tied to wire that bound the end of the willow splint. The top of the splint was forked and braced into a sling about her hip. If this failed, we would have to kill her. We moved her out of the tent and onto a clean bed of spruce boughs under a tarp. It was all we could do for her.

We sought our bags early that night. The air had that cold, crystal quality that promises frost—stinging into our nostrils even before the sun had faded. About midnight we woke with our usual need to visit the outdoors and discovered the northern lights. At first appearing as a green-white luminous cloud, the bright curtain crept toward us, poised and then lunged across the sky, trailing green fire in cold, aloof splendor.

Together we stood, shivering and hugging one another against the night, reluctant to retreat into the closeness of the tent. How expansive and glorious it seemed, that silken display put on for no one at all.

Jeanie holds Net-Chet while the Indians take us upriver.

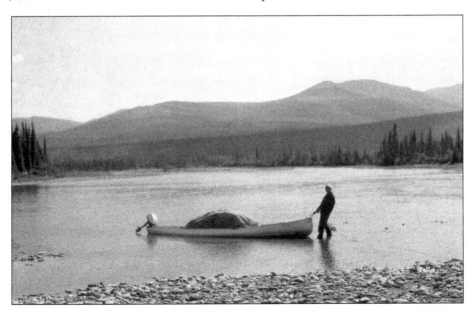

At last we enter the foothills of the Brooks Range.

Phil's twenty-fourth birthday.

Jeanie brings home a snowshoe hare.

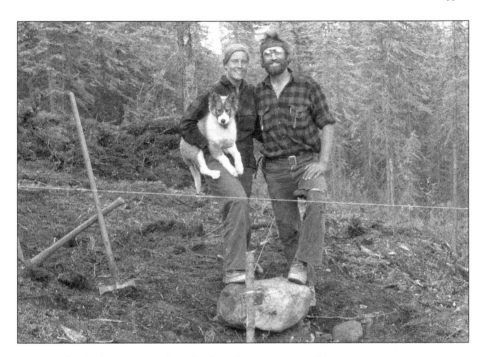

Happy to be off the river, we clear the foundation for our cabin.

Phil unloads the river moose.

Jeanie hangs a moose shoulder.

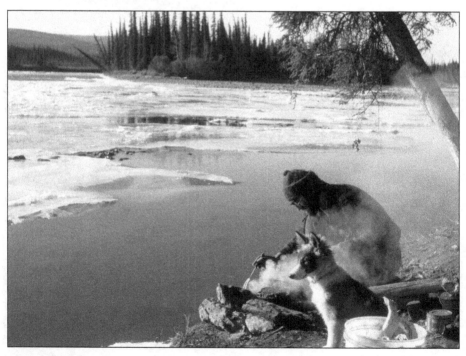

Freeze-up closes our exit, but we have food for winter.

CHAPTER 5

September arrived under icy rains and overcast skies. A few hardy mosquitoes remained, although less active. Occasionally we found cold and stiff caterpillars, hatched perhaps too late. Around our camp there was a brief frenzy of gnats mating in the ashes of our fire, drawn to the warmth. Spider backs were furry with their many-legged young. Soon all were gone, vanished with the summer.

I think I secretly hoped that winter would pass us by this year. How could it snow after the tropical days on the Yukon when my hair bleached white and my face burned brown under that endless summer sun? Now ice crept out at night, skinning over puddles.

Birds grew restless, gathering into flocks and talking excitedly of far-away southern places. They made trial runs up and down the beaches, testing themselves against the long miles ahead. No longer did the Bohemian wax-wings dot the exposed river rocks in the evening. The bright and noisy king-fishers were gone too, as was their faithful enemy, the Swainson's hawk. One day a great band of small birds raced twittering through the yellow trees and out over the water. It seemed to me that I detected a new note in their voices. With a sense of loss I watched them disappear into the southern sky. A longing stole over me: we too should be winging our way southward with the birds.

Hunting took on a new urgency for us. Soon the moose would begin to rut, running off their summer fat in search of mates. From dawn to dusk I wandered through the falling leaves, rifle in hand, praying for food. It seemed somehow wrong that I should ask the Creator for the death of another living being, but I did. The largest animal I had ever killed was a rabbit.

To our great relief, Net-Chet began to recover, but we had lost precious time in her care. She learned to walk again, using the splint as a crutch, screaming whenever she entangled it in brush. We knew she would make it when she reinstated her old whining, picky, nagging, complaining ways. Dogs have individual personalities, just like people. I must admit a grudging admiration for her tenacity. I have never met a more stubborn dog. She always had to have the last word.

It was a bleak and windy afternoon and I was cold. I had been walking all day, following the river, looking for game. Moose season was open, and we could legally take two apiece, including one cow. We could kill six black bears at any time of the year and unlimited caribou. I reached into my wool coat pocket for sandy crumbs of jerky, which I sucked with satisfaction, chewing them slowly to savor the taste.

I emerged from the horseshoe swamp onto the beach. The swamp was an old river bend, now partly silted in, stubbled with cotton grass and sedges. The mud of the shore was imprinted with my old tracks. I found them every-where—hopeful wandering feet. Sniffing the icy wind, I looked upstream and down. Might as well cross the river, I decided. I trudged into the crystal water, feeling it tug at my knees. Cold billowed sharply to my waist.

I climbed the cliff above the rapids and sat searching the colorful terrain. Across from me a yellow expanse of willows and muskeg butted into the mountain feet, clear and perfect across the distance. I leaned my rifle against my knees and watched, wondering if I had knocked the sights out of alignment in my travels and occasional falls.

Scanning the thickets, I pretended to see big dark forms moving in the brush. I sighted at my imaginary moose, thinking how I would shoot him in just the right place. Then I would swim the river above the rapids . . . there . . . and, let's see, how would I gut him? I would have to gut him of course, to surprise Phil. I smiled privately.

It was almost dark when I plodded into camp. Phil was bent over his logs in the fading light, skinning off the bark with a drawknife. He smiled when he saw me and stuck the blade into the butt of a log. He greeted me by bounding down the hill like a puppy. I had to laugh. Phil could be very silly and it touched me to see the effort he put into the display. Net-Chet sniffed cautiously then broke into a little dance of her own, dragging the splint loudly over the rocks. Phil took my hand and pulled me up the bank to the campfire. Gently he pushed me onto my sitting log and handed me a steaming mug of tea. Then he knelt and began to remove my soaked boots.

"Oh, Phil, you don't have to do that," I protested.

"Hush, now. My hard working L'ammal deserves a little care," he answered using a nickname we had started calling one another. It meant "little animal."

I dug into my trouser pocket and found a brightly colored stone and handed it to Phil. "And a dead vole I found for Chet," I tossed it to the pup. Phil received the stone like a treasure, turning it to study the markings. We often brought one another such gifts.

"See the red vein?" I pointed out. He licked the stone and rubbed it with his thumb. "I watched a wolf hunting across the river today. I sighted on him for some time, but he seemed to be having such a hard time. I felt bad. He was checking all the ground squirrel holes and not catching anything. How would you like to hunt ground squirrels with your teeth?"

Phil wrung out my shapeless socks and flopped them limply over willow twigs near the fire. We hadn't washed our socks all summer, merely wringing them out evenings. In fact they rarely dried. I wriggled my bleached and wrinkled toes over the flames. I was tired and discouraged. Phil had a pot of jerky on the fire and steam filled the air as he lifted the lid with the point of his knife and set it before me.

"Last squeezings of the moose," he said cheerfully.

"It's getting pretty grim," I acknowledged. "An old trapper once told me that the difference between what he would and wouldn't eat was twenty-four hours. I hate to bring this up, but if we don't find something soon, we may have to eat Chet. Not that she'd make much of a meal, but not having to feed her would buy us time. Starving won't be any fun for her either. I love her too, but we need to be realistic." I stroked the soft, trusting head that pressed into my lap. Phil glanced away.

"If we don't start getting a lot of something soon, we're in big trouble," he agreed. "We can't make it on small game. It just takes too much energy hunting, and there's no fat on it."

"It's not fair to her either," I continued. "She's trying to grow up on a poor diet. No wonder her little legs are brittle."

Phil sighed deeply. "Well, maybe the moose will start moving soon and ..."

He stopped in mid-sentence, following my gaze across the darkening river.

"That rock. . ." I whispered, pointing. "I don't remember a rock there, do you?"

"Could be a bear!"

Phil grabbed his rifle and sighted through the scope at a sandspit island we called the "Snack Bar," because we planned to put moose guts there, when we shot one, to attract a black bear.

An explosion startled me as Phil fired his .30-06. The dim shape seemed to melt in the gloom, sinking to the ground. That was all.

Phil grinned, exalted.

"Think he's dead?" I could hardly make out the spot in the shifting light. I blinked and squinted.

Phil peered through his scope a long moment. A scope concentrates light. "Hasn't moved. L'ammal, I think we got ourselves a bear!"

I danced around Phil in my cold, bare feet then snatched my freezing socks from their sticks, all weariness forgotten in a rush of sheer happiness. There is no feeling like a reprieve, even if temporary, from starvation. Impatiently, I thawed my socks over the blaze.

Phil was already loading the tethered canoe with teapot, skillet, knives, steel, whetstone, buckets, tarp, and packframes. I could hear the metallic thump as he set them into the empty craft. "I think Chet better stay here," he said over his shoulder. "She'll just be miserable over there and we'll be back soon enough." He paused a moment and gave me a triumphant hug. "We got one!"

Within minutes we were underway, skimming easily across the glassy river in the empty canoe. Behind us, Chet set up a howl of protest. I leapt ashore with the bowline as the boat grated to a halt in the shallows. Phil followed, his arms loaded. Together we pulled the 110-pound freight canoe far onto the gravel. No moon tonight, I thought: it would be very dark. From out of the blackness overhead came a first soft whisper of snowflakes.

We were reluctant to approach the silent form—that ominous lump on the beach, a black puddle within the blackness. "He can wait," I assured Phil. "Let's build a fire." We had no flashlight, it being another item we decided to do without. It is surprising how rapidly darkness claims this land once it arrives. Only a brief time since we had seen our first stars, and already there were several hours of real night.

Across the river, Net-Chet wailed her loneliness. I grubbed about in the dark, searching for something to burn on the barren island and with difficulty kindled a fire. A dry wind froze my wet jeans stiffly about my calves and kicked sparks into the rattling sedges. My feet burned with the cold. I stamped them and bent low over the flames to warm my fingers. Steam rose from my thawing trousers.

The bear was dead. Phil began skinning and gutting him while I scrounged for firewood. Watching Phil illuminated by the flickering, I felt suddenly weary. Behind him the circle of light was swallowed up by the night. I should be over there helping, I thought guiltily. Only a moment longer near the fire.

There is something spooky about bears. He was powerfully built, the snout and teeth menacing even in death. His claws and thick arms seemed almost human as we bent over him in the darkness. He was a small animal, perhaps only 350 pounds, but rounded with fat for the winter. Here was the energy we needed to get our moose. A sweet, cloying smell rose from his open belly like fermenting blueberries. The stomach was full of berries, branches and all. The meat was dark and greasy. His lovely golden coat gleamed in the firelight. A grizzly!

We hadn't known, of course, but I think we would have killed him anyway. We were beginning to feel endangered ourselves. Grizzlies are rare and not generally considered good to eat. The season for hunting them was a single month in the spring. They, like the wolf, are one of the last vestiges of truly wild country. Neither can survive crowding by humans. Grizzlies and wolves need big, healthy tracts of land. A world without either of them would be an impoverished place.

"Want some fresh meat?" I asked, looking up from stripping the congealing fat from the intestines. I longed for an excuse to return to the warmth of the fire.

"Good idea. And some tea. Think you can find the river and fill the teapot?" he asked. It certainly was black out, not even stars. Suddenly a chorus of deep answers broke Chet's mournful soprano in mid-screech.

"Now see what she's stirred up," I said wryly. "I hope nothing gets her."

We worked through the night. Gray streaks of dawn lined Phil's face as together we loaded the canoe, heaving aboard the icy bear meat, buckets of organs, and hide. To the north, the morning star glimmered in fading purple velvet. Gradually, we worked the craft out from shore as the weight increased.

Lady Grayling slipped over the dawning water, our paddles dispersing the mirror of autumn mountains as we glided across the stillness. Strands of fog lingered, snagged in treetops beneath a clearing sky. We scraped bottom over the shelf into our harbor, leaving silver streaks on the rocks.

It was September 5, a cold and misty morning with fine snow powdering the frozen mud where intricate patterns of ice had formed during the night. We blew life into the coals of our home fire and squatted near it in the growing light, frying bear meat and fat while we comforted Net-Chet.

Phil sat on my log. He had his boots off and was flexing his stiff toes over the blaze. I could sleep for a week, I thought. My body was sore, my pants caked with blood. I glanced fondly down at the loaded canoe a few feet away. The first jays were arriving. Groaning upright, I knocked Phil's rifle over with a thud and hobbled toward the river to toss the nylon canoe cover over the meat. I spun back in surprise. A moose!

Chet saw him at almost the same moment I did and began a frantic baying. Phil was instantly up, grabbing his rifle from where it had fallen. His bare feet flew up the beach, leaving no trace in the frozen mud. I crammed on my socks, ice and all. In panic I closed my hands around Chet's muzzle to shut in the noise. Damn her! Damn! Damn!

I galloped after Phil, boot laces dancing, rifle bouncing on my shoulder. Far upstream a great, dark wraith stepped from the misty river. He poised a moment on the far bank, looking back. I was praying and running as fast as I could. Phil came panting back, cold and sore footed.

"Go up to the lookout rocks at the bend and see if you can spot him!"

"Get your boots on and cross over," I answered back. "Work up the far side!"

"Okay!" He was off in one direction, me in the other. Chet was still shrilling the alarm.

I rushed wheezing over the mile of broken ground, scrambled up the cliff at the river bend, and stood gasping. Rapidly I scanned the land across the river, seeking out a big, dark shape back in the bushes. Then I ran on. Around the cliff tops I scurried, knowing every step, through the bushes and now down the rock slide, stones scattering beneath my feet and . . . then! I stopped. My mind came sharply into focus. Directly below me was a bull moose.

Unafraid he stood, knee-deep in the rapids, watching me from fifty feet away. His body was massive and strong, a yard across at the rump, his shoulders close to seven feet high. From just above each eye a great antler curved outward forming a vast spread of flowing bone. There was a sense of power and majesty in his presence that altered the very scenery for me. This was no longer my familiar river bend. How often I had imagined this meeting, but how different it was! I had been looking for a big, brown target browsing in the bushes. Now I confronted this majestic Being.

I slipped to a sitting position, sending another shower of rocks down the slide. My rifle heaved with each breath and heartbeat, and shook violently to the tremble of my hands. Calm down, I commanded myself. There is time. Don't shoot him in the water. My mother had drilled that into me: never shoot a moose in the water.

He turned and slid from me, cleaving through the roaring current of the rapids like a long-legged ship. Where shall I shoot? I looked down on the smooth ripple of his great shoulders and back. I had never thought of this position. He's going! He's going! My mind cried out as I wavered in indecision, frozen. He clattered out on the far shore and flashed between the high bushes, floating easily away, leaving only a memory.

Stupid! Stupid! I grieved in silent rage. He was everything, and now he's gone! I scrambled down, knees still shaking, and circled above the rapids, wading the river. How slow and clumsy I seemed compared to him. On the far shore I thrashed through the dense brush, sweeping back and forth to check for tracks. You would think that tracks as large and deep as those made by a moose would be easy to follow, but it isn't always so. Heartbroken and exhausted, I started back for the river in the vain hope of seeing him once more.

I was flailing through a willow thicket when a rifle went off a few yards away. I wanted to scream, "Don't shoot!" but clung to the knowledge that Phil would not fire unless he had a clear view of the animal. I pushed through to the river bar. Phil was there. He waved me toward him and then plunged into the water. The moose had crossed back over. Ice water plowed into my chest, dragging me downstream as I fought for the far bank. Phil was ahead of me and vanished into the forest before I reached shore. Then came another shot. And another. Oh, please God! Don't let him get away wounded! I prayed silently.

At length Phil reappeared, a big grin splitting his tired face. He spread his hands like antlers, fingers sprouting from his scalp, and stamped his feet, grunting.

"You got him!? You got him!?"

"The biggest bull moose you ever saw! Twice the size of the other one!"

"I want to see," I insisted.

I followed him through a jungle of alders and into a sudden clearing where a deep pond and muskeg pushed back the trees. There on the only piece of dry land lay an enormous animal, his belly as high as my waist. He was still breathing, shuddering founts of steam into the air. Looking queasy, Phil fired into the back of his massive head. The long legs thrashed a moment then the thick neck relaxed. Smoke blew out one ear and drifted into the morning.

I went for the canoe, leaving Phil to begin butchering. First I unloaded the bear, heaving the heavy pieces onto the hide laid fur-side down, and covered them with the tarp. I was fatigued in every muscle of my body, my movements slow and leaden. It was almost noon by the time I lined the canoe upstream to the moose. I axed a trail through the dense alders and found Phil bent over the giant carcass. A wholesome, almost milky smell filled the clearing. Sunlight had burned away the morning mist, and popcorn clouds scudded in a rich, blue sky. The sun was warm, and in the dazzling light the mountains stood forth in purest colors, brilliant with fall.

Despite our weariness, we were festive. Here was meat in plenty, and Phil gaily pointed out the two-inch blanket of fat over the haunches and the lacy caul fat about the paunch. White and brown velvet still hung in tatters from his antlers and the full stomach showed that he was not yet in rut. I built a fire and fried another breakfast of liver sautéed with generous nuggets of kidney fat.

Butchering an animal of this size is an enormous task. First we had to heave him onto his back, which took all of our combined strength. We skinned the hide back from the belly and carefully slit the abdomen, allowing the contents to billow out. Opening the rib cage at the brisket where the ribs join, we cut the ligaments that attached the internal organs to the spine, and severed the intestinal tract at both ends. Only then could we drag the voluminous stomach, or "paunch," out, taking care not to rupture it or the attached intestines.

We ran a seam up the inside of each leg, and worked the heavy hide down the animal's sides until he lay naked on his own skin. The front legs were removed by slicing the muscle between the armpit and the ribs. The hindquarters were heavier, perhaps 175 pounds each, but the ball joint pulled open as we severed the muscles at the groin. The trunk proved harder to section, but we cut it into four pieces using only our pocketknives: the pelvis, two rib sections (one attached to the backbone), the neck, and the head. We then had nine pieces weighing from 100 to 180 pounds, plus the hide and assorted organs.

It was growing dark as I lugged Mightypot full of liver, heart, and kidneys to the water's edge. Dully I dropped onto a boulder and gazed back into the woods. Phil emerged, slid down the short cutbank, and started over the rocky beach. He had a five-gallon bucket of blood in one hand and one of gut fat I had stripped from the intestines in the other. He moved like a sleepwalker, stumbling over the stones.

"Hi," I said.

"Waste not, want not," he answered, heaving the blood-bucket in the canoe. "For Chet."

I struggled to my feet and picked up the packframe. Phil took my free hand and plodded wordlessly beside me. It was one hundred yards to the moose. We made the trip fifteen horrible times, stumbling along through muskeg. Supporting the slippery meat between us on a packframe, we crashed through bushes in pitch darkness, caught in an endless nightmare. We would rest a moment and start back for another load to the squish, squish, squish of sodden boots, our clothes drenched in freezing blood.

The last thing we took was the hundred-pound hide. Hauling its stretchy bulk into the river, we secured it by rope to the canoe. The entire moose weighed perhaps fifteen hundred pounds alive, and our load floated very low in the water.

The route home was hazardous even by daylight. We had to run the rapids above our still mile of water. In total blackness, we walked the sagging craft out from shore, then climbed aboard and paddled frantically for midstream. We could see nothing as we spun along in the quickening current, wincing when we slammed into rocks. The roar increased as we shot into the main channel, adrift in the night. We were in deep water now, funneled into a narrow shoot. Waves smacked into the bow and coursed into my lap as we swept through.

Then we were past it, the sounds diminishing behind us. Soon we floated homeward on a quiet ghostly river, lost in the daze of our own fatigue.

Now that we were fed, we seemed to reach a slump. Like runners who have sprinted the last mile, we had no more to give. We had perhaps three months food, but our "cabin" remained a pile of skinned logs. We moved slowly, as if in a dream. It took a long time to get anything done. We were indecisive and spiritless—no longer able to think clearly, to act, or to choose. Winter was coming. Daily we watched it close upon us, hypnotized by its rapid descent. Still we floundered ineffectually.

Why hadn't we put up the shed roof as planned, or even unpacked our warm clothes? All I can say is that prolonged stress, like semi-starvation—both of which we had known—undermines judgment and ability, engendering a state of apathy. We didn't realize this at the time, but we knew something was wrong. We didn't seem to be able to prioritize our efforts and we moved sluggishly.

I worked quietly rendering gut fat, cooking it until the water evaporated. When the oil emerged and the dry "cracklings" floated on the surface, I poured the golden liquid into five-gallon cans—moose tallow in one, bear lard in another—where it quickly cooled in smooth, white layers. I munched raw moose fat as I sliced and stirred, sitting cross-legged on the freezing ground before the fire. I had craved fat all summer and it tasted marvelous.

The wind hadn't stopped in days, blasting endlessly across the fire where Mightypot bubbled. Our cabin site was set back in the protection of the trees a few yards up the hill, but our camp was on the riverbank. The hill was steep and there really was no other place to pitch a tent. We lost all interest in spicing our food. Too much bother. After a diet of drymeat, we were accustomed to doing without salt. Sugar tasted almost bitter now. Our urine turned green from a diet of liver, and still we had not finished it all. Organ meats differ from muscle, containing concentrations of vitamins. Large quantities of liver can even be toxic, something we didn't know then.

The time to hunt was passing. It had been four days since we brought home the moose, and we needed perhaps three more to safely make it until summer. The bulls were moving now, running off their summer fat in search of cows, and would soon be well into the rut, a time when they cease eating and the meat becomes strong. In three weeks they would be thin and stationary, hunkered down for winter.

Every night the ground froze and the river temperature plunged to just above freezing. We had counted on Net-Chet developing a thick winter coat while sleeping outside, but I was awakened again by her shivers. I reached out and stroked the trembling bulge in the tent wall.

"Phil?" I said softly.

"Ummm . . . ?"

"I can't sleep thinking of her out there night after night, shaking like that."

"If she were still in the village . . . " he started.

I cut him short. "Maybe so, but she's our dog now."

"Don't you think we should give her a little more time?"

"No. Look at her. She's so skinny and she has her little broken leg. She can't even curl up properly. It isn't fair."

"She needs to be cold to grow good fur," he insisted.

"What if she doesn't grow any more?" I asked. "There was quite a mixture of dogs there. No telling her genetics."

"All right," he gave in. I was already half out of the bags, pulling the surprised puppy into the tent. "But she sleeps at the foot of the bags."

"Now, you slept with Junior for eight years," I teased him as I made a nest for Chet. "Your mother even had special sheets for your bed."

"That was different," he retorted. "Junior was a house dog. Chet is a work dog."

Net-Chet snuggled happily beside my feet as I dove under the covers. Our heads were close to the open door and looked out upon a pale gray sky that promised another overcast day. It was still windy. The tent rustled and popped while the black trees sang to themselves.

"I'm going to zero my rifle today," Phil decided, peering out. "I think my scope is out of alignment again. May as well be ready." We each had a .30-06. Mine was from my mother, but Phil had carved his stock from a piece of black walnut and fitted the pieces together.

We rolled over and he curled around my back. I slid my foot between his knees and pulled them tight against my legs. "We have a great start, but at the rate we eat, we'll be starving by midwinter when it's cold and dark," I said. "My parents ate three moose, a bear, and a whole pile of caribou their first winter out, and they were starving by March. Spring is a difficult time when the snow is deep and the animals are thin."

"I sure hope the caribou come through here this winter," he said, "but we can't count on them. I've heard we're on the very edge of their migration."

Chet had begun a slow upward migration of her own, creeping onto the sleeping bags and crowding my feet.

"They still had meat in March," I continued, "but were starving for lack of fat. Like us when we were living on dried moose."

"Which is another reason we need to push ourselves now," he agreed. "Those moose are getting skinnier by the minute." He sat, spilling cold air into the bags, and began rummaging for his clothes in the growing light. Chet, already accustomed to her new status as tent dog, complained as he pulled his trousers from beneath her.

"I'm going to check the overlook and then pace off a range at the river bend," he said. He was sitting with his feet out the door, lacing his boots. "I'll eat later."

I watched him disappear up the beach, red-checked mackinaw closed tightly against the biting wind. Slowly I groped about for my clothes and began to dress in the bag. Then, fully clothed, I drifted back to sleep.

Some time later I was startled by Net-Chet's vigilant "Woof!" She was very bright, if stubborn. After the episode with the moose, she never again barked at game, giving only a single low note to alert us. I grabbed my rifle and bolted upright. A cold, plaintive "meow" drifted from the Snack Bar, and there stood Phil. He stomped his feet and made antlers of his hands.

"You gotta be kidding!" I yelled across the river.

"Big as the last one!" he called back. "Come and get me."

Poor Phil is wet, I thought as I paddled. The empty canoe was unwieldy for one person in the wind. My teeth were chattering. Behind me, Chet started to wail. I hoped the moose was near the river.

The canoe grated on a shoal and Phil waded out. Shoving us back into the current, he grabbed a paddle and pulled for home. He looked cold, his lips thin and blue above his ragged beard.

"Well, tell me!" I sang out as I jumped onto our two-foot cutbank, pulling the bowline ashore and tying it to a stump. I began to search through storage cans for dry clothes and long underwear. It was time we got them out, having worn the same outfits all summer. It was turning into a bitter day, a good time to switch from jeans to wool pants. The water measured thirty-six degrees and a south wind gusted past at twenty to thirty-five miles an hour.

"I was up on the cliff when I saw the flash of antlers near the hill across the river," he started excitedly.

I groaned. Two miles of leg-breaking muskeg: it might as well be on the moon.

"Now wait," he commanded, enjoying his story.

I had finally located the can with the wool caps. I stuffed the other contents back in and pushed the lid down.

"I swam the river and stalked him, unable to get close enough to trust my rifle," he continued. "Then I lost him and cut back to the river bend, looking. I peeked through the willows and there he was getting ready to cross. He gave a grunt when he saw me, and started for the water. I nailed him behind the head and he went down like a rock. Then I saw that he was *in* the river—about eighteen inches of it." He shrugged.

"At least we have more food," I said. "That's all that really counts right now. The wind whipped our light canoe upstream at a good rate as we paddled. This moose lay above the rapids, directly across from the last one. The shoreline, a long muddy bar, sloped from a thicket of yellow poplar into the channel where a dark form protruded from the river. The icy stream flowed steadily over his submerged head and neck, around his belly and away. There was nothing to do but butcher him where he lay in the cold, rushing current.

All day the wind blew, kicking spray over us as we worked. Feet and hands burning with cold, we sliced away underwater, blood from our nerveless fingers often washing downstream with that of the moose. We tied the canoe to the inverted head, using his big antlers as an anchor, and loaded the quarters as we cut them free.

He was a big bull, perhaps a bit younger than the last, judging by his teeth and antlers. He had less fat across the rump, but more gut fat: individual variation. His antlers were free of velvet, polished and dry, but his stomach was still full, showing that he hadn't started to rut.

Cold dusk fingered us while I held the straining canoe and Phil heaved the head—the final piece—aboard. It was an awkward thing, antlers jutting like wings from either side of the craft. At the stern, the hide and guts floated in the river, tugging on ropes.

Gingerly we walked the craft downstream over the riffles, hauling her through the shallows around the rapids. No point in running them if we could avoid it. They were becoming more difficult each day as the flow decreased with coming freeze-up. If the water dropped much more, we would have a hard time getting a moose down from above. The upper river was now peppered with large boulders.

We arrived home in the purple of evening. Tying the canoe securely in her harbor, we left the moose aboard and rekindled our campfire. When we thawed our feet over a blistering fire, we found them drawn up in unyielding tension, almost as if the tendons had shrunk in the cold.

I was concerned as I massaged my rigid feet. "Do you think we are damaging them in some way?" I asked Phil. They looked unpleasantly white and wrinkled, dead almost.

"We've had them in cold water all summer," he reasoned.

"Yeah, but not this cold. That water is almost freezing."

"But it isn't," he reassured me. "Moose do it all the time. You can't get frostbite above freezing."

I wasn't so sure. At the time I didn't know about countercurrent heat exchange in moose and duck legs. Arteries running to the feet heat blood returning to the body cavity, conserving energy while maintaining circulation. Humans don't have this adaptation. Cold can injure people even at temperatures well above freezing, especially if combined with dampness. Called "immersion" or "trench foot," extreme cases may lead to gangrene. Unlike the moose, our bodies conserve core heat by shutting down circulation.

After a big meal of rib steak, we hobbled off to bed, leaving our boots, socks, and pants to freeze by the fire.

Dry leaves whispered past as I sat on the frozen earth and sliced fat for rendering. Two days before, we had unloaded the latest moose, hanging the water-bleached quarters with lengths of rope on a log propped between two stout tripods. We no longer feared spoilage or flies, and merely tacked the hides on the southern exposure to exclude direct sunlight. Now we had food into the new year.

"I'm really going to zero my rifle today," Phil announced, untying the canoe. It was late afternoon and the sky was clear despite a nagging wind. He hopped aboard, sending the slender craft over the water.

"Just don't shoot any moose," I joked.

"I'll be over on the Snack Bar," he called back, paddle flashing.

I had done a majority of the hunting and he all the shooting, which was fine. It was food that mattered. My mother told us that when you are in the country, you are always "hunting." The game is moving, and eventually it comes to you. This was why we brought two large rifles, even though we left out rain gear, flashlights, lifejackets, and winter boots. I had reasoned that if we got moose before winter, we could make boots; if we didn't it wouldn't matter.

I sat rendering fat and skinning leg bones. We planned to make mukluks from this slick-furred hide. I laid aside a cold shin bone and hoof, stacking it with seven others, and flopped the hide onto a pile. Across the river, I could hear the thundering boom of a heavy rifle and I automatically counted the shots. Every animal within miles is leaving, I thought sourly.

When Phil appeared on the far shore bellowing and making with the antlers, I didn't believe him. Curiously, I watched him paddle home.

"I really did!" he said defensively. "I shot another bull."

"I don't believe it," I replied flatly.

"I can't either!" He laughed aloud and snatched up Chet in a little jig. "We're all going to make it! We're really going to live through the winter!" His voice sounded surprised, exhilarated. The voice of one who wins the lottery or is pardoned after years in prison.

I was gathering up buckets, dumping fat and livers onto the moss. My feet were still sore, yet I hobbled happily about, filled with a sense of thanksgiving. Another moose! Salvation.

Phil grabbed me up in a hug for a moment. "I paced off a seventy-yard range and lay down to shoot, using the cutbank as a backstop," he said excitedly. He stooped to fish the packframe out of the river where it had been soaking off gore, secured by a rope. "After a few rounds, I reloaded. When I pulled the rifle down on the target—through the sights, mind you!—I saw this set of brown legs!"

"Just walking?" I asked incredulously.

"Trotting! I was so surprised, I completely missed the first shot. He broke into a run and the second round caught him in the diaphragm. The third one broke his back."

"Phil, nobody, but nobody, fires six shots at a target and then has a moose walk in front of it!" I danced him about. "Oh, L'ammal, we're almost home free! Three moose. How good the wilderness is to us. Is he big? Is he still fat?"

He grinned happily. "Sure looks it to me."

Evening was rapidly overtaking us as we started out. The water was very low, and we couldn't get clear across the river. We pulled the canoe up on the Snack Bar and waded the freezing shallows, splashing over the rocks the last fifty yards to the mainland. The moose lay on a four-foot cutbank. He stood out plainly on the exposed, yellow muskeg.

We gutted him by firelight, releasing his warmth into the frosty air. Even in subzero temperatures, an ungutted animal of this size will begin to rot overnight. We worked by feel, reaching into the cavernous belly in the dark. Thank you, thank you, I silently told the moose and the spirit of the land that had raised and gifted him to us.

This level of killing may seem greedy or uncaring, but it was necessary to our lives. Like the wolf, we needed food from this land to live, and like him we were part of this great cycle. In some ways, we were far more conscious of and grateful for this supreme Gift, for we saw the price paid by the moose that we might live. When I open a package of hamburger, it is anonymous and sterile. There is no opportunity to thank that life or acknowledge its contribution. We say grace over meals, but have lost touch with what it means. I was learning the meaning with my hands in blood.

This time we brought the tent along and pitched it nearby. I could hear Net-Chet making herself comfortable by the door as we ate a midnight meal of boiled tongue, brought from home. She wasn't allowed in the tent without us, and an occasional loud moan issued from her direction, urging us to come to bed.

"I think he'll cool all right now," Phil said, accepting a mug of tea. "What say we hit the sack?" Another insistent groan came from the tent, and we grinned at one another.

"Why don't you get out of those wet socks and give your feet a chance to thaw?" I suggested. I already had mine off.

"I broke the bladder in the dark and I want to rinse him out before we turn in. May as well do that before I get too comfortable."

This isn't much fun for him either, I thought, as I cut off a piece of tongue and held it on my knife to cool. "I don't think he's quite as fat as the others," I said. "But it's hard to tell with his stomach empty. Notice the smell?"

A faint odor, like fallen willow leaves, clung to the surrounding night. "That must be rut," Phil answered.

"It's not a bad smell." We had been told that rutting moose were almost inedible.

"I think he's an old man moose," he continued, taking a long pull on his tea. "He has spinal arthritis or something. Anyway, the disks are solid. I couldn't get my knife between them. His hooves are worn through on the bottom, like holes in his shoes. Also there is a healed broken rib, did you notice?"

I shook my head, no. "Old battle scar, I suppose." I could just make out the stiff form a few feet away, legs up. "You know, all the time I spent hunting and praying, Phil? Maybe I thought I'd get my orders in early—like maybe God wasn't listening. Then, we get food as fast as we can handle it. Rags to riches in eight days! A week earlier, and the meat might have spoiled. Two weeks later, and the moose would have been thin. It makes me wonder why I worry so much about things I have no control over."

He smiled at me. His face was haggard in the firelight, almost eerie. He put his dirty mug down in the withered cotton grass and got painfully to his feet.

This cold water is crippling us, I thought, watching him disappear in the night. I heard him stumble down the cutbank and then the crunch of ice when he broke the water free. I stared quietly at my stiff fingers, caked with blood, sore from numerous cuts—ugly slashes in my flesh. They hurt less than it appeared, as if my body had forgotten them with its attention on survival. The little diamond hung loosely under my skinny finger. No sparkle. Were these the soft, plump hands I remembered? Alligator hide, bones, and tendons.

Rags to riches, I mused. We were down to squirrels and dead voles. Now look at us. How wonderful life is! Of course, it is a matter of perspective. Most people wouldn't have envied me just then, but being wealthy and not knowing it is a form of spiritual poverty. Life close to the bone puts things in perspective.

From the Snack Bar sixty yards away came the long, low call of a wolf. We had left moose guts there days before, but they had just discovered them. A higher voice answered from upstream and the first one repeated its message.

Phil appeared, squatting quietly beside me. I heard Chet retreat further under the rain fly. The stillness was broken again as others arrived. We could clearly hear the young voices exclaiming over our treat, punctuated by the deeper tones of adults. Wolves live in highly social family groups. A single mated pair have pups within a territory, older siblings often helping to raise them. I felt guilty that we had murdered one. They had undoubtedly never seen people before.

"The neighbors," I whispered, as we listened into their darkness.

"Hope nobody raids camp while we're over here guarding this moose," Phil said in a low voice.

"Spooky, isn't it? They know we're here, of course."

"It's their night and their valley," he replied quietly.

That night I dreamed I was cutting my way out of a cavernous corpse. I was smothering in folds of fat. Pushing upward in a struggle to breathe, I sliced and hacked in mounting panic. I awoke bolt upright in the little tent. Phil had his arms about me in the cold air saying over and over, "Shush, L'ammal, it's okay now. Shush."

Two days later I was back hunting. Almost home free was not good enough. We might not get another chance before spring. Once the river froze—as it would any night—there would be no way out for us until breakup.

I stepped softly, rifle slung over my shoulder, my mind as hushed as the swirling snow. All day I had traveled a shifting land of black, white, and gray.

I searched the bleak water, the drifting flakes, the dark trees. Only I, in my red wool coat and blue cap, was in color; the only sound was my breathing and the muffled tread of my feet. A few withered leaves rattled against the bare alder bones, slapped by the drifting air, but this too was sucked up into the great, whispering silence.

I cut quietly through the horseshoe swamp, frozen yellow tussocks hard beneath my boots. Vole trails stood out under the dead sedges, vulnerable in the scanty new snow. Ahead, the river bent back upon itself and I turned to follow it homeward.

A dark phantom stood suddenly before me, stepping from the falling snow. He was talking to himself, grunting softly as he drifted toward me along the far shore of the river. I dropped to my bottom in the snow, looping my elbow through the rifle sling to steady it across one knee. My hands were shaking. Traitors! I thought, desperately. Calm down. Sight. It's a long shot in this light. Take your time.

The moose entered the river, preferring the icy swim to sharp rocks along the bank. I galloped forward, bent double, hidden by branches. My shore had a willow bar into which he would vanish. I dropped down and fired. On he sailed with graceful strides. Again! Water sprayed up and he jumped. Then he was ashore and gone. I crept through the dense brush, seeing nothing. God, no! I thought in panic. Oh, please, NO!

I emerged from the dense poplars to see him seventy yards away, standing indecisively near the river. Down I plunked and fired, and over he went. So easy.

"Take your time and let him die quietly," my mother's voice admonished me. "It takes awhile."

Carefully I crept over the rocks, my eyes intent on the moose. But no! He began struggling, long legs flailing the air. He would be up any moment! I sat, grabbing bullets from my pants pocket, dropping them in the sand and snow. Then he was swimming. Shoot! Shoot! Why won't he die? Blindly I tried to knock him over. See? I thought miserably. I knew mere bullets wouldn't kill a real moose. Again I shot into the chest. Hadn't I always imagined bringing him down with a single shot? Just like big rabbits, my mother had told me. Yet he plowed steadily on. I knew he would reach shore and dissolve into the afternoon.

Finally it was over. In slow motion the big animal pitched forward into the river and was still. I had forgotten the freezing water. I traveled slowly upstream in search of a shallow place, looking always backward at him. But he was dead. In my mind I saw a living moose, talking to himself, lovesick. My world had been brushed by magic for that moment, and now in my triumph I knew also a great loss. I had killed the thing I loved and in some way that I could not define, I would never be the same.

I crossed the river, water to my chest, holding the rifle over my head. Down the beach loomed a dark carcass. A raven swooped from the gray sky, and then fluttered away with a musical "Plunk!" I waded out, my sore feet burning as the shore-fast ice crunched against my shins.

The moose was sprawled in shallow water ten feet from shore. He was smaller and younger than the others. From him rose the autumn smell of willows, that now familiar scent of rut. His velvet nose lay in the mud, eyes open. I touched his head and wiggled an ear. They let you down, fellow, I thought. Tears seeped through my lashes. I must build a fire, I told myself. Glancing about I saw only soggy driftwood frozen into the mud. I decided to skip the fire. My teeth were chattering loudly.

I wrestled the big head, turning it to plant the antlers. I could not roll him alone, but tied his front leg back to an antler with a bit of parachute cord to expose the deep chest. Then I heaved the dripping hind leg over my shoulder. Moose have cold legs. His abdomen was soft and warm. I pulled my large jack-knife from its holster, working the blade up with stiff fingers, and made a timid slice. Cutting into a newly dead animal was different from helping Phil with one already in the process of being butchered. The chest muscles quivered as I made the incision.

It was nearly dark when I left the gutted moose to cool. He had not eaten on his journey, and his stomach was empty, reducing my task considerably. I swam the river, ice water invading my armpits, and took the shortest route home, pounding my feet over the stones. I began to warm a bit, pain returning slowly to my feet as I hobbled. Water spurted rhythmically from the holes in my boots. Before me, fresh wolf tracks dotted the new snow, and I quickened my pace.

At camp, Phil hurried about, building up the fire, making tea, and fussing over me. I savored the moment, and when he started to strip off my wet boots, I said casually, "No, we have to get back to the moose." We laughed and hugged one another in chilled delight. How often I had planned that!

First we needed to unload the last moose, pulling the rigid pieces from the frozen blood in the bottom of the canoe onto the hide. The moon had returned, and by its half-light we toiled slowly upstream lining the canoe until after midnight. We pitched camp in the snow and went to bed, too tired to eat. Unable to get warm, we chattered together through the endless hours until dawn, a tense knot of misery and muscle cramps.

In the morning, we squatted over our breakfast fire, grimly appraising the day's task and chewing boiled flank. Flank is tough but easy to get. It had taken me much time and pain to force my tender feet into frozen boots, which were hard as steel and would not bend. I thawed Phil's over the sluggish fire that I managed to start with the available wood.

It was snowing lightly. Already an inch of white sifted onto the exposed bar, smoothing out the wrinkles and frosting the stiff and twisted carcass of the moose. He was frozen into a film of ice that had grown out from shore. The mountains were lost in gray, the trees faint and unreal.

"What time do you think it is?" Phil asked. He was squatting by the fire, hands cupped around a mug of mint tea. Not even a bright spot betrayed the position of the sun.

I studied the sky a moment. "Morning."

"Shall we?" he asked, indicating the moose.

I shrugged. "May as well." I set the pot back on to boil and stood up. My knees were stiff from squatting, but there was no place to sit. "How long do you think we can stand in freezing water?"

"Until the pain gets too great," he answered, starting for the river.

"Won't our feet freeze or something?"

"Not before the river does."

Things are the way they are, I thought. There's no point in resisting them or wishing they were different.

Snow fell softly all day. I might have smiled at the thought of us, ice freezing around our knees as we struggled with that stiff carcass. Moose revenge. But it wasn't funny.

The work went slowly. We left the water frequently to gallop clumsily along the beach gathering the firewood and restoring pain to our feet. We kept the pot boiling and devoured quantities of meat and broth while thawing our numb fingers. By late afternoon we were ready to load the moose.

Phil started with the canoe, dragging it along the freezing channels. Chet and I plodded beside the river with the camp gear. As he dwindled into the mist, Phil seemed to shrink before my eyes, adrift in the falling snow on a black river. Alone he fought the canoe, helplessly splashing through the water, yanking the bow, slipping on the rocks.

He could hardly move when I pulled him from the slowly drifting craft and pointed him to shore. Numbly I climbed aboard. The river was unbelievably shallow and sluggish. At once the canoe grated to a halt and I leapt over, smashing my nerveless legs into boulders. Water seethed around my knees. Phil stumped up and down the beach, trying to restore circulation. I was misery beyond all misery. I had never been so cold. My legs were asleep to the thigh, my hands useless, my feet dead. Time lost all meaning. I was emptied, sucked down and down until nothing remained but that terrible cold.

Just above the rapids the canoe hung up badly, water driving her sideways onto the rocks.

"I hate it! I hate it!" I screamed into the evening, my voice lost in the roar of water. I could see myself as if from a great distance, jerking at the bowline, sobbing hysterically, but no tears. Dimly I saw Phil drop the pack and begin splashing toward me, scrambling awkwardly over the slippery stones. But I couldn't control myself.

"I hate it! I hate it!" I kept shrieking repetitively.

Phil ordered me to shore. No legs. Where were my legs? They had lost all sensation. Violent shivers wracked my whole body. Phil was in the rapids now, the water rushing over him as the canoe jammed sideways onto the boulders. I stumped out to help, pitching into the swift current to my waist, smashing into rocks. He was fighting vainly, waves cascading into the swamped canoe, rolling her and spilling the meat out. He yelled at me above the roar. I strained with all my strength, praying. Slowly the craft pivoted.

"Get on! Get on!" I shouted. "She's moving!"

"I lost a quarter!"

So what's a quarter? I thought. "Never mind! Jump!"

It was too late. As the canoe picked up momentum, he was dragged down through the rapids like a sea anchor, directing his course by snagging on boulders. The trailing moose hide whipped around my legs, yanking me under.

"Here it is!" he yelled, gesturing at the quarter.

I was washed down after Phil. The water looked black in the fading light. It doesn't feel cold, I thought as it swept me through the foaming shoot. An odd light spot appeared just below me, and I tried to kick as I was carried upon it. I couldn't feel my leg connect, but my body slowed and the quarter lifted and moved in the current with me. Slowly, I worked it toward shore. In quiet water now, I ducked down and encircled the meat with my arms, my nerveless hands useless, and tugged it onto the rocks. Then I pulled myself from the river and started back for the pack, spasms convulsing me.

Phil deserted the swamped canoe, leaving it to drift down the deep mile alone. Together we stumbled homeward, hurrying as best we could, holding to one another for balance. At camp, he grabbed the other packframe and started back into the darkness for the lost front quarter.

"Get into dry clothes," he told me, hobbling out of sight. "I'll be back in time to catch the canoe."

I nodded numbly. But how? I couldn't get my wet clothes off, working with fingers like sticks. My hands were useless and my body was shaking violently as I fumbled in the dark. A fire! First a fire, I thought. The coals had gone out in our absence. How I chattered and blew as I knelt shaking in the blackness, matches grasped clumsily between my palms! I would have tea for Phil, dinner for my brave Phil.

"Get off me!" I yelled at Chet.

I held the matches until my nerveless hands were burnt. Finally the damp spruce twigs caught and smoke billowed harshly into my face. I pressed my mouth close and blew softly until a healthy blaze crept up. It was life to me.

Within minutes I was able to slowly pull off my clothes, standing naked in the freezing night. Shivering violently, I crouched next to the fire, hoping to warm enough to be able to dress myself. I was chilled to the bone, my core temperature dangerously low.

Then out of the night sailed the canoe. I could see its half-submerged form drifting relentlessly toward me in the starlight. I fought free of the shirt I had pulled about my shoulders. A breeze played over the little hairs on my back. I stuffed my dead feet into wet boots and wrapped the laces around my bare ankles, unable to tie them. Naked, I entered the freezing water again.

Phil rushed into camp as the laden craft collided with the reef. I was holding the bow, but couldn't see to maneuver into our harbor. I backed it up, fighting the current. He dropped the pack and stumbled into the black water to help me. Together we hauled her over the rocks and safely to shore.

He was bruised from falling down with the quarter in the dark. He had tried to run on numb feet, fearing that the canoe would escape into the night, with our final moose. But we had made it, somehow.

The next morning the river was running ice.

CHAPTER 6

I t was clear blue out, and the bright morning sun streamed into the entrance of the tent as I dozed in the warmth of compressed bodies. It had taken us nearly all night to regain normal body heat after the cold water. I was dreaming of food, reluctant to awaken, but a nagging sound pulled at my consciousness. I opened my eyes, visions of pudding dissolving into the orange nylon walls, and listened. A merry tinkling of tiny bells was followed by a grating sound, then a swish and more bells. I pulled my shoulders from the bag for a look outside.

"Phil! You've got to see this!"

The yellow sunlight had already driven yesterday's snow into hiding behind rocks and under trees, but the river was a dazzling sea of moving ice—cobalt water offset with sun diamonds. Big islands of ice drifted silently up and grumbled to a halt on our exposed reef, where slush piled until it was forced musically over the barrier.

The first chore of the day was to dry our clothes. My feet were blanched and badly swollen. With pain and difficulty I finally crammed them into my thawing boots. Phil's were no better. In flimsy night things we limped about camp, gathering our frozen clothes and propping them by the fire. The day was beautiful, not a breath of wind, and seemed warm despite the 24°F temperature.

Camp was cluttered with animal parts. In ten days we had cut up and carted home almost three tons of live animal, or about three thousand pounds of food, figuring that half of an animal is guts, bone, and hide. Besides the hanging quarters and two moose still unhung, we had buckets of fat and organs, sixteen lower legs, twelve shinbone skins, various cans of tallow, three antlered moose heads, and sacks of cracklings. One moose head still had a tongue, two had noses, and one had been cut up for boiling. We had eight kidneys left, four and a half hearts, one hundred pounds of liver, and five large hides. At least it wasn't likely to rain again, I thought, but the meat was beginning to drip in the gentle sun.

Fondly I patted the big, cold slabs. I haggled a neck into thirds and put one into Mightypot to boil, then settled myself near the fire for a day of moose-sorting. About me a chaos of caked and filthy utensils were scattered. I had already rendered over a hundred pounds of tallow, insurance against winter.

During the fall rains, the mud bank behind our cabin foundation had caved in. Phil started fires to thaw the hummocky ground so that we could dig drainage ditches and fill them with rock. Soon we would begin transforming our accumulation of crooked logs into a home.

The following day was also sunny, but the river was slushed over and no more rafts of ice came down. The day after that, it froze. A sparkling road now joined the two lands. Only the rapids remained open, pouring dark blue from under the white ice. After breakfast that morning I decided to visit Chris Olson's cache for a load of tools.

The country was beautiful as I hiked along, the red autumn peaks now capped with white, the ground strewn with birch leaves. Muskeg potholes were covered with ice as clear as glass and dusted with snow. Twigs and leaves encased beneath the surface stood out in color against the black water.

It was warm when I reached the cache and I spent some time going through it to see what we needed. Olson Creek was a fairyland of sculptured ice where spray from the tumbling current had coated the shoreline in a fantasy of white, while a lazy trickle still gurgled unseen beneath the ice. The frosted cranberries edging the stream tasted delicious, and soon my fingers and mouth were stained red as I poked among the ruined structures.

I glanced up from time to time while tying things on my packframe, half expecting old Chris. The clearing was haunted by his work and dreams, and I felt somehow an intruder, even a thief. It was afternoon when I hoisted my pack and started for home. On it were strapped the stove, stovepipe oven, and assorted tools. As I reached the edge of the clearing, I stopped and turned around.

"Thank you," I said softly into the still air. "You don't need these things anymore, and they mean a great deal to us. Thank you."

I covered the mile home in good time. Phil bounced up the trail to greet me, pulling the awkward pack from my shoulders.

"Gee, you've done a lot," I said, looking around. The sill logs were in place, saddle notched together in a rectangle and firmly planted on a foundation of rocks. It was easier to visualize a cabin now, laid out neat and square. I thought it looked odd, that one spot in the wilderness so defined.

Neither of us had built a cabin before. Phil had examined several, and his general experience with tools put him in charge of construction. We designed it together, and he figured out how best to build it. My mother's advice was of little value here, for she was remarkably helpless in some things.

"I'm starting to notch the floor joists into the sills," he told me proudly, as we headed for the fire. "We'll nail the boards to them after the cabin is up. Here, sit down and have some hot soup. I put dried vegetables in for a special treat. To celebrate the sills. What do you think?"

He scooped two mugs into the small cooking pot and handed me one. We walked back up to the cabin and sat astride a sill, basking in the afternoon sun. Below us gleamed the strange, white river.

"Thank you for making the cabin larger than you planned," I said. It would be twelve by fifteen feet inside, and at least six feet from floor to roof so that we could stand upright "in the warm," as we called it.

"I think we'll be glad we did," he answered. We drank our soup, admiring the sills. "We're a few logs short. I'm going to cut some green ones," he said. "There just aren't any more dead trees worth taking close by. I'd rather put them on the bottom. They're twice as heavy and they'll drip sap. They'll shrink some too as they dry out."

"They're all a pretty twisted lot," I said, looking over the pile. "And small. It'll be more like a moss cabin held together by a grid of sticks."

"I thought we could put every other row in with scrap pieces on the side with the door. They'll be doweled to regular ones to hold them in place. It won't matter because we'll saw out the door hole. A lot of these old places fall down because they aren't doweled under the eaves or by the door and window openings. The guys who built them just framed in the door to hold the walls straight."

"Tomorrow I should start gathering moss to chink," I said. "Once the snow is deep, we'll never find it." I drained my cup and fished out the last pea, thinking again of my mother picking every grain of a spilled bag of rice out of the sand. Food is unbelievably precious. How had I ever taken it for granted?

"We'll need moss under the floor too," Phil told me. "I'm banking the sills with dirt on the outside to keep the wind out, but we'll need insulation from the ground."

"It'll help keep the permafrost intact," I said, "so we don't melt into the mud." After a moment I went on, "Maybe a moose hide rug is in order."

The sun was low and already an evening chill began to settle. "Let's continue this celebration down by the fire," Phil suggested. He stood and began to coil the hauling rope, slinging it over a branch. "I'll cut some tenderloin and we'll have a feast. With salt and pepper," he grinned wickedly.

I smiled and got stiffly to my feet. They were very sore and inflexible. Phil took my hand and together we hobbled down to camp.

"I think we should have treats every Sunday once we're in the cabin," I suggested. I squatted to build up the fire, blowing gently on the embers.

"Treat? Treat??" Phil went wide-eyed, making me laugh. "Treat!" he demanded, pretending to shake me. Net-Chet caught the mood and began to sing shrilly. She never really learned to bark.

"Hush!" we snarled in unison.

Phil picked her up a moment and petted her. "Now that's a good girl."

I sat on my log and Phil squatted flat-footed by the fire. We were eating our fourth course of fried meat and fat as twilight dampened the woods. I stopped chewing and extended my greasy hands to the flames.

"It'll be such a dream getting into the cabin," I said, shifting my weight to the other icy cheek. The temperature had dropped to around zero the moment the sun was gone. Only six weeks after our first star, and now we had thirteen hours of darkness. "Just think what it will be like getting dressed in 'the warm.'"

"I want to place the stove so we can light it from bed," Phil told me.

"Maybe in the middle of the cabin," I suggested. Arranging the cabin was a major topic of our conversation lately.

He tossed a bone to Chet and reached into the skillet for a fresh helping. She withdrew her nose from under her tail and sat quietly gnawing, snugged up close to the blaze. She had recently been liberated from her splint, having outgrown two of them. The fracture was reduced to a bony prominence, and her foot was a bit crooked, but the leg had healed. It had atrophied and she ran with a crooked little hop, but she was learning to use it again. To sit, she would swing her foot up in the air as if still wearing a splint, a habit she would keep for life.

"You can always tell when Chet's around," Phil observed with a grin, "by the smell of singed fur." At her name, Net-Chet thumped her tail over the coals. A flame flicked along it and Phil patted it out.

"I spend more time beating out smoldering dogs," he continued. "She won't have a hair left by the time we get into the cabin." Net-Chet sniffed the tail as if it belonged to someone else.

"I don't think she feels it through her fur." I reached across and stroked her. She looked up with her slanted, brown eyes. "Do you know that she sometimes digs up the coals and sleeps on them when the fire dies down? Not that I blame her." I hugged my knees.

All that remained of day was a lingering yellow streak over the southern peaks. Stars appeared like jewels in the deep, velvet blue. Life is good, I thought, when the wind drops and you're well-fed.

Phil licked his fingers and wiped his knife on his pants. "I'll go first," he offered, rising. While he arranged himself in the tent, I squatted over the embers, roasting my haunches. My rear was chilled to the bone, as dead as moose meat. He called, "Ready," and I gave my left side one last turn and bolted for the tent. Away from the fire the below-zero air bit sharply.

Net-Chet whimpered miserably while I slipped off my boots and stowed them under the tent fly. My teeth were clashing together as I pulled off my clothes and fumbled into the thin, ragged pajamas that Phil had warmed next to his skin. I spread out my clothing and called the grateful dog onto them then partly zipped up the door, venting the tent to reduce the snowstorm of condensed breath. Submerging in the icy folds, I balled up near the bottom of the sleeping bag, where I found Phil. Net-Chet began to creep upward from the foot almost at once.

❄

Phil's patience paid off as we fitted the twisted logs together, customizing each. First we would lift one into place to measure and mark. Because the curves gravitated downward, I clamped it between my legs while he chopped the notch. We pinned the tiers on either side of the door, solidifying the otherwise flimsy front wall by drilling down with a T-handle auger and driving inch-and-a-half pegs made from small, dead spruce poles through the layers. It was a cold, tedious job, for the auger jammed easily, filling the space between logs with chips. I spent many hours twisting it.

For a week winter relaxed its grip, gathering force for the final onslaught. We worked always under the weight of it, afraid of the cold and dark as we watched the snow creep down the barren peaks. The leaves and gay colors were suddenly gone, the willows transformed into lifeless sticks in the frozen mud. At night, our sleeping bags became rimed with ice. Crystals grew down the tent walls, cascading upon us whenever we moved. We ate enormously as autumn yawned, but far from gaining weight, we were still on the decline. At least now that we had fresh, fat meat, our diarrhea resolved.

With freeze-up, our backdoor slammed shut. We were truly committed; no longer could the river carry us downstream to safety. The ice was never really silent. Occasional slow motion waves rumbled through it, buckling the surface as pressure ridges stirred momentarily. We became almost accustomed to the startling groan and snap of the river resisting its bonds. Then the snow came. For two days it piled steadily upon our icy corral of logs, accumulating as we worked. The familiar outlines of camp vanished under inch after inch of fluff.

It was September 29. I huddled in the sleeping bag, writing in my journal with numb fingers, reluctant to rise. Nearby, Phil wrestled the rock-like quarters, trying to saw off a slab for breakfast. It was ridiculous to be surrounded by tons of meat and unable to eat it. He gave up and set Mightypot full of meat on the sputtering fire to thaw.

At last I could put off getting up no longer. The temperature had risen to 15°F, but a wind was picking up. Cold need not be extreme for a person to suffer severe exposure. Even a relatively mild temperature coupled with wetness or wind has great chilling potential. It seemed too cold even for breakfast. My feet were soon numb in their worn, summer boots. I shouldered my pack and set out at once for Chris Olson's to get floorboards.

By noon, snow was falling thickly. Wind whipped it up my sleeves and down my neck as I trudged homeward, trailing the boards. My world faded to a few yards and I fought along beneath the swaying trees, Net-Chet close to my side. One end of the lumber was lashed to the packframe, but the other end dragged behind me, snagging on every lump. It would catch and then snap forward, driving the load into the back of my head. A human pack mule, that's what I'm becoming, I thought as I staggered along.

I left the trail just before Cranberry Hill, taking a shortcut across a frozen pond. Away from the trees, all was silent but the hiss of wind and the bat of snowflakes against my stinging cheeks. I reached home to find Phil thoroughly chilled. Falling snow obscured the river beyond, leaving him adrift atop the unfinished walls. There he sat in his own little world of wind and white, faithfully twisting the auger.

We adjourned to the tent away from the pitiless wind, taking Net-Chet and a steaming pot of moose neck. There we crouched, the center of all things, the three of us alone in the white world, and gnawed bones while reading aloud about ballooning in Africa. Outside our little tent, the wind increased, shaking it as snow streaked by. A sober, quiet feeling invaded our buffeted little shelter as darkness settled and the snow continued endlessly. Gradually, we came to realize that here at last was winter.

Morning light filtered dimly into our tent, for we were snowed under. The wind had stopped, but falling flakes continued to rush out of the colorless sky. The nearby spruce trees stood in ghostly silhouette. All was silent, except for the lonely groan of branches settling under their burdens. Outside lay an alien land, lost in formless gray—an eerie world without dimension, no up or down, only falling snow.

What a beautiful world to play in, I thought, as I dislodged an avalanche of snow from our sagging tent. This is a day to be a child and run through fluffy mountains of white. I reached through the doorway and dug for my boots. I had placed them beneath the fly, but it too was buried, collapsed under the weight of snow. A day to come inside laughing and red-cheeked, stamping feet and shaking soft hair. A day to sit by a crackling fireplace and drink hot chocolate. I kicked at the impossibly soft drift that blocked the entrance. The flakes were almost half an inch across, six-sided, and as perfect as pictures. No way to avoid getting wet.

I waded to the fireplace and fished around for lost pots and utensils. We could lose things, I realized. From the trunk of a nearby spruce, I snapped off dead twigs for tinder. Buckets of snow emptied from the patient tree with each one plucked.

Snow woman. Icicle lady.

Already my feet were cold and wet, the new snow melting into the leather of my boots. I sniffed the thick morning air; my thoughts fingered the sleeping land, feeling the slowing pulse of life as blankets of winter were pulled on. I listened into the stillness. After the throb of summer and the autumn battles of wind and ice, this was something new. It wasn't the silence of a void, but the minute whisper of countless hurrying snowflakes. Every noise was sucked up and swallowed by this imperceptible rustle of stillness.

And where are all the people? I wondered, gazing into the empty, gray valley. It was a dream world. The far shore drifted momentarily before me in the soup. My eyes could not focus on the featureless ice, and it seemed to shift and change as I stared. I stood knee-deep in powder, twigs grasped in my bare, red hands. Strange to be so alone after a life built around people, defined by people, hemmed in by people. And where are they now? I stamped out a small circle and squatted to light the tinder. People are my boundaries, I realized, my points of reference. I could be anywhere. It really didn't matter in a land of no people.

Above me on the hill was our unborn cabin, an illusion of warmth and comfort. I studied it as I fed the small fire, seeing only a lonesome pile of logs, half-buried in snow. I shuffled and slipped my way through billowing clouds of powder, climbing the slope to stare into the bleak structure: a three-foot corral with joists. Net-Chet burrowed unhappily up beside me, tail drooping. She climbed through the door hole, her thin legs resentful of the deep snow, and sat in anxious confusion, looking at this thing that demanded all my time. I know how it is supposed to look, I thought wretchedly, but I just can't picture it.

Phil was bent dejectedly over the sputtering fire, blowing, as I skidded back down the hill. Steamy smoke marred the snow, dissolving it like cotton candy.

"You don't like snow," I stated.

"Not to work in," he replied. He was rearranging the damp sticks. The snow was too deep even for squatting—like knee-high feathers.

"I remember how we loved it as kids," I told him. "It so rarely snowed in Tucson that any flake was cause for joyous celebration. Then the adults would grump."

"Now you know why."

"Because they were grownups," I stated flatly. "Is it really necessary to become so joyless? To lose your sense of play as you age?"

"Well, grownups have to work in snow," he answered.

I stooped to remove the little teapot that was suddenly boiling over and poured tea for both of us. The pot was blackened and dented. "The first snow I remember was when I was six years old," I said. "I was spending a month or two with a sitter, a strict Baptist, while my mother was on a lecture tour. It was Sunday. I looked out and saw tiny flakes in the rain. It was snowing! Really snowing! She simply couldn't understand how important that was. For her it was just something that happened. By the time she herded me into that bleak old church, snowflakes were streaming down. All I remember is looking back at the glorious snow as those heavy doors closed behind me."

Phil took a pull on his tea. Despite the new food, he seemed somehow gaunt and frail, backlit in white. "When I was in high school it snowed once. They turned the sprinklers on and melted it all."

"Joyless creatures."

"And now you're a grownup," he finished mischievously.

"What could be more important than enjoying our glorious planet?" I answered, ignoring his comment. Love of adventure was a gift from my mother. For her, living was a smorgasbord—a banquet of opportunities to be eaten and enjoyed.

It snowed all day. We worked quietly, Phil on the cabin, me unearthing the sphagnum moss for chinking. Moss was plentiful and thick, and it would have been an easy job without the snow. Now it was hard to find. The last thing we talked about as we drifted off to sleep was our first Sunday celebration in the cabin, planning the menu in detail. Snow was still coming down.

❀

The following morning the sky was clear but the temperature had dropped below zero. A numbing wind sprayed powder through the air, stinging my cheeks. Snow had melted into our summer boots and they were frozen in grotesque shapes. I peeked from beneath the stiff folds of down, watching Phil struggle with his boots. I could see his chapped hands strain with the unyielding leather, and I knew that his feet, like mine, were tender and swollen. Our feet never really warmed, but when sensation returned during the night hours, they ached and itched unbearably. To add to our nighttime misery, we were now beset with muscle cramps.

I ran my fingers down my contracted legs and gently twisted one foot. It had lost much of its flex, and the skin protruded in painful lumps over the joints. I hadn't seen it in days, for I dressed in bed. I pulled it up for inspection. It looked pale and bruised and I kissed it tenderly before tucking it back under the covers, acutely aware of loving my body and all its familiar parts. How unkind, I thought, to send my feet forth in frozen boots for yet another day.

In the tent entrance Phil was working with growing despair, forcing his wretched foot into the frozen boot. I knew he was wasting precious heat in this twenty-minute ordeal, but could offer nothing. Finally, one at a time, the poor extremities were crammed into the unyielding leather and he hobbled off to build a fire. Before I had completed dressing, he returned with my boots, damp but pliable, from the fire.

I was lame and my feet were cold almost at once. I hurried to the wind-blasted fire and squatted over it in the frigid sunlight. The flames gusted to and fro, singeing hairs from my numb fingers but warming them little. Phil looked the picture of misery. His eyes had a lusterless, sunken quality in a dark, weathered face. His nose was running into his mustache, freezing icicles above the cracked lips.

"L'ammal, you go back to the tent," I said. "I'll finish breakfast. There's no sense in both of us being out here."

Phil nodded unhappily and handed me the warped Teflon skillet. He fumbled his pocketknife from meat he had been trying to pry apart and finally snapped it shut against his leg.

"It's so frustrating to order your fingers to do something and they don't," he apologized, turning for the tent. I watched his woolen back recede, so vulnerable. He was staring at his feet as he placed them cautiously. They looked stiff and wooden. We have to finish the cabin! I thought desperately. Then everything will be okay. Yet I knew in the dark, unspoken back of my mind that not all stories have happy endings. When you're young you feel invincible, but it's an illusion.

I scurried to the tent with a smoking skillet of meat. Phil was buried in the sleeping bags, his boots tucked beneath him to keep them from freezing. I zipped the tent shut behind me and pulled the bags over my lap. The tent snapped about me in the wind. Phil raised up on one elbow.

"Hurry now," I said, pushing a filthy fork into his hand. "The fat is already solidifying." My feet were in agony. I loosened the boot laces and worked them free. My socks were frozen to the inside of the boots and I pulled to get them free. Phil put my stiff feet through his shirt and pressed them against his bare stomach.

"I wonder how our meat will hold out at the rate we're eating it," I said. We were wolfing the meal, careful to share the fat chunks that made up a third of its volume. "I bet we each eat six thousand calories a day."

"Don't cut against the skillet," Phil intoned as usual. "I don't know how we'll sharpen the knives. I tried this morning, but ice sheeted over the stone too fast to work. The ax stone has shattered from water frozen into the pores."

I was eyeing the last piece of fat.

"Go ahead," he told me, receding into the covers, still chewing. "It's yours."

I finished and began scraping the burned grease from the pan, eating it off my knife. "I always wanted to be thin," I complained, "and now I don't enjoy it. It's uncomfortable. Even sleeping. Sitting on logs while you chop a notch is bone-shattering. Every time I slip in the snow, I fall on one skinny hip or the other. I'm bruised all over. My butt and legs are black and blue. I almost wonder if I haven't frosted the skin or something."

"Can't you squat? That would be warmer than sitting."

"Not while drilling holes and holding logs. The circulation in my behind has always seemed poor. Remember how cold it got even in mild weather? Now the old body is shutting off service to the suburbs. Well . . ." I decided reluctantly. "I'll go fry us a couple more pans of meat and then we'd better get to work. The cabin won't build itself."

I pulled on my frosty boots and crawled from the tent, zipping it behind me. Our precious structure loomed above me, completely uninhabitable. It was colder inside than out because of the shadowing walls. I dreaded another day of digging through the snow for chinking moss or straddling the icy wall, drilling holes for pegs. I hate it, I thought resentfully. If I ever get out of here, I'm going to spend my life inside—warm and well fed. I used to think of myself as the outdoors type. But I'm not!

"I agree with you, if that helps any," Phil told me as we again gulped the unattractive food. It had cooled on top while the blasting fire burned the bottom. "This is the sort of 'character building' experience that I would like to have had long ago. I think it will be good for us . . . if we live through it."

I understood what he meant. "Hardship puts life in perspective," I remarked. "It knocks the pickiness out of you and teaches you how strong you really are. You can quit almost anything. You can drop out of school, get divorced, go AWOL from the military, run away from home, give up your job. But we can't quit. We have to finish that cabin."

"Oh, I suppose we could just die," he answered. He looked so lost that I studied him awhile, before answering.

"No," I said at last. "There have been times in the past that I considered suicide, when I felt overwhelmed by the complexities of that other life and my relationships with people. But this is different. My body was designed to survive, honed by conditions like these through millions of years. It won't give up without a good fight. It's interesting to see, when really threatened, how hard I will fight. That's something I didn't know about myself."

The sun had almost reached the zenith of its low swing across the southern sky before we left the tent. Daylight was sliding rapidly now, deserting us at an accelerating pace.

What followed were some of the most difficult and miserable days of my life. We felt a desperation waking each morning in frozen sleeping bags at temperatures of fifteen and twenty below zero to face another endless day toiling in the wind and cold.

The cabin walls became more stubborn as they rose. First we would wrestle a log into place for fitting. Then, gripping it with icy thigh bones, I straddled it in the proper position while Phil sat astride a side wall and chopped the notch. Turning and shaping the logs, we settled them one by one into place. Then I would chink the cracks, using one frozen hand and then the other to pack moss between the logs, pounding it snug with a chip of wood. The hardest task, however, was to straddle the icy wall slowly turning the auger down through the layers of logs and jamming chips. When we reached window height, there were five holes to drill with each tier.

Looking back it seems strange that we did not get out our winter clothing. True, there was little to be done for our feet, yet long after the rains ceased, we continued to wear our summer woolens. Our down parkas and pants remained in five-gallon cans, buried under the snow beside the tent. We didn't even sleep in long underwear. We knew enough to remove our damp day clothes, but night after night we chattered into filmy night clothes and rattled bones together in the middle of the sleeping bag. And bones they were. Although Phil was bundled in wool by day, at night I could feel sharp ribs and shoulder blades protruding through his thin T-shirt.

We were obsessed with the cabin and nothing else mattered. All our thoughts were of warmth and shelter. All our sentences began with "When we get into the cabin. . . ." Just as our numerous knife cuts from butchering were nothing in our battle for food, now other pain was ignored by brains engrossed in staying alive.

The hardest thing I have ever done was to face those mornings: putting on my twenty-below-zero clothes and frozen boots and climbing out of the tent. My previous life of comfort and plenty seemed a dream, a fairy tale from another century. How had I ever taken such abundance for granted? This was the natural state of existence. *This* brutal effort for life was the way it had always been. My world narrowed to the moment. Past and future dissolved as I struggled through the eternal present, caught up in an endless reality of pain and cold.

Each night, chilled and exhausted, we crawled into our sleeping bags and shivered together in the blackness beneath frozen layers of nylon. Seldom did we move, reluctant to waste heat despite the discomfort of the hard, lumpy ground. We developed sleeping postures that gave maximum body contact. Phil would curl around my back, folding one arm under his neck and wrapping the upper arm and leg about me. Sometimes I slept on top of him, chest to chest, braced off the ground on my knees and elbows.

During the night, layers of ice from our breath formed on the sleeping bags. Frost rained from the ceiling each time one of us rose to pee, chattering barefooted in the snow beside the tent entrance. In the cold, dry air we were tormented with thirst and consumed great quantities of hot broth during the day. We kept water in the tent by sleeping with an old syrup bottle from the village until it froze and shattered one night. Then we took turns when we woke at night, melting snow in our hands for one another.

Net-Chet crept resolutely upward until the three of us were condensed in a tight, little knot in the center of the tent. By midnight, thanks to the gift of Phil's stomach and legs, my feet and behind would begin to warm. How wonderful to be warm! We had one place to crawl into and raise our body temperatures—one place in all this frozen, uncaring world. How good the comfortable smells of our own unwashed bodies, the warm smells of life!

Net-Chet was miserable too. She spent most of each day curled wretchedly against the south wall of the cabin, out of the wind. Although she had put on a few guard hairs, she was slender of build, thin and unhappy with her arctic lot in life. Her lovely, curly tail hung limply between her legs and though she seldom whined now, she was not doing well. It hurt to see her silent misery, but we could no more help her than ourselves.

The strain was showing on all of us. Phil looked thin and pinched, his great, green eyes pits above his ragged beard and its mask of icicles. We wore our wool caps continually. Every few days I discarded mine to brush out my long, matted hair, which came out in handfuls. All this, and I'm going bald too! I thought in desperation. But it didn't matter anymore. Only the cabin mattered, that cold, useless edifice to toil—our haven to be.

We gave up trying to saw the iron-hard meat into pieces for frying. I chopped a hole in the ice and filled Mightypot with gallons of water and big hunks of frozen meat and fat. This bubbled all day over a listless fire. We ate continually and without interest, replenishing the pot as we worked. We even gave up tea as too much bother.

Work on the gables went the slowest of all. They were high and exposed to wind. It took effort to climb the walls, and balance to hold the short, loose logs in place while securing them with pins. We counted our progress in two or three logs a day. But gradually the gables grew. We rolled the first purlin into place and then the second, securing the gables. A purlin is a roof support log, similar to the ridgepole, but not at the peak. Our roof was constructed off center, its peak four feet from the long south wall where the windows would be, and eight feet from the dark north wall. The windows all faced south to catch the winter sun.

One afternoon we set Chris Olson's heavy sheet metal stove up on coffee cans balanced over the joists and built a fire in it, abandoning the windy fireplace down by the river for good. We should have moved long before. The cabin remained a roofless ice cave, impossible to heat, but now we could easily break from a task to stand for a moment out of the wind, drinking hot broth and warming our hands. Falling snow hissed onto the warped stove top. To celebrate the installation of the second purlin and the stove, I sawed a giant round steak for dinner and fried it up "inside."

The following day, Phil finished drilling and placing the last two gable logs while I cut and hauled rafter poles for the roof. We would need over a hundred rafters, but some long-ago fire had left acres of small, dead spruce trees standing between the mature hardier ones: nature's way of pruning. By evening we were ready for our triumphant placement of the ridgepole—a great log that would form the peak of the cabin and extend beyond in a meat rack. This would be supported on one end by the stump of a tree that grew eight feet from the east wall.

Next morning we heaved the massive ridgepole onto the butt ends of plate logs that capped the main structure below the gables. Then slowly we rolled it up the gables and into position. It was hard and dangerous work, balancing aloft as we carefully notched and fitted that log. When it was done, Phil sawed the top from the nearby tree, and we scooted the end of the ridgepole onto the high stump, securing it in place with a metal strap. Our cabin suddenly looked real! We measured the walls. Phil's "almost level" had broken weeks before when the water in the little bottle froze, but despite this, the cabin was accurate on every measurement to within a quarter of an inch.

Infused with new hope, we retreated to the tent for only a brief foot warming session. Then Phil chopped the gable logs to pitch while I headed up the hill to the Cathedral Grove for more rafters. My skid trail was now a smooth chute of packed snow, worn slick by the passage of many logs.

We missed the deadline for celebrating our first Sunday in the cabin. Still, it was with much enthusiasm that we attacked our growing roof the following day. Phil pinned a rafter-retaining log over the butt ends of the plates and sawed my poles to fit using Chris Olson's bucksaw and laying them side by side over the purlins. I felled the dead poles and hauled them as rapidly as Phil could place them. Gradually, the sky disappeared from inside our home. At last! Our cabin was becoming a shelter! By midweek, a pole ceiling spread over the entire cabin.

When we finished laying the rafters it was late, but we set off together for Chris Olson's place and more boards. This was Phil's first trip over my route. Despite a new snowfall, the trail I had broken two days before made the going easy. The temperature was below zero; my feet were numb and my body tired from the long labor. Nevertheless, the woods were beautiful—a wonderland where every creature left its story in new snow. Here a lynx had caught a luckless rabbit, discarding its hide and feet for Net-Chet. A squirrel had eaten a spruce cone, scattering reddish scales over the snow. I spotted the little animal next to a tree trunk at eye level. He churred sleepily at us, flipping his tail. I watched him a moment, grateful that I no longer needed to eat little squirrels.

Net-Chet bounded ahead while we wallowed through the knee-high snow. The bushes were loaded, and cascades of snow dumped on my back as I passed beneath them. It is hard to pick a straight trail through timber, but now that snow marked my passage, I would blaze a path and then clear it, I decided.

By the time we reached the cache, snow was again falling thickly through the purple of evening. We wasted no time in dismantling the crumbling outhouse, nailing boards together into packets. They were rotten and warped, stained and dirty—and oh! so beautiful. Phil and I helped one another into our cumbersome packs and, trailing bundles of boards, set out for home.

We trudged up the ridge, lurching through the mist and thickening darkness, pulling our boards. What if we should lose the path? I wondered suddenly. Ahead of me, Phil plodded like a patient shadow, a dark form in the drifting snow. The familiar mountains were gone. Strange creatures of the twilight we seemed as we thrashed through a silent, fuzzy world.

I was drenched with sweat and melted snow when the lone spruce that marked our home trail appeared in the gloom. The boards crowded close upon our striding legs down the packed chute, around the toilet hole, and into camp.

We helped each other unsaddle. I propped my packframe against the front wall and ducked through the door hole. Inside it was black. Slits of gray light beamed between the rafter poles overhead. The door and two front window holes were also winter-evening gray.

"Look Phil, a real house!" I spread my arms. My shoulders ached with the released strain. "Hey, the meat I left on the stove is thawed."

"Watch your step," he warned. "I think I'll light the lantern." Between the joists, the frozen mud was mounded and slippery with snow. Cautiously, we stepped over the knee-high joists as we moved about the room.

We had a single gallon of white gas for special occasions. It took time to find and fill the lantern in the dark. I prepared dinner in that unreal white glow, and we ate sitting on the joists as snow sifted between the rafter poles. The door and window holes loomed ominously black in the strange glare that now separated us from the rest of the Arctic. In camp I had always sensed the land about me, but now I was limited by these walls, cut off from the night by my dulled perceptions.

After dinner we turned off the lantern and sat by the glow of the stove. It was cracked and bolt holes emitted a dancing light with occasional showers of sparks. I stood up to warm my bottom, as I had seen my mother do since childhood. She would pull up her skirt, and with her hands behind her back, toast her fanny near a stove.

"Have you noticed the way Chet's new teeth are popping in?" I asked. "Our little girl is growing up."

She was snuggled in Phil's lap as he leaned against one wall, cleaning his teeth with dental floss. He always kept a string of it in the compass case he still wore in his shirt pocket, using each bit of floss until it was frayed. Dental floss is important to meat-eaters, we had found.

"Oh, she's a clever one," he laughed.

It sounded good and I realized that it had been a long time since I'd heard him laugh. He tugged on the end of Chet's nose and she rolled her belly up, bicycling with her legs.

"And hair!" he continued. "She just wanted to be a house dog. She waited until we let her into the tent." It was true. Net-Chet had turned hairy overnight, submerging beneath luxurious blankets.

"Maybe she lost faith in our cabin," I suggested, rotating before the heat. My feet were cold in the slush a foot below the joists. "I did myself."

"She's just stubborn," he countered.

"Really now, can you imagine our little family alone here—you and me inside and her left out?"

Phil was noisily driving the end of Chet's nose, her "squelch knob" he called it, and shifting gears with her legs. She rolled and growled happily. It was good to see them play.

"With those shiny new teeth and winter outfit, all she needs is a furry squelch knob, don't you think?" he asked. "How would you like to have that cold, wet thing on the end of your face all winter? Ouch! Don't touch me with that!"

"You're silly." I smiled, watching them fondly.

The next morning we awoke in a mess of sagging nylon and melting snow. Winter had abated. Leaving the little tent frozen sadly under a burden of new snow, we abandoned camp and hauled our soggy sleeping bags into the cabin to spread on boards laid over the joists. The thermometer soared to thirty-four degrees, and falling snow melted into our clothes on contact. Even our meat began to thaw. In many ways, we had been better off when it was colder.

There was compensation, however. The frozen mounds of dirt from beneath our cabin were now soft enough to hack into lumps and shovel onto the roof. Phil tacked the tattered plastic tarp over the rafters, and the cabin began to warm almost at once. I could hear the rhythmic thumps of falling clods as I prepared breakfast of fried liver. I nailed plastic flaps over the door and window holes. Soon water dripped from the frosted walls. Warm! I took off my red wool coat and spread my arms like a child. For the first time in months I was warm.

Invigorated by hope and this brief reprieve, Phil and I toiled into the half-light of a snowy afternoon, lifting the stacked sods and placing them onto the roof. With this completion, a remarkable peace began to settle upon us.

We yearned to remain inside and celebrate, as we had long planned, but there was still much to do. The cabin had no floor, windows, or door, and the upper half had yet to be chinked. The next day, I set out to grub up moss for insulation. It would require forty-four duffel bags full, or about 120 cubic feet of sphagnum moss, to chink the walls and insulate under the floorboards. This may seem like a lot, but the following spring I couldn't find where I had harvested it.

It was late Saturday afternoon and I had been gathering all day, making trip after trip into the forest. Using Chris Olson's shovel, I rummaged through drifts until my two duffel bags were packed, then I turned for home. How strange it was to see a cabin perched there where none had been before. It was the same beach, same trees, same hill, same forlorn little tent—yet now a cabin stood there!

As I mounted the hill, Phil met me and took my bags.

"Wait'll you see how it looks with a floor!" he exalted, swinging the plastic door flap aside for me. The doorway was tiny, only four and a half feet high—made to conserve heat and boards. I ducked through, stepping over the sill log. Inside, Phil had been laying out boards, patching Chris's old planks into a floor and tacking them down with straightened nails. He came in behind me, rearranged the flap, and dumped the moss between two joists.

I held my cold fingers out to the stove and looked about. Our very own floor! For half a year we had lived outdoors. Now the whole world was snowed under, and we had a floor—flat, clean, and warm. It was hard to believe. I hugged myself, smiling. I would bathe, and wash dishes, and someday have a table! Erecting these precious logs between ourselves and the Arctic had made all the difference.

"Only about three more loads for the floor," Phil said, dropping the empty duffel bags by the doorway. He bent over and smoothed the moss between the joists.

I groaned and reached for the bags.

"No, wait and warm up a bit," he suggested, putting his arms about me.

I smiled and shook my head. "I want a floor for our first Sunday, and we still need to bring up all the supplies." Everything we owned was piled by the overturned canoe: all those precious items chosen so long ago and carried so very far. "I'm going to clean out the plastic bucket and fill it with water. I don't want anything to spoil tomorrow."

Phil was carefully straightening rusty nails as I dropped the door flap and plodded out into the snow. The world was the soft, blue-gray of snowy evening as I stepped noiselessly along the familiar beach, headed upstream. As I passed the forlorn tent, a bird called from the spruce above me—strange and wild in the twilight. I listened, caught by a memory from my childhood. I knew that bird . . .

The roar of wings startled me. Then I placed it. "Phil! Bring the .22!" I called out.

He appeared beside me, unlaced boots filling with snow, eyes alert.

"Up there." I pointed. "A spruce chicken. See the dark outline near the trunk? Want me to shoot?"

"No. I see him," he whispered.

The short "twhinggg!" of the .22 was swallowed in the flutter of wings as the heavy body plummeted. Phil started forward.

"Wait!" I called in surprise. "My bird is still there!" I could see the shadowy form turning its head in agitation. The movement caught Phil's eye and there was a second echoless shot. Two spruce chickens for Thanksgiving dinner! Life is so good.

An hour later we were sitting on our partial floor, savoring chocolate pudding—our first treat in weeks—by the light of the open stove door. "Did you ever taste anything so good?" I asked.

"Never." Phil had his eyes closed as he rolled the pudding around in his mouth. In the darkness I had used cornmeal instead of sugar, but it didn't matter.

The fire cast strange shadows on the walls and my eyes danced over the logs in childish awe. How had we come to be here? I couldn't quite remember. Something about walking and wind and cold. A dream, I thought. A beautiful dream. My home.

"Just look! Oh, not you, Chet," I stroked her basking head. She was enjoying the cabin as much as we were.

"You have to be careful around a dog that speaks people," Phil told me in a serious aside.

It was true. Net-Chet followed our conversations carefully and was able to pick out many words. Perhaps she was unusual in this, certainly our circumstances were unusual, but I think humans often underestimate the non-human world.

Net-Chet settled her golden head into my lap and stretched her toes luxuriously. "Our cabin," I whispered, still unable to believe it.

Phil was also gazing about the room in wonder. "You were right about making it big," he acknowledged. "There were times I had my doubts." He took my hand and we laughed in delight. Our cabin! We had cut and dragged every log here with our muscles, shaping each one just so. How solid and strong they all looked, this product of a dream—this triumph! Our life, restored. For the first time in weeks I dared hope we could survive winter.

I touched a log, sliding my battered fingers over the honey-colored wood. "Remember?" I whispered. This log had once been as crooked as a caterpillar. The surface was decorated with intricate tunnels made by spruce beetles that had killed it. The grain revolved in a corkscrew. There were fresh stripes of exposed wood where we had peeled the bark away with a drawknife. How well it carried the hours invested!

Phil was caressing the walls and ceiling with his eyes, remembering our struggle. Then, suddenly we were both laughing. We toppled backwards onto the sleeping bags, giggling and pointing out logs. Each had its story. Overhead, the sturdy rafters flickered in the amber light, and joy welled up within me— pure childish joy. How lucky we are, I kept thinking. How wonderfully privileged! Not just to have food and shelter, but to know its worth.

Later that night I lay comfortably half awake, stretched full-length in our warm bags beneath Phil's arm. It had been a long time since I had stretched out.

"Phil...?"

"Ummm..."

"I had a fantasy of spruce hens for Thanksgiving dinner, and now we have them. Just like that. I don't know why I worry so much. When the time comes, we always have what we need. Do you notice? Like the floor. Or moose. Phil...?"

"Ummm...?"

"There really aren't any accidents. Phil...? Are you awake?"

"Uh huh."

"Then why are you snoring?"

My only answer was a gentle snore. His arm twitched a moment, drawing me in. The stove on its gallon cans glowed a lovely cherry, sending out occasional sparks. The walls wavered in the light of the dying fire.

Outside, I sensed the weight of frigid wind, black against the cabin, ladened with big flakes. They swam through my sleepy imagination in flurries half seen, tons of frozen water. On they came, a white flood pouring southward over the drowsy land, pulling me with them. Flung onto my well-known river, I became a snowflake . . . no . . . a leaf! A dried alder leaf. Lightly I danced, skipping and skating over the wind-rippled snow.

How different things were out here. How vast! Dried leaves don't mind the cold. And the music! I paused against a dune to listen to the tinkle and whisper of crystals, but the next gust threw me upward, twirled on the singing wind. On I shot, past the burl tree, past the large, white rock that looked like a molar, past the deserted little tent. I caught a glimpse of the cabin as I hurled into the bigger world, tumbled southward on the rising crest of winter. I lost my vision somewhere in the mountains as sleep claimed me.

I woke the next morning with a feeling of complete peace. Gradually my surfacing mind constructed the cabin about me, and I opened my eyes and stretched. No icy tent walls.

"It's Sunday!" I remembered, sitting up.

"Hi, sleepyhead." Phil had a fire going and was reading a book about tanning hides, his head pillowed beside me on his old, patched boots.

I slipped from bed, feeling the forgotten sensation of warm air on my skin.

"Oh, wakin' up in the Warms,
In the Arctic in the winter.
It's a whole new kinda feeling,
Wakin' up in the Warms.
In the Arctic, in the winter, in the Warms!"

I sang out, to some long forgotten advertising jingle, ending with a little dance routine. Phil laughed and dropped his book as I pulled him out of bed and together we leapt about the cabin singing made-up songs to made-up tunes. Chet danced with us, making little dashes at our ankles, while a fly resurrected from the moss bumbled about in confusion, thinking it was spring.

The cabin was a jumble of possessions. When Phil asked for a treat, I searched for our two twenty-five-pound bags of flour. We had forsworn opening them until this day, living almost entirely on meat since August. After he soldered the holes in Chris Olson's flour bin, we poured in the precious powder. The cloth bags were moldy and crusted from their long journey in the bottom of the canoe. I set them aside, planning to soak the flour from them to use another time.

Phil brought in fat bear flank. This I sliced thinly and sprinkled with salt and sugar to make a sort of bacon. We had been planning today's menu for weeks: a breakfast of pancakes, blueberry syrup, and bacon followed by lunch of T-bone steaks with as much fat as we could eat, biscuits and gravy.

"Maybe 'vegetable meef stew' for dinner," I decided. I would make it with a few dried vegetables, moose meat, and beef bouillon.

"And applesauce ice cream?" he hinted. We would open the gallon of dried applesauce.

"And applesauce ice cream. We can eat all day and never go outside."

"Oh, this is the day we change clothes," he sang out. "From now on, I think we ought to change underwear every Sunday, whether we need to or not. Look how clean!" He held up a pair of panties we hadn't seen since that long ago Yukon day.

I had forgotten clothes could be that clean.

"I'm going to make a bookshelf so that we can look at all our books whenever we want," Phil declared. He was dancing over the floor in his bare feet and ragged T-shirt like a dirty, bearded scarecrow. Except for our rifles and sleeping bags, books were our most prized possessions. Now that we were safe, we yearned to look at them.

"Maybe you'd better wait until we finish chinking," I suggested. "They might get snowed on and warp." Phil looked so disappointed that I amended, "Well, it won't hurt to make the shelf. Maybe I can finish chinking that wall today."

It wasn't a cold day, but we kept a fire going. Sky showed between the upper logs and ice still hid between the exposed joists. I lifted the door flap and stepped into a foot of silvery fluff. My bare toes sank through the stinging softness and I stood listening. What a different world! I had forgotten this place. Suddenly released from the cabin, my mind expanded. The Arctic was everywhere, as far as my thoughts could travel.

Inside I could hear Phil hammering away and humming an unrecognizable tune in some key of his own. About me the trees moaned softly, their tops rocking as they guarded the cabin from the cruel wind that streaked down the river. I watched sheets of snow sweep our old camp at thirty miles per hour. It drifted like sand over the ice, building dunes, burying the tent.

How glad I am not to be down there, I thought. I wondered suddenly how the animals were faring. It wouldn't be a fun day to be a wolf. I breathed happily of the falling snow, standing contentedly in my bare feet and tattered pajamas. Let it snow.

CHAPTER 7

I stretched and pushed back the covers. Phil was already up, and the roar of the glowing stove filled the cabin. Two weeks had elapsed since we moved in, but much work remained before our home would be safe and comfortable.

"It looks pretty hot," I said apprehensively. The stove was a cherry red and sparks flew from cracks in its warped old top. I reached over and flipped the draft shut, but it did little good. The stove was balanced on coffee cans, and the boards below it were smoking. Occasionally the whole stove had pitched forward, filling the room with cinders and smoke.

"I need to install a damper in the stovepipe," Phil said. "I'll get to it when I finish the windows." He poured water between the floorboards as another rain of sparks descended.

"That layer of moss would make dandy tinder," I commented. "Not to mention all these wood shavings. It'd be terrible to burn the place down." The temperature had dropped to thirty below zero, giving us a taste of what life without shelter might be like.

"I should be able to start on the stove stand tomorrow," he told me. The stand would include a small table with a storage shelf beneath. It would secure the stove and lift it above the floor.

"You really think you can finish the windows today?" I asked in excitement.

"I think so," he grinned.

Real windows. I smiled to myself as I pulled on my daytime long underwear. We each had a pair to sleep in and one for days. "Where's Chet?"

"Playing 'Wild Dog of the North' down on the river."

I threaded between the clutter and pulled aside a plastic flap that covered the window hole. On the riverbank below sat Net-Chet, attentively watching. On windy days she chased stray leaves that drifted past. Her gait was strong now, but she still had a few odd habits acquired while her leg was splinted.

I finished dressing and sat on a wooden crate to brush my hair. It was still coming out, though at a diminished rate. It felt remarkably soft since I had washed it. I recalled my mother saying that you never get any dirtier after the first few weeks. That may be true, I thought, but my standards of cleanliness had changed. Daily bathing is very hard on skin when you live outdoors, especially one's face and hands. Washing removes the protective oils.

"We need wood," I commented. "It's scary facing winter without a woodpile. We really don't know how dark or cold it will get."

Phil stepped outside for firewood. I looked around the room. The stove had slowed, and already a chill was returning. A damper in the stovepipe would help. So would windows. I glanced fondly at the new door, thinking what a difference it made closing the Arctic out. It took a long time to build things using an ax and jack plane. The cabin was piled with our belongings; the sleeping bags, already filthy from the summer, were still underfoot on the floor. But the windows and stove came first.

He returned, stamping fresh snow from his feet as he closed the door. It was frail and covered with plastic to keep out the wind. A double plastic window filled the top, constructed to let in more light and conserve lumber.

"I want to try trapping this winter," Phil said, dumping the wood by the stove. He removed the pot of boiling meat and set it on a five-gallon can. "It would be good survival knowledge and teach us about animals. Besides, the price of fur is sky high."

"I've been thinking about setting a couple of rabbit snares up on the hill," I told him. "I'd like to make us fur caps. It would be fun to see if I can catch a snowshoe hare." We hadn't seen one since they had turned white. "While I'm out, maybe I'll backtrack the caribou we saw yesterday and see where they came from. It would be good to know."

The day before, Chet had proclaimed the arrival of caribou to our valley. While we scuttled for coats, mittens, camera, bullets, lenses, and rifles, they had trooped by our doorstep in tireless migration. It was a little band of perhaps forty, all bulls, the fringe of a tide of animals. Their trotting feet soon carried them behind Timber Island and away.

"Do you want to shoot any?" Phil asked. He was blowing on a chunk of meat, skewered on his fork.

"We can always use the food," I answered. We didn't know how much meat we would need to see us through winter, and we had already eaten most of a moose. "Caribou might make better mukluks," I said as an afterthought. We were still wearing our summer boots. "Moose hide is really too thick. I'll leave Chet here and take my rifle, just in case."

Phil chewed contentedly. I sat down near him and stabbed into the pot. The meat tasted very good. Everything did. The bland diet had sharpened my sense of taste. I could tell within a few inches where a piece of meat had come off the animal. Although our consumption had dropped dramatically since moving inside, we were both putting on weight. It felt good to fatten up. It felt like success.

I chuckled and Phil glanced at me over his fork. "We'll be too fat to get out that little door soon," I commented. He grinned.

After breakfast I ascended the hill, snow billowing about my knees. Shafts of noon sunlight streaked low between the trees casting long, blue shadows over the sparkling crystals. Each day the sun fell in its arc across the southern sky. It was so weak now that only a few clouds on the horizon were enough to obscure it altogether.

I studied the tracks of the little invisible folk of the forest. Intricate paths marred the perfect snow, telling stories of the night. Hidden tunnels mined the drifts and I stepped cautiously, my unseen feet punching into convoluted mansions buried beneath the surface.

Bunny "runs" were everywhere. Young trees, bending under the weight of snow, were nibbled by the hares. Even spruce trees. A rabbit trail zagged under a fallen tree and I stooped to peer in. A foot of snow covered the trunk, raising the surrounding terrain and leaving a secret depression. With an exit. Rabbits never forget they are rabbits—fair game for every predator from owl to wolf.

It will be time to put on snowshoes soon, I thought, as I waded through knee-high crystals onto a ridge that paralleled the river. I paused to check the wind direction. It was strange how erecting walls had separated me from the rest of life. I had never awakened in the tent without knowing the direction of the wind. How easy it is to lose track of the wilderness from inside a cabin. My life was now defined by a few logs. Somehow I had exchanged this vast wilderness for a safe and comfortable enclosure. There seemed no way around that. How fragile is appetite; how easily lost, appreciation.

Ahead of me I spotted the caribou trail, a single deep set of tracks, wending through stunted spruce trees. Their hooves were nearly as large as those of the moose and very round—snowshoes for an animal a fraction the size. Apparently they had all stepped in the same tracks to conserve energy breaking trail. I could see where they plunged for the river, and I followed the path down through the thick aspens. It ran steep and straight, avoiding the worst thickets until it emptied over a ledge, sliding to the river below. I could not climb down the icy cliff, but sought out the trail with my eyes, tracing it downstream, out and around Timber Island. I could see where they hit overflow and the single track split to forty, joining again on dry ice. I turned back to find where they had come from.

Their broken trail was easy walking, the prints placed at close to my natural stride. It carried me overland above Olson Creek, choosing always the best ground. Before me a vast tundra opened, climbing westward. Caribou know how to walk, I thought. Down one mountain and up the next. They are designed for a country where food grows slowly. My mother once told me if you see a caribou that's not moving, it isn't a caribou.

Turning my back to the bitter breeze, I stopped to take in my valley. How big it looked from up here! Away from the sheltering trees, the wind was strong, burning my cheeks. The private sound of my heart thudding inside its warm ribcage and my gasping breath brought a feeling of comfort. I stared south into the ruby sun, watching a sparkle of falling frost squeezed from the clear, yellow sky by dropping temperature. Downstream a faint mist clung to the river where water had seeped from under the restless ice. The sun slid sideways, rolling along the crest of the southern peaks, until it glimmered out.

I gazed over this formidable expanse—home of the caribou. Again I faced the wind and continued up, up, hearing only the crunch of my feet breaking through the crusted snow, the wild song of my heart and breath, the fierce, cold wind. What was it like to roam without possessions through this land? Finding food everywhere and a shelter within one's own hide? How limitless the horizon! I was caught for an instant in the flow of my stride, feeling the muscles contract rhythmically as I placed each hoof, hearing the familiar rustle of the other deer about me as we scaled the mountain. I lowered my head against the wind, steam ripping from my frosted muzzle as I climbed. Up one side and down the other, entranced by the simplicity of owning nothing—even in this unforgiving land of extremes.

The sky was brilliant in flaming clouds scattered over a flawless, distant gold, but the land was dissolving into purple and blue. I glanced about, shrinking into my own puny body wrapped in clothing. I remembered my cabin and fire. Shoving my hands deeper into the pockets of my down parka, I turned from the stinging blast. Tears of cold were frozen to my lashes, and ice sheeted the collar of my parka where the wind crept under to burn my ears. I wiped a mittened hand across my dripping nose and looked about a last moment before starting home. Back to the cheery little haven of warmth and food. Back to the small space that made my life possible. I was only pretending to be free. I left the winter tundra to the caribou.

Phil and Net-Chet danced out to greet my return. This was the first time we had been separated in many days.

"You just sit right there," Phil said, pushing me onto a crate as he stripped away my mittens and cap. I had to laugh. It was our usual routine, but had lost none of its charm.

"Oh, look at the windows!" I exclaimed, hopping up half shod. Despite having worn Phil's larger boots with extra socks, my feet were burning with cold. "Why, they're beautiful! Just look at the view!" Two 18-by-34-inch Plexiglas windows of ten panes each now graced the south wall of the cabin, allowing the mountains to pour in. They were set in whittled frames of willow, snug and tight, and combined with the window in the door to brighten the cabin considerably. With the peeled log walls, the place looked very inviting.

Phil beamed as I examined the windows in delight. "Now sit down," he insisted.

"Oh, Phil, you shouldn't have," I protested, as he placed a cup of REAL hot chocolate into my numb hands and knelt to unlace the remaining boot. "Such a treat. You drink half." I tousled his silky hair. What a difference a bath makes.

I took a sliver of wood and lit a tallow candle from the stove. It had taken awhile to work out a good system for making candles because tallow melts more readily than wax. This candle had been cast in a tin can, removed, and rolled in paper. The paper held the melting fat so the candle would last longer. After an hour, we usually extinguished the flame and lit another.

"What'd you see?" Phil asked as I sat again upon the box.

"They came down Olson Creek, like we thought, cutting high and straight for the river. Phil, they just walk right over mountains. They take the shortest route."

I sipped the scalding cocoa while he removed the felt insoles from my boots and hung them up to dry on the ridgepole. I stretched my cold, stiff toes toward the stove. There were only three pieces of wood inside, and I opened the stove door to push one through.

"Firewood gobbler," Phil teased.

"I'm going to be warm this winter," I declared defensively.

"We'll both keep warm—you burning wood and me chopping it."

"Okay, I'll get wood today. Well, tomorrow," I amended, glancing around the darkening cabin. Living from hand to stove worried me, especially with so little daylight. At least the windows were finished and I had almost completed chinking under the eaves. We had made a mistake in not laying moss between the rafters and plate logs when we put the roof on. The cabin leaked air, but there was nothing to be done now. It steamed like a kettle along the roofline, forming white mounds of frost outside.

"I'll spend the whole day tomorrow adding to our woodpile, such as it is," I promised. My thoughts, however, were back on the darkening mountain with the caribou, caught in the ceaseless ebb and flow of their endless journey, hypnotized by the rustle of countless hooves.

The cabin glowed with rich tones in the dancing light. Exaggerated shadows bounced over the uneven logs, causing them to waver and bringing designs to life. Each log was unique—a living statement of its history, imprinted with weather, sunlight, bark beetles, water stains, and ax.

"When I delivered flowers in high school," I stated, "I realized their value is in their beauty. Because I enjoyed them, I 'owned' them as much as the people who paid for them."

Phil was silent, accustomed to my monologues. He picked up the pot of boiled meat we had eaten for breakfast and placed it on the stove. The floor was cold, despite the warmth of the room, and the meat had frozen. I sat looking into the candle. Tallow had melted around the wick, forming a dark pool inside the paper. I took scissors and trimmed the candle wick.

"That's the way I feel about land," I went on. "At best you get a lifetime tenure—and what's a lifetime to this Earth?" Through my thoughts like a whispered mantra stirred the wandering hooves.

I stepped to Phil's new window. Stars glimmered above white peaks in a periwinkle sky. "Why is it," I asked, "that I stay inside so much? I should be out climbing mountains."

"Or chopping wood," he countered.

I glanced at him and returned to the mountains, resting my elbows on the windowsill, my breath fogging the panes. The peaks were turning silver against the darker sky. A plump moon sat in the lavender east, lighting the world below. I felt Phil's arm slide around me. Together we watched. Color faded from the land and sky. Deep shadows striped the hillside as the cold moon climbed slowly, luminous white against the royal blue.

"I could shoot two hundred yards by such moonlight," Phil said at length. It was true. The brilliant moon highlighted the snowy ridges, etching in every tree. The mountains gleamed like white satin beneath an inky sky. I could feel their call.

"All my life I've been seeking the 'essence' of experience," I said wistfully. "It's that elusive something that makes the world sparkle. Sometimes I can almost smell it, but I reach out and it dissolves. It can't be held." Down the silent valley wafted the voice of an owl. Another answered from upriver.

"Sometimes I want to run out and embrace the Arctic," I went on after a minute. "I can see it over there, so clearly, way up where the mountain meets the sky. Calling . . ." I ran my fingers over the panes, caressing the peaks. "Surely *there* is the real Arctic." We were silent for a while, watching the faraway pass, so near in the moonlight. "But what would I find? More wilderness miles," I answered myself, "and the essence on the ridge somewhere beyond."

"You'd be cold," Phil said.

"It isn't real, is it?" I asked. "The essence? It's more like a memory of something. Like a memory of a smell."

"And that's not real?" He seemed to be trying to understand me.

"Well, it's not something I can discover out there."

The owl continued his monotonous song. "Hoo . . . hoo-hoo . . . hoo . . . hoo."

"You think too much."

I glanced back fondly at him—my friend, Phil, the spruce tree. He rested his chin on my shoulder and I pressed my back into his warmth. Moonlight filtered over the hushed valley. An element of sadness had stolen upon me, a strange nostalgia for this very moment as if I were remembering it from some distant future.

Taking him by the hand, I stepped to the door and opened it. Night suddenly flooded in—cold, vast, and real. We closed the door behind us and entered that different world, shrinking to specks in the Cosmos. The owl had ceased calling; I heard only the squeal of snow underfoot and the quiet hiss of my breath freezing and falling like snow in the subzero air.

"How silent it is," Phil whispered. I started to shiver. The smoke from our stovepipe cast crazy shadows on the moonlit snow. "Come, let's go back in," he said softly.

"Listen," I requested. The silence beat upon our empty ears. Not a sound. Nothing! My mind stretched into the wilderness night, listening. It was different from the muffled silence of falling snow, which sucks up every noise. Neither was it the silence of plugged ears. This was the clear, cold music of thousands of miles of *nothing* to hear.

We lingered, breathing it in. "It's the silence of a million ears," I said at last. "Of life, waiting."

❀

A few days later, I climbed our steep hill to check my snares. In the frigid dawn, the snowy mountains above Olson's Creek stood out sharply against a pearl-gray sky. I gripped my wood-hauling slings and ax loosely in one hand and smiled to myself, thinking of my mother's words, "Never return to camp without a load of wood." I suppose every daughter gets advice upon leaving home, but mine seemed more practical than most. "Pets and children tie you down," she had warned. She also said to never pee on a fire, but it seemed I needed to find things out for myself.

With the rapid descent into winter, collecting dead spruce was now an important focus. We burned much of a tree each day, but had cleared the surrounding area of snags while building. I wanted a stockpile of firewood before the deep cold and dark arrived. Sunlight, when we saw it, lasted only a short while each day, though we still had several hours of twilight. We didn't know how dark or cold it would become.

I felt strangely happy as I entered the Cathedral of Trees. I turned from the packed trail, my snowshoes sending up billows of white as I climbed. I stopped, knee-deep in morning-blue snow to view my world. Overhead boiled the flaming clouds of dawn. The mountains floated like strawberry ice cream—islands protruding from a pink sea of mist. How big it all looked! The sky stretched forever up, bordered with clear horizons and inked-in spruce trees. Naked birch trees stood silhouetted against a canary yellow sky. Somewhere below, our tiny cabin was nestled, folded into the hillside and hidden by the size of this land.

Tired of waiting, Net-Chet floundered by, stepping onto my snowshoes as she plunged into the deep, soft snow. She was trailing harness from the leather work collar given to her by Chris Olson. She had business of her own, searching out secrets with her licorice-tipped nose. She told me a good deal, pointing out the doings of our neighbors.

Between the trees, I could see the river. I spotted a dozen caribou crossing the ice below the islands. Phil had shot one the day before, a poor animal infested with parasites and devoid of fat. We decided not to take any others. Phil was already working on the hide to make mukluks.

"Okay, Chet. I'm coming," I told the impatient dog.

It was the last day of October. What does that mean? I wondered. A moose, a sunrise, a storm. The leaves fall. The ice goes out when it's ready. We divide up life and call it "time." With subtle currents, this wilderness was drawing me into its seasonal rhythms, days spreading before me—almost as in childhood—unstructured and undivided. Now.

I climbed the ridge and Net-Chet fell in behind, allowing me to break trail yet impatient with my progress. She was almost helpless in deep snow, and I wondered how the wolves managed. The land was softened in smooth undulations—snow blanketed over bushes or lifted against the trunks of trees. Across exposed muskeg the trees were stunted; the wind had packed dunes that I alternately clumped over or plowed through.

I came to a stand of spruce trees and stood a moment, studying them. They were all probably the same age, though they varied greatly in size and shape. Some had grown too close together. Others had been broken under snow, gnawed by animals, or damaged by bark beetles, accounting for the differences. They were too old to benefit greatly from thinning; still it wouldn't hurt to remove the dead and dying. I enjoyed my role as tree friend.

One had died the summer before, though a few yellow needles remained. Life was hard long before insects finished the job. I scraped my ax over the dry bark, peeling it easily away. Stepping back, I planted my snowshoes and swung from the hips. The double-bit sank deeply with the solid "thunk!" of a green tree. I looked up in surprise in time to catch a face-full of snow. Yes, there was one green twig. I shrugged and swung again.

The next tree was truly dead—naked and practically limbless. The wood was twisted, weathered grain spiraling upward. I was reluctant to clear brush for a good swing, but it was better to kill willows than feet. Besides, you can't kill willows; they would spring up stronger than before from the pruning. I knocked the snow free, butting the head of Chris Olson's double-bit ax against the trunk.

The familiar ring of dry wood echoed across the valley as I penetrated the years, scattering yellow chips in the snow. I tried to imagine what this old tree had witnessed through the seasons. I pictured it as a green shoot, a sapling, a struggling pole. At one point the crown had been broken, but it had gamely sent forth three more, crooked and spindly, in a determined push for life. Growth here is counted in inches, not feet; decades rather than years. What could I learn from trees? Were they conscious of me? I imagine we are too skittish to attract the attention of trees. I would need to sit for a month beneath one to be noticed. Life wasn't easy here. Maybe it never was. Hardship keeps a species strong—and individuals too, I decided. Hardship is Life's ally.

I finished my main cut, and then called Net-Chet behind me while I sank a second notch on the opposite side. The sun was already disappearing sideways into the southern peaks. The clouds were brilliant red in its last rays, reflecting off snow. The butt of the tree was rotten, making it tricky. After a few swings, I leaned on the tree and pushed. It heaved to and fro then sheared forward in a loud twisting of splinters. It hung up in another tree while I flopped about, tripping over my snowshoes, trying to free it. *This is life,* I thought, as I grunted and strained. All the little failures and triumphs. No heroic leaps, no mighty lunges. Real heroism isn't heroic.

I limbed my downed trees, cutting the larger one in half. The top I fastened to Chet's harness and took the heavier portion for myself. My sling was a simple strip of nylon webbing sewed to form a circle. By looping it under one end of a log and through itself, the sling tightened into a handle enabling me to drag logs weighing several hundred pounds. Together Chet and I hauled our loads back to the Cathedral Grove where I had set my snares.

At first I thought the hare had gotten away—so complete was his camouflage. Then I saw the bloody, trampled snow and the frozen, white carcass. I could reconstruct the nighttime struggle of a frightened creature. This had happened while I was busy elsewhere, and yet I had caused it. The rabbit had its head and both front feet through the snare. It had strangled slowly, tearing the skin from his slender legs—my cunning prey diminished to a terrified bit of life.

I picked up the body, retrieved my ax, and started homeward, dragging the firewood. I didn't reset the snare.

Dusk was descending, shadowing the valley below in blue-gray. I could see the frozen river through the treetops and the silver mountains beyond, light against a darker sky. The cold air was as quiet as only arctic winter can be. I paused, listening into the vast wilds. I knew that there was nothing but wilderness forever. Man had never been here. I was alone—perhaps on the planet.

Yet I was not alone. I was suddenly aware of another presence in the glade; I felt Chet stiffen behind me. Together we watched the white form of a wolf emerge from the snow, making itself known to us as if by choice. The wolf, parent of one I had eaten, studied us: human and dog. In the gathering gloom we three faced one another until the wolf, finished with the encounter, turned and melted like smoke into the dusk.

Coming down the skid trail was easy. The packed trough opened the land before me through the deep snow and laden trees. I felt like a sled as swiftly I descended with my dragging log, rounding one smooth turn after another. The trees grew taller and closer together as I neared the river. I rounded a corner and saw the meat racks. A hard turn around the toilet hole, and out of nowhere there appeared a snug cabin, cradled in the hillside. Smoke puffed from the stovepipe into the still evening, and outside a man was splitting wood.

I was somehow surprised to see them there, the man and the cabin. The scene was so comfortable and homey, it seemed out of place in this wild spot. I greeted Phil and we went inside together and lit a candle, for already the darkness of a Halloween night was upon us.

Phil sat on a corner of the stove stand. On one side of the cabin, the birch skeleton of a high bed was taking shape among knee-deep piles of shavings. Underneath would be Net-Chet's nest and a wood bin. The bed frame was mortise-and-tenoned together and pinned into the back wall and joists. The surface was of spruce poles planed on three sides and precisely fitted, representing days of work.

We had decided to celebrate Halloween with "cranberry upside-down cake." We looked forward to such treats, for the vast majority of our food was still meat. One of the nicer gifts from old Chris was a stovepipe oven. A rusted metal barrel about sixteen inches in diameter, it fitted between the sections of the stovepipe. Inside this was a smaller barrel, forming a flattened donut. Smoke traveled up the pipe, between the barrels, and back into the pipe. It was an ingenious device that baked food and added heat to the room.

"I've been thinking we should take a trip when the sun comes back," Phil said unexpectedly.

I looked up quizzically from cooking.

"There are some old mines on the map and we might find one in operation," he continued. "Most are at least forty miles away and far above timberline, but maybe we could mail out some letters—and get some treats."

"I know where your mind is," I laughed. "My poor, starved L'ammal." I reached over and pinched a roll. He squealed indignantly and lunged for mine.

"Not fair!" I shrieked, batting him off.

Soon a tempting aroma enveloped the cabin. As Phil lifted the hot cake pan with his pliers, it slipped, landing upside down on the floor. Undaunted, we sat on the floor, spoons in hand. When the last wood shaving had been spit out, Net-Chet was allowed to polish the boards with a quick, pink tongue.

Phil tried to look bashful as he suggested another helping. "After all, it is Halloween," he argued.

While he read aloud by candlelight, I put the old flour sacks to soak. Chet was attempting to nose into the sleeping bags with Phil. He scratched her ears absently as he read. The greenish lumps of flour gradually softened and I worked them free with my fingers, kneading them into a thick paste. I added baking soda to sweeten the glop that reacted with the cranberries. Soon the oven was filled with bloated sludge, bubbling and burning. We choked it down, smiling at one another and declaring how "not too bad" it was, our eyes smarting from the reek of ammonia that almost masked the taste of mold.

"We must be getting spoiled," I commented, an unwelcome burp rising in my throat.

Phil stretched and loosened his belt.

Outside, the low howl of a single wolf echoed down the river. I trimmed the paper about the candle, and lit another. We sipped tea into the evening and played chess on a miniature board.

November descended in gathering darkness—crystal days of pale skies and flamboyant clouds backlit by the vanishing sun—days as soft as goose down. November nights were long and sharp, as clean as glass beneath the dazzling moon or bathed in the silky blackness of stars and aurora borealis.

We filled these nights with talk of new adventures. From our very doorstep ran a great highway, a river now stilled in winter's sleep, that would carry us over the earth. In dream it stretched before us, south to the Yukon River and thence to the Bering Sea, then on to the world. Our minds traced other arteries that, with years of toil, would lead at last to Hudson Bay and the mighty Atlantic: the inland Northwest Passage. We were tireless those long nights, hauling our austere outfit over passes and up nameless rapids through the years ahead, as snow drifted on our doorstep and the candle burned low.

"We could get by on much less than we had this time," one of us would say.

"We would have to," the other would agree. It seemed easy now, with our lives warm and our stomachs full. On we dreamed, making lists of equipment and plotting routes. Our biggest frustration was having no access to information. Like food, it was something I had always taken for granted. The only references we had were stored in our heads or in the cherished few volumes of our library.

We spent much time together—one of us crafting furniture or mukluks and the other reading aloud by candlelight. To our surprise, we found much pleasure in the dictionary and almanac. Hardly a day went by that we did not settle a question with the "answer books." It was amazing how many topics arose in conversation and, like Pandora's box, once the books were opened all sorts of things popped out. We finished the New Testament, but were finally lost somewhere in Israel with Moses and his Arc of many rules. No, that was not what I sought—not straight lines and a packaged system of belief.

When I stepped through the small doorway that separated our cozy world of candlelight from the blue expanse of wilderness, I felt as one awakening from a dream. The mountains whispered of majesty and power, while the spreading sky arced to infinity over my head. I could fall off the planet, I thought, and wander among the stars. It is so easy to become lost in the human story, forgetting how to fly . . . and yet the Truth is everywhere. Some memory teased at me, under that sky. There was more. I knew it. I had come seeking to the end of the earth, and yet the pull persisted. Well, seek and you will find, I thought. Don't and you won't. Some of us seemed born to the Quest. It was a part of me that Phil could not understand.

Vaguely we recalled that November is the month of national elections and wondered idly who had run and who had won. It didn't seem to make much difference in our world. We talked of many things as the sun dropped from sight and snow drifted in ever-changing patterns over the river. Then one day it didn't appear, and we entered the arctic night—a time of white moons and northern lights, of frost flowers on windowpanes and bitter cold. The day, unborn, became a dawn where the sun burned its fiery path forever out of sight, setting flame to the clouds for hours at a time while it slid from east to west below the southern horizon. Peace settled upon us, and like the tiny things we are, we walked under that great, painted sky, gathering our firewood and dragging it home.

Beneath Phil's patient hands our bed grew, one hand-planed log at a time, until a waist-high platform emerged. I read aloud while he worked, sitting among the mounds of wood shavings and speaking above the rhythmic swing of the plane. Net-Chet would lie with her head in my lap, honey eyes watching everything. She had become quite a beauty, her gold and white fur now tipped with black, the showy coat reaching a billowing length of ten inches in places. She was usually too hot inside, but endured it for our company.

As she entered adulthood, we decided to feed her once a day. She responded by promptly exhuming a quarry of ancient bones, many left by an unfortunate cow moose some time before our arrival. These proved devoid of all but moss. She nevertheless greeted them as old friends. Even the wolf bones returned from their resting place on the Snack Bar, proof that she sometimes strayed, though she knew better.

She had settled comfortably into our lives, deciding when we should awaken mornings. At night she became our shrew trap, thundering over our sleeping bodies in pursuit of her tiny prey. By day she watched for hours outside the door. As patient as a glacier, she waited for something to move. Her lonely vigil wasn't always in vain. While some animals sleep away the cold night, most travel the land in search of food. Sometimes we would see a lean wolf slipping along the far shore. More often we would hear them talking across the distance. Who am I to say that wolves do not care about one another or that they do not say so? It was a wild and beautiful song to hear at midday dawn, cutting through our conversation in deep and haunting tones.

How did they make it? I wondered. Finding and catching food in the deep snow, traveling forever in the cold? And the tiny chickadees in the dark: what do they eat and how do they keep their matchstick legs from freezing at fifty and sixty below zero? How do fish breathe under the thick ice? What do they do down there in the dark all winter?

There was a fox whose rounds took him along the distant bank. After alerting us with a low "Woof!" Chet would watch him, her tail twitching like a cat. The fox appeared almost to glide over the shoreline, cocky in his feather-weight.

Rabbits are never cocky. Sometimes they would venture onto the exposed river, humble frightened creatures, but curious nonetheless. I never actually saw one out there, for they were scarce and invisible in their snowy garb, but I often saw tracks. Once I trailed a brave hare onto the ice. The tracks were followed closely by leaping prints of an ermine. A fresh page of river snow told of the ermine's sudden veer—and then nothing. Owl wing tips touched the snow where the hunter had become the hunted and the trail vanished.

Most of life went on quietly, hidden from us by darkness and the deepening snow. In nocturnal visits out-of-doors, I would stand gazing into the galaxy, where stars like searchlights flashed colors from the velvet of space. Shivering in long underwear, I stood barefooted on the packed, subzero snow, the breeze on my behind reminding me of my mortality. We were timid nighttime creatures. I would glance into the shadows, feeling soft and fragile without clothing. Edible in my nakedness, I faced this Arctic with humility.

Like soundless music the northern lights rippled above me. Awed by the vast stillness, I strained to hear. Curtains of flame leapt across the night to stand trembling for another whiplash or to fade and reappear somewhere else. Castles of green and red would burst like flowers, sending stairways of light tripping across the stars. How could I hold it? I felt my body heavy upon me, the weight of gravity forcing me down. I would fly, soaring with the auroras this night, swirling joyously into the misty light, dancing over the earth, expanding into nothing and everything. I could almost remember . . . when was it? Like a sparrow I flitted inside my head, searching, searching until the cold ache of my bare feet reclaimed me. Then I would scurry back to bed filled with happy wonder and a great sense of loss.

I recall standing one morning in the lee of Timber Island. It was snowing—the valley a misty gray about me. The only sound was the hiss of wind-blown snow. Before me a packed trail, drifted and marked with sticks, led into the falling snow toward home. Then the faint, peculiar tone of Phil whistling "Summertime" came to my ears, so out of place. Far upstream a single wolf called, pulling me into kinship. I stood listening, reluctant to turn homeward with my load of firewood. The call did not come again.

As I neared the cabin, twenty caribou caught my eye, sprinting downstream behind Timber Island. I dropped the wood and headed for the island hoping they might afford me another look. It was difficult traveling off the trail in the deep snow. Wind had packed the dunes just enough to make me lunge forward before I punched through. How do the caribou manage? I wondered. Slowly I circled the island, seeing many tracks, but no deer. They had all come down Olson Creek, heading east. Had our cabin been a mile upstream or down, we would have missed seeing them altogether.

I rounded the last island and faced homeward into the wind. Soon overflow forced me to retreat, my feet wet by the treacherous water that can seep invisibly over the ice, hidden by snow. I cut between the two downstream islands, walking cautiously, my cap pulled low over my ears. I could see the tiny cabin ahead far away in the driving snow—so distant in all that space. When I arrived, my boots were full of slush, my socks frozen to them.

Our long-awaited Thanksgiving Day dawned warm and snowy. Phil organized the cabin while I set about the last minute preparations for our royal dinner.

I had never had a real Thanksgiving before. Not that I hadn't eaten myself into a yearly stupor, but it hadn't meant anything. Why should it? For weeks we had rationed our treats to make this a true day of celebration. We put on special shirts for the occasion. We set out Chris's enamel plates and silverware. The cabin was tidy, belongings now stashed on new shelves or in bins.

I had baked beans, bread, and blueberry pie the day before. Cooking on our stove and little stovepipe oven required time and patience. I worked happily preparing gravy, rice, dried vegetables, and cranberry sauce while the two stuffed grouse baked. I thickened the cranberries with flour, turning them an odd color, "like a lung-shot moose," as Phil poetically put it. Our treats would probably not have excited most palates. We often conserved sugar by substituting saccharin. Bear lard was our butter. The little oven didn't bake evenly. Our fresh foods were meat and berries, and we had little in the way of spices or variety. "Cranberry upside-down cake" was cranberries sweetened with saccharin and topped with a "cake" of cornmeal, flour, bear lard, and baking powder; "chocolate moose" was made of tallow, sugar, powdered milk, and cocoa.

Last of all, I mixed up blueberry ice cream using berries, powdered milk, and a lot of fresh, fluffy snow. We set all the food on the new bed and lit the lantern ceremoniously for a picture. Whenever I see that picture now, what I notice is that the ice cream is pushed to the front of the pan to make it look larger. We had wanted to capture the thankfulness we felt.

We ate slowly by lantern light, reluctant to finish, recounting our blessings aloud to one another. Only a few weeks before we had no home, no winter food, no place to get warm, and a dog with a broken leg. Now we were blessed with this abundance and we felt *truly* thankful. Of all the people sitting down to dinner this day, perhaps we were the most fortunate.

December came, cold and dark. Like children Phil and I awaited Christmas and—more important to us—winter solstice, when the sun would begin its journey back. We were making presents for one another, sewing down booties as much-needed indoor footgear to protect us from the icy floor. When we wore boots in the cabin, the inevitable perspiration made for cold feet outside. I was knitting us each a new pair of socks and mittens for Christmas. Phil had almost completed mukluks for himself. I was to inherit his summer boots with plenty of room for extra insulation.

As Christmas neared, we set out to cut a tree. We climbed our hill and entered the Cathedral Grove. The land was muted beneath the exquisite serenity of new snow, trees bent with its weight. Within a few days a wind would free them, but now the woods were buried in white. I studied the frosted alder catkins in the blue twilight of December noon. They hung like tiny pinecones on bare sticks. Already the virgin blanket of snow was decorated in the minute train tracks of voles—in one tunnel and out the next.

"I hate to cut one," I admitted, knocking a load of snow from a small spruce tree with my mittens.

"We don't have to," Phil answered.

"No," I insisted, resolutely. "We're going to have a Christmas tree. We can find a group that needs thinning." I wasn't certain where we would put it, but we would find a place. Phil had planed the thirty-second and final board of our bed and we had moved our sleeping bags up to that warm and lofty place, leaving additional room on the floor.

"We've got a yard full clear to the horizon if you want, and we don't have to cut them," he said reasonably.

"I want something I can decorate." I had crocheted colored yarn ornaments, which I planned to unravel and knit into mittens and socks after Christmas.

Phil was studying the grove. White ice masked his face and only the eyes peered from under his hoary brows. Chet whined and I leaned sideways to let her scoot past. She burrowed by me along the waist-deep trough left by Phil's snowshoes. Abruptly she stopped and plunged her head deep into the side of the trail, leaving me her furry, wagging behind for company. Satisfied with the news, she withdrew and wallowed up the hill after Phil, curly tail plume marking her progress.

I breathed happily of the cold air, rubbing the frost from my sticky eyelashes with my mittens. It was forty-five below. Christmastime. How are you, dear ones? Where are you today? I wish I could tell you what became of the two who set forth on the Yukon in an overloaded canoe that summer day so long ago. How I long to share it all with you!

I trudged through thickets of young trees, studying their tops. The best ones, of course, didn't need thinning. A trail of broken spruce tassels marked our progress up the hill, for trees are brittle at very cold temperatures. It's surprising how much colder minus forty is than minus twenty.

"How's this one look to you?" Phil asked when I came up to him.

I smiled. "Better a scrawny tree," I agreed. "No reason to take the best." None of ours would have been considered down south. Chet curled up and began chewing ice balls from between her toes as Phil cleared the deep snow away from the base of the little, sleeping tree.

"Oh, what the heck, Phil," I said suddenly. "You're right. We've got a world of living trees. Let's just enjoy them."

We grinned at each other, Phil over his ice beard, me with my flaming red cheeks. "We're old softies, both of us," he told me.

Hello out there! I thought joyfully. We linked arms and descended homeward, clouds of new powder billowing about us as we cascaded down the slope. I hope you're as happy as we are this Christmas. From my window I will have the world with thousands of Christmas trees, no two alike, each one decorated in purest white.

CHAPTER 8

January was the month of cold.

The early Norsemen are said to have had a calendar consisting of ten months with thirty days in each. The remainder of the year didn't count. Having neither fuel nor food to combat winter, families spent much time sleeping, not unlike some arctic animals, until the sun returned.

It seemed like a reasonable system to us.

As darkness claimed the frozen land and the thermometer plummeted, layers of ice built upon our windows and white frost crusted the lower walls inside the cabin. Because of poor chinking under the eaves, we lost much heat into the vacuum-like cold beyond our door. Wary of this hungry cold, we stayed close to home. It was an unknown—a temperature ranging perhaps 150 degrees below that of the human body, cold that could suck the animal warmth from a creature in minutes, leaving a lifeless shell—a vast, waiting, all-devouring cold.

Late dawn would steal upon us, sometimes soft and poignant as a distant and solitary flute, sometimes with the grandeur of a full orchestra. Daily we made our little excursions for firewood, always together now. We would put on our down britches and parkas and set off hand in hand into the great, pastel twilight.

At fifty-five below zero each breath comes like a drink of ice water. Snow squeals underfoot and axes are brittle. I was making trips from Timber Island with Chet, hauling small, dead snags as Phil cut them. Net-Chet enjoyed the work, throwing herself gamely into the harness when I called out "Move!" She struggled along the packed trail, pulling more than her weight in wood, pausing now and then for me to catch up. A puff of wind, a breath too faint to stir a dried leaf, trailed from the north, and I stopped a moment to warm my cheeks in my wooly hands. I must knit more mittens soon, I thought. Logs are rough on yarn.

When I faced the breeze again I could hear the familiar hiss of my breath colliding with cold air and see it falling in a fine snowstorm around me.

I bowed into the breeze, pulling against the weight, and resumed trudging. Chet turned without a word from me and pulled for home.

The cold made me uneasy. There's a deadly seriousness about fifty-five below. It was the ultimate test of our cabin and our woodpile. Still, we had passed the solstice, the darkest part of winter, and although I couldn't see it, we were on our way back into summer. I glanced back at the island, a frozen still life in pink and gray, trying to remember the sounds and bustle of summer. I shook my head, doubting if warmth would ever again penetrate this land.

At the base of our hill I unhitched Net-Chet. She bounded before me heading back to the island, eager for another load. Ahead of us I could hear the steady, clear knock of Phil's ax. The land lay soft about me; in the distance the pearly peaks stood light against a deep violet sky. The moon, three-quarters full, hung low in the northeast. Net-Chet rolled happily in the snow, toboggan- ing along, propelled by her hind legs as she rubbed the frost from her snout, dry-cleaning her coat. Then she shook to fluff the fur. Her fur always smelled fresh, as did her breath, the clean land and meat diet keeping her in top health.

On the open river, snow was drifted in scalloped dunes, frozen waves built by the wind. Despite the line of upright sticks, the trail was difficult to see. Blowing snow had obliterated all trace, but beneath the waist-high snow lay a packed ribbon. Chet leapt sideways and bucked forward a moment in the deep snow, then galloped playfully around me, traces whipping out behind.

We found Phil back in the forest, limbing an old, dead spruce. He was swathed in an orange down parka, blue wool cap, and red down pants.

"My feet are cold," he told me. He severed a branch with a final swing of his double bit and smiled at me through his glacial beard. "Let's head on in." Only the big, green eyes gazing from beneath the white eyebrows were famil- iar. His long, dark lashes were frosted exotically. I could see mine too—white with growing crystals. They felt gummy and glued together. I rubbed them a moment with a mittened hand and blinked to clear my vision.

Already dawn was fading into winter dusk. A shifting land of purple snow lay before us on the trail home. Across the white desert—once a river—I could just make out a cabin tucked back in the dark trees. I located it by the sluggish puff of smoke. Chet whined impatiently, holding one foot and then another off the snow while I prepared her load.

"Move!" I called, and she threw herself forward. The log snagged in brush and she glared back at me. I kicked it free. "Move!" I sang out again, and off she struggled.

Looping my sling about one end, I tugged a log out into the open and plodded slowly homeward across the ice. Phil fell in behind, hauling the heavier butt end of the tree. His ax was stuck in the top of it and it plowed into the snow as the log twisted. He stopped to reposition it.

"Good dog," I told Chet as we reached the cutbank before the cabin. I unhitched her and started back to help Phil. Together we pulled, and the big log slid quickly after us. We arrived home panting. I curled my tongue over my front teeth and the frigid air whistled around it, warmed on the way to my lungs.

"You have a white spot on your cheek," Phil said. Frostbite looks dead and waxy, a peculiar color of gray-white.

I held my hand over it a moment. Phil had given up wearing glasses and his belt buckle because of frostbite. Any metal next to the skin conducts the heat away. I had removed my little gold earrings and Phil had threaded a piece of fishing line with a couple of beads on it through my ears to keep the holes open.

Frost swirled about our legs as we entered the cabin, clouds of snow born as warm air collided with the cold. Phil shut the door behind us just as Chet decided she wanted in.

"You moaned?" he asked with exaggerated politeness, opening the door. He had been training her to shake before entering. It is equivalent to teaching a person to sneeze. She would twist her head from side to side, trying to work up to it. Chet wagged in with another burst of frost and looked about for her dinner.

"Not yet," I said. "Go to your corner." She trudged sullenly to her stall under the bed, looking back to see if I was watching. With an elaborate sigh, she dropped into the shavings and sat licking the ice from between her toes while we shed our parkas and "hot pants." The windows were darkened with gray sheets of ice. When Phil lit a candle, the three green-cut logs used in the back lower wall sparkled white with frost.

I built up the fire and put Net-Chet's bowl on the stove to thaw. Anything left on the floor froze solid. Then I reached into Mightypot for a frozen slab of ribs and placed them in a pan in the frail stovepipe oven. Phil was perched on the bed removing his canvas and moose hide mukluks.

"I think we should bring in a moose hide to carpet the floor," I said, climbing onto the bed. We sat up high much of the day, reading and working on projects. Chet snaked her head out from under the bed and whined irritably, wanting to be up with us. I glanced at her and she turned away meekly, folding one ear back. Then she shot me a petulant look and whined again, very softly.

"Those skins are as hard as plywood," Phil answered, ignoring the dog. "We'll have a hard time fitting one in. But it's a good idea. I need some more rawhide too. I'm going to build a hand sled for our trip to the mine. I'll make the frame from birch and stretch the hide over the bottom."

To make rawhide, he soaked a piece of moose skin until it softened and began to rot. Then he could scrape the hair off, stretch, and dry it. If he was making rawhide lacings, he cut this in a diminishing circle, creating a continuous string and soaked it again.

The teapot soon began to boil, spouting steam. I put on my down booties and hopped off the warm bed to make tea.

"I have no idea how we'll soak that much hide," Phil said.

"We could use the water bucket and hang it from the ridgepole so it won't freeze," I suggested.

Phil took his mug and sat thinking. "We're going to need pemmican for the trip, too," he said after a while, "and packsaddles for Chet." Pemmican is a trail food Indians had used—pulverized dried meat, tallow, and berries.

I peeked into the oven then shut the flimsy door. Returning to the warmth of the bed, I crossed my legs under me. It was growing dark in the cabin. The only sounds were the crackling of the fire and the occasional pop of burning wood. I sighed, staring into the yellow candle flame.

Another low moan came from under the bed. I looked down to see Chet staring impatiently up. "Her food is probably ready," I said to no one in particular, and slid from the bed, clicking my tongue for her.

I studied the cabin, wondering where we could dry meat for pemmican. The bed and kitchen shelves were aligned against the east wall, Phil's shop area took up the southwest, and the stove was in the middle. Underfoot were piles of shavings, for Phil generated them faster than we burned them, making fire a constant danger. We'd had a close call once when the gas lantern was knocked down, breaking the glass chimney and shooting a jet of flames into the shavings.

"We can string the meat between the purlin and ridgepole," I decided.

Phil glanced up, obviously caught in other thoughts.

"If we use a darning needle with heavy nylon twine, we can sew it through the meat so it won't fall. Then we can hang the string from nails in the rafters."

❊

The "way-belows"—as we called temperatures lower than forty below zero—broke in mid-January in a snowstorm. Severe cold rarely lasted more than a fortnight. Within the warmth of our cabin we made plans by candlelight and talked of our coming journey to the mine while outside the trees sang and bent beneath a thundering ocean of wind, and snow drove tirelessly over the river in a blizzard that raged for days.

"I never thought a windy twenty below would seem balmy," Phil said, shutting the door behind him. I caught a glimpse of dove-gray before the cabin returned to the soft browns of kerosene light. He dumped an armload of firewood on the floor with a crash. He had been out splitting it in shirtsleeves, but his beard was frozen. He came toward me, a look of innocence on his face.

"Oh no you don't!" I warded off icy whiskers. "If you enjoy 'em, fine!"

I was leaning over Mightypot, scrubbing clothes. Our seven-gallon kettle served for cooking, bathing, and washing clothes—which was a hard job with little detergent and scarce water. Because we had few clothes, we were loathe to part with them and they became very dirty. Unlike Chet's fur, grease permeated the material even in the clean snows of winter.

"Holly's back," Phil said, indicating the window, which was clear of ice. I left the clothes to look outside. Phil started for the door to bring in more wood.

"Stay in a moment," I entreated. "Let them play. Ravens are shy of big people."

We crowded at the window, watching the daily spectacle. The great black bird sailed slowly upwind, just over Chet's nose, alighting heavily. Net-Chet charged and the raven beat ponderously aloft, midnight wings inching upward a bound ahead of the dog. This game would continue until Net-Chet tired of it. At first we had worried about Holly, for his act was excellent—the moves deliberately clumsy and his getaways painfully slow.

Net-Chet sat down, eyeing that elusive bird. Holly stalked forward, short legs stepping precisely over the packed snow. No response. He looked thoughtfully at some invisible tidbit, cocking his thick head to one side, and pecked. That did it. Off they went again.

I know why a dog would play with a raven, but why would a wild raven come daily to play with a dog? I watched the big bird, sensing the rush of wind and snow. Above the storm, I seemed to hear the whistle of air through his coarse pinions. Long had Net-Chet awaited a playmate, watching by the hour outside the cabin door. Now the sky had sent a raven.

Phil was talking of our trip to the mine. "I'd like to take a trial run when the sun comes back," he said. "We can leave the meat outside for the two days, but we should bring it in when we leave for the mine. This summer I want to build a meat-house so we won't have to worry next year."

We had puzzled over the low structure in Chris Olson's yard until we designed a meat-house. As big as his cabin, it was spanned by stout poles and latched from the outside. I smiled at the thought of my anthropology teacher and his "ceremonial structures." Until you deal with problems in an environment, the purpose of a tool may not be apparent.

Holly circled, gaining elevation. With a musical call like running water, he allowed the wind to catch him and sailed out over the river, rapidly dwindling. Then for an instant he seemed to wink; I thought I saw him slip through the gray sky in a playful wingover. I stared, but could see only a raven dissolving into the streaking snow.

Reluctantly, I returned to doing laundry. Phil stepped out to retrieve a tallow candle he had put on the woodpile to harden. He ducked back inside and ran into a line of wet jerky, hanging from the rafters.

"I'm ready to rinse," I said, wringing the last pair of long johns. They weren't exactly clean. Together we descended to the river carrying a pan of clothes and Chris's large teakettle. Phil had chopped a hole through four feet of ice and I stooped to skim out a bucket of water. With bare fingers I brushed the floating chunks of ice over the edge, new ice forming even as I worked, and added a few cups of boiling water. This brought the pan up to ice cold. Quickly we rinsed and wrung the clothes. Then another pan and another. By the time we started back to the cabin, my hands were stiff and blue.

The cabin was steamy with wet laundry. I set Mightypot on the stove to heat and then took a bath, washing my hair first and working down while squatting in the big kettle. Then I heated a fresh pot of water and ordered Phil in. His distaste for water had increased with cold weather.

Clean and dry, we turned out the kerosene lantern and lit a tallow candle. Darkness was again settling over the wilderness. To the hypnotic bluster and howl of wind we ate a quiet dinner and curled up in bed together to read aloud by its flickering light. After the candle was put out, I lay for a long time, listening to the wind and thinking about our coming trip, wondering if we were making a mistake. I was in no hurry to leave this refuge. Phil was breathing in the steady cadence of sleep, at home on the hard press of our narrow bed. I heard Net-Chet circle once in her nest of shavings, then settle with a sigh.

As my mind swirled down into sleep it was caught by the roar of wind. I drifted in a stream of voices, faint and rapid, yet distinct, as if I were eavesdropping on the Universe. They pattered through me, light and quick as rain, old and young in everyday mood, touching me here and there like feathers. I floated in a warm bath of Beings: tiny sparks within my mind. Then faint upon the wind I thought I heard a wolf call. I searched the ragged clouds for him, but the cry was not repeated.

A few days later the temperature dropped again, and through the melted space at the top of one window I could see livid clouds of dawn streaming along the southern mountains. Any day now we will see the sun, I thought. It had been gone two months. I yearned for it. I fantasized about swimming pools and tanned skin and the taste of sweat upon my lip. Of green leaves and oranges and the dazzle of a summer afternoon.

"Well, we'd better go get wood," I sighed, reaching for my hanging boots. Chet flung her front paws onto the bed, smiling. She was always on the alert to unspoken commands and invisible signals. The slightest click, snap, whistle, or tap would suffice. Even an eye cast in her direction was invitation enough.

"You wanna go outside?" I asked, deliberately misunderstanding her.

She flashed me a meek "No," dropping one ear and turning her head to the side.

"Chet, you wanna go for a work?" Whenever we went out, she hauled or carried something to teach her to enjoy work.

Oh, yes! Yes, yes! She sailed happily about the cabin, sweeping the furniture with her tail.

I pulled on several pairs of socks and Phil's big summer boots. Then I damped down the stove and ducked through the tiny doorway, fastening my parka. Maybe today we'll see the sun! Exalted by the thought, I sucked in the subzero air. Phil was already outside gathering snow in Mightypot to melt for water. The river had frozen to the bottom. He reentered the cabin and set the pot on the stove, then joined me.

Along the rim of our valley a curtain of clouds roiled, molten flame igniting its hem. Suddenly a ray of sunlight leapt over the ridge, licking past the edge of the world. From beyond the Yukon it shot, northward over the frozen land, pressing back the arctic night as it stretched a finger out from the blackness of space. Up the river, past the old gold town, beyond the nameless rapids and bars, over Chris Olson's place it flooded, filling our valley with golden light. It was only the merest of slivers, but it signaled the end of the long dark: sixty sunless days.

"The sun's back! The sun's back!" we shouted joyfully.

Phil squatted in his slick-soled mukluks and slid down the hill. He sailed over the bank and landed on the dog, where they rolled happily, legs and snow flying. He was dusting off when the bright ray dipped away, leaving us bathed in familiar pastels. It had edged up for only a couple of minutes. Net-Chet's face split in a grin and she dashed around us as we headed for Timber Island. Phil smiled at me through his powdered beard and took my hand.

"Ow!" I complained, switching hands.

"I forgot your sore finger," he apologized.

I laughed. Odd to be troubled by a cut. Last fall we had hardly noticed injuries.

The island was deep in snow, trees bent and buried. Usually storms were ushered in and out by fierce winds, but this time the cold had returned in silence. Small spruce sagged earthward, and I wondered how any survived to maturity. The majority seemed in various stages of tortured decline.

"Have fun," Phil called as I plodded into the trees.

Net-Chet followed in the swath of my snowshoes. I had to lift each foot to my waist and it was slow travel. I was looking for dead trees and taking pictures while Phil bucked up the first log. I wanted to photograph Net-Chet burrowing through the deep powder, but she was helpless off my broken trail and was content to plunge her icy nose into the tunnel wall. I plowed through the snow over a tangle of naked branches. Many sprang up as I shook them free but others were snapped off or bent. Birds had been among the alders, knocking seeds from the catkins and feeding, the snow printed in their story. With my eyes only two feet above snow level I could easily pick out details. Rabbit tunnels dove under submerged logs into hideaways created by the rising drifts. Snow had swirled into dunes creating false topography over the familiar landscape. It was hard to recognize.

I came upon a clearing where trees were felled a long-ago winter day. The stumps wore big caps of white that canted out of the wind. Such clearings are common on northern rivers. I have seen small valleys denuded of trees for mine timbers and firewood. Men burned the trees to thaw the ground for gold. Long after the gold was spent, the scars remain. On tundra where plant growth is slow, this bare ground absorbs sunlight and melts the permafrost, creating sores in the land that can ooze for centuries. This is true whenever the fragile sod is disturbed. Even snowmachines injure this land.

I stopped and listened. Out of the south came a low whistle of wind. To my right, a burst of spray plotted the wind's course through the treetops. Another gust hit near me and I shielded the camera under my parka. The air was suddenly filled with flying crystals as the trees about me flung off their burdens. I was deluged in snow. Fascinated, I watched this air-made-visible, touching the trees and shaking them free, one by one. The sky had turned a delicate salmon color. I retraced my steps, shooting film between bursts of wind.

"What say we head for home," Phil called as I came into view—abominable snowwoman, my hair thick with snow. "I think we're in for a blow."

We labored across the river on our familiar skid trail, dragging logs. Behind us in the southern sky, a single blood-red cloud hung suspended in yellow. Out of the west came a vast shape of flying snow, whipped from the mountains and obscuring everything as it flew toward us. It was coming fast, raging hundreds of feet high, a roiling wall of gray, devouring the valley. As it hit the nearby peaks, it ripped the snow from their flanks and plumed it high aloft. Like rabbits we scurried for the shelter of our nest.

The day of our trial expedition dawned clear. We would travel upriver with the dual purpose of breaking trail and seeing how well we held up before setting off for the mine. It was not a direct route, because steep mountains ranged between us and the dots marked "mine" on our map. Long before first light we were up, tending to last details. By candlelight, we stuffed sleeping bags and balanced the dog's packs while she watched with anxiety, never letting us out of her sight.

Sunrise found us a mile upstream. It was late February and the sun was rapidly returning. The day dawned crystal blue and about twenty below—sharp and bright beneath a pale sky. We left the wind-packed river at the bend and labored up the drifted cutbank into the dunes that covered Horseshoe Swamp. We were each packed heavily, prepared as for a week on Everest.

I was breaking trail. When I reached the top of the cutbank, I stopped to catch my breath. Before us lay a quarter mile of muskeg cutting across a loop of the river. The deep snow, folded and dipped about scrawny trees, was crusted just enough to upset my balance. I needed to raise my feet almost thigh-high and lunge onto the crust, only to break through with each step. Hidden sticks punched up snagging my snowshoes and tripping me. Net-Chet was impatient behind me, frequently stepping on my snowshoes.

"Okay smarty, you break trail," I said, stepping aside to let her pass. She bounded ahead but was hopelessly bogged in deep snow and soon had to fall back.

The land ahead looked soft under the snow, rounded and mellow. We hadn't been upstream since freeze-up. I made it to the far bend without falling down, wading through snow to my hips. Windblown, it had metamorphosed into coarse crystals that sang and crunched underfoot like glass beads. When I came to the river again and started down the drift that packed against the bank, I floundered on my big feet and pitched facedown. My hands never hit ground, and it was some moments before I could shift my weight enough to lever myself upright.

Our shortcut across the bend had saved perhaps a mile, but taken time and energy. Down on the windswept river, the going would be easier. Below us, the blue-shadowed river wound like a desert—quiet beneath the sterile dunes. I tried to recall how it had looked in summer, where the water ran. There was overflow down there, a turquoise streak of ice staining the center a hundred yards upstream. I sniffed uneasily, studying the silent snow.

I stood looking at the towering peaks, feeling small and bogged in snow. There are so many levels to view things from, I thought. No matter where you stand, you can't see it all.

"Maybe going straight over the mountains would be best," Phil observed, catching my glance. That was the shortest way, and the driest. Before us waited the deceptive ice.

"Well, let's put in this upstream trail anyway and see how we fare sleep-ing out," I suggested. Other people camp out in winter, I reminded myself. Phil led down the embankment and onto the river.

Carefully we clumped along, sometimes backtracking from overflow. Where water had gushed onto the surface cracking the ice under its weight, the exposed seep was often solid despite its malevolent appearance, but the innocent-looking snow nearby could disguise three feet of slush. Snow insu-lates these seeps even in the coldest weather, and often the only clue is the for-mation of ice feathers over the dunes or a faint uneasiness along the back of my neck.

I stopped and looked back questioningly at Phil. I was again in the lead as we switched off breaking trail.

"I think we should cut inland here," he answered.

I nodded in agreement. Another sweeping bend lay ahead where the river almost doubled back on itself. Cutting across the bend would be a hard trudge. I stood, breathing into my mittens to warm my cheeks. Impatient at the delay, Chet was tromping a circle in the snow. She glared at me and whined.

"I'll break trail awhile," Phil offered.

I fell in behind him, scanning the landscape. It was difficult to pick out the lay of things under winter's disguise, but a muskeg must drain down through here. My elongated shadow stretched before me, undulating over the smooth frosting. Here and there bits of cotton grass poking through had drawn circles on the dunes where the wind had whipped them around. Stunted trees sprouted from the thick blanket and many more snoozed out of sight, waiting to trip us. Ptarmigan had been feeding in the willows near the bank, and their feather-footed tracks were scattered in the softer snow of thickets. About them the big prints of snowshoe hares touched lightly.

Phil thrashed on, cutting a trail inland. I fell into the steady swing of my stride and breath, my ears muffled by my cap: the mantra of movement. There is a place of quiet between steps where the mind ceases to chatter and each rhythmic contraction is sufficient.

"Doesn't look good," I observed as we again gazed upon the river. "I'll go first."

Low sunlight danced over the sleeping islands as we studied our options. The dunes lay still and blue before us, the sky a deeper blue above. Snow was piled high against the cutbank and it was a slow process descending to the river. Net-Chet let me break trail onto the packed dunes of the river and then jumped in front as I paused. In a few steps she sprawled abruptly on the scalloped snow, spread-eagle, and began to wriggle backwards. Her feet had punched through to unseen water.

"You stay there," I ordered Phil as I dropped my pack. Wearing his old boots with extra socks, I was less vulnerable than he in his canvas mukluks. "Wait'll I cut a path clear to the island."

I tried several spots along the shore as evening deepened. There were big trees on the island and we didn't want to camp in the open. Net-Chet, now wary, stayed behind me. Softly I stole over the dunes, the unmarred white drifting beneath my scrutiny as I placed each foot. I was just congratulating myself on crossing to the first island when I noticed that Net-Chet had deserted me. Glancing back, I saw my big snowshoe tracks filling with cold, gray water. Only a bit further, I thought, and I'll reach shore. Suddenly I went in!

In panic I struggled to free my snowshoes, slush to my knees. They were caught under the thin crust and ladened with saturated snow. I lost my balance and pitched forward onto the snow. For the moment it held and did not drop me into the water. I fought free and crawled forward, dumping mounds of slush onto my down pants as the snowshoes flipped back on my heels. I scrambled to my feet, shaken but not seriously wet, in time to see Phil heading for me.

"No! Not here!" I waved him back.

When I reached the shore, I trudged downstream looking for good ice before starting back. My snowshoes were crusted with freezing slush that picked up snow, becoming heavier with every step. Still the ice below me held as I cut over to my old trail, satisfied that it would hold. Net-Chet might punch through in spots, but it would probably sustain Phil on snowshoes.

"I'm okay. Now give me my pack," I demanded. Phil was preparing to carry both packs and looked doubtfully at my frozen pants and boots. "That ice won't take you with two packs," I countered. "I'm not badly wet."

We reached the island without further mishap. It was well timbered with large, somber spruce. We set about making camp in a sheltered hollow among their feet. Chet was disgusted with the idea of camping out. Relieved of her packs, she trampled a nest in the snow and glared at us as she chewed the ice from her paws and legs. Phil dropped a big, dead tree, building a fire on a bed of logs. Then he placed me before it and told me to change socks while he cleared a place for the tent. I put a pot of snow on the fire to start supper while my bootlaces melted free. It certainly was turning colder. A deep, blue silence flooded the land and a piercing chill that the blaze pushed back only a few feet.

Phil joined me by the fire, squatting in the snow, his arms resting on his knees. We had stamped down the deep crystals with snowshoes, but still his feet were buried. I offered him a scalding mug of tea. He cupped his mittened hands about it, sipping. In the fire warmth his frozen beard began to drip.

"It must be thirty-five or forty below," he observed, sniffing the calm air. The first star of evening glimmered low over the mountains to the north.

My bottom was getting cold despite down pants. I slipped a heavy down parka over the everyday one and shifted my weight on the log. Nearby, my thirty-pound snowshoes leaned sadly against a tree. I thought for a moment of working with them, but decided on supper first.

"We didn't come very far," I said, lifting the lid from the boiling pot to stir. In fact, we weren't far from where I killed the moose last fall, though you'd never recognize it. The fire crackled merrily, sending clouds of steam into the darkening trees. There it clung in tiny crystals, frosting the needles in misty white. The old trees seemed to lean close above us, like sleeping sentinels, enclosing our camp.

"Too far for her," Phil smiled, indicating Net-Chet. She was curled in the snow, wrapped in the fur stole of her tail. Lengthy fur britches combined with her tail plume to cover her feet and nose so that little heat was lost. She withdrew her long face to register a sour complaint. I got up to dig out drymeat for her dinner.

Net-Chet was not a wolf and she knew it. She might play Wild Dog of the North, remembering perhaps some racial heritage as she stalked voles, but her ancestors had relinquished their power to survive alone in trade for a relationship with mine. She finished her meal and sat grumpily by me a moment. I noticed that snow was melting into her fur. She wasn't designed for fires either. The cold bit deeper as darkness thickened about the three of us, age-old companions in a wilderness.

"Why don't moose get frostbite?" I asked suddenly, breaking a long silence.

"Or do they?" Phil countered, raising his head from some reverie in the glowing coals.

I had to think about that one. The lives of wild animals are not easy. They probably never die of old age. "The ones I really admire are the mammals that live under ice," I said. "Think of it. Seals live most of their lives in darkness, under ten feet of ice, yet they are warm-blooded and breathe air—just like us. They find their way between breathing holes and keep them open by gnawing. You wouldn't believe it was possible."

"What about polar bears?" Phil asked. "Living on seals that live under the ice. Emerging wet into subzero air. And why don't they get snow blindness? Why don't eyes built for hunting in winter darkness burn out in the glaring white of summer?"

I looked long into the fire, thinking. "There was a point," I began at length, "that I believed there were answers. Do you know what I mean?"

I glanced at Phil. He didn't.

"I studied biology because I thought it would give me the *answers*," I said. "I collected facts, hoping to piece them together into answers, but the deeper I look into anything, the more there is to see. I sometimes think our pretense of labeling—all those neat boxes of facts—blind us from seeing beyond our beliefs."

Phil was shaking his head mutely.

I began on a different tack. "Physics is that way. For years people thought they were rounding up the last few great facts that would add up to the *answers*. Then along came quantum mechanics and the uncertainty principle, and we're back in the twilight zone. That doesn't refute everyday Newtonian physics, but the *nature* of reality still eludes us. We are so permeated with our sensual data that we cannot even ask the questions.

"Once my universe was a logical structure, a little yellow box. There were shelves for each opinion. I could touch the walls and ceiling. Occasionally I heard noises outside, so one day I pulled up a floorboard and discovered space beyond. I began to decorate my box with new ideas—and they ripped it apart."

I glanced at Phil, but he was lost to me, a stranger who I loved. He was uncomfortable with my need to examine life. He took life at face value. What a paradox, I thought. We are each inseparably mingled in the life of a teeming Cosmos and each totally alone in our experience of it. Every organism belongs wholly to itself, even Phil. He was not mine, and never would be.

"What an adventure life is," I smiled, releasing him. "What a wonderful game. Strangely, I think the saving grace is that we all die in the end. That takes away the significance. We've already lost so we don't have to be so careful."

I sat awhile, watching the fire and thinking. Then I continued, "Life isn't a book that starts and goes somewhere and ends. I keep waiting for it to all turn out. It's an experience—an adventure. If there are answers, they can't be taught—only discovered. Whether we find the meaning or invent it, life forms a complete whole because we are the end product of our choices. Things don't turn out. The sun comes up and goes down. I remain right here, right now, in my life, forever. It doesn't go anywhere. This is it."

Phil was silent. I gazed a long time into the fire until it filled all my world. There was a glowing cave, surmounted by a castle with a flaming stairwell among the embers. A log broke suddenly, collapsing the roof and sending up a shower of sparks into the keen blackness. The shadowy trees seemed to bend lower as if drawn to the warmth.

"Did you lay out the sleeping bags?" I asked, breaking the spell.

"No. I meant to, but got sidetracked with food."

"You stay there," I motioned him back. "I'll only be a moment."

It took me much longer than I had planned, for the Ensolite pad was curled into a rigid sausage and would relax only after I worked with it near the fire. Away from the warmth, the cold descended, penetrating my clothing. It was hard to pull out the stiff sleeping bags and zip them together in the familiar little tent. I had an apprehension that the night would be most unpleasant.

And it was. Net-Chet deserted the tent early in the evening for her own spot in the snow and seemed to have fared somewhat better. As for me, I was never so glad to see dawn in all my life.

❀

In the bright, cold sunlight of early morning, I hung the frozen sleeping bags over bushes. Phil and I had retreated to the bottom of the bags, and our breath had frozen within them as well as sheeting the surface with ice.

"Other people sleep out at thirty and forty below zero," I complained as I stooped over the morning fire warming my stiff hands. "There must be a way."

"You're still alive," Phil reminded me sweetly. He was running in place by the sluggish blaze, trying to thaw his feet. Chet glared out from her nest beneath a big spruce and moaned loudly.

"Barely. And to think our lonely cabin waited all night for us and we slept over there!" I pointed to where the tent had been: a little hollow showed how our compressed, shaking bodies had melted into the packed snow.

"Next time we'll scrape down to the moss," he said.

"If there is a next time," I answered. My joints still ached from the miserable night.

"Maybe the only way to travel in arctic winter is like the old-timers did. Fur parkas and bedrolls of caribou don't frost up. Canvas wall tent and stove to dry out. We'd need more dogs to carry the outfit . . ."

"And more moose to feed the dogs," I interrupted. We were at an old impasse. "And who said it was ever easy or comfortable?"

As the sun swam higher in the blank sky, the temperature climbed to minus thirty.

"Shall we spend part of the day snooping upstream?" Phil asked from the bottom of his tea mug. We had voted to cut the excursion short. "With a broken trail, it shouldn't take us long to get home."

I agreed, and we began the prolonged process of breaking camp, interspersed with many fireside sessions. It seemed warm out now. With our bellies full of hot broth, we laughed gaily in the morning brightness, congratulating ourselves on surviving the night.

It was almost dark when we got home. The log walls had lost their warmth and the cabin seemed a dim and frosty cave. Still, we greeted it as an old friend as, tired and chilled, we stepped from the purple dusk, hauling our packs in after us. Phil lit a fire at once and I pulled out the bedding to dry while I started supper. Net-Chet whined until she was put on the bed. It wasn't warmth she wanted; she liked to be included.

We kept a hot blaze going until we went to sleep that night. Outside the temperature was back to forty-three below zero with a slight breeze trailing from the north, and the black sky was pricked with frozen points of light.

As the season advanced, we spent much time in tedious projects of preparation for our long journey to the mine. We could count on making only four miles a day breaking trail over the mountains, and because we might not find people, would go prepared for three weeks without resupplying.

"March ought to be a good month for travel," Phil said. "We have a lot of daylight now."

It was warm in the cabin. Late February sunlight slanted mellow through the windows, and outside a squirrel churred in the still air. I glanced up from pounding drymeat into a fibrous meal for making pemmican.

I grinned at him, saying, "'In August was the jackal born.'"

Phil looked at me, puzzled.

"Oh, it's something that my mother used to quote. Kipling:

In August was the jackal born;
The rains fell in September
"Now such a fearful flood as this,"
Said he, "I can't remember!"

Phil smiled broadly, but I persisted. "I don't trust this weather. 'In like a lamb, out like a lion.' March is famous for change. And wind."

We were silent for a while, each with a task.

"Do you know that I wanted to be a hermit when I was a kid," I said. "And now I am one!" I pushed meat crumbs into a cup and poured hot tallow over them. I had mashed the old horse jerky into the mixture for salt. We'll get rid of that stuff yet, I thought.

From the window, I could see that the spruce forest across the river had taken on a greenish blush as if it too was beginning to awaken. Net-Chet was outside stalking squirrels. They were busy scattering the snow with spruce tassels, pruning trees for a cone crop they might never see. It takes two years for cones to come to fruition.

"Come on, Phil. Tell me about some of your daydreams. Everyone has them."

Phil was making a spare set of mukluks, softening the heavy moose-hide soles with bear lard—"Rhino leather" he called it. He hung the sole on a peg and leaned back in Chris Olson's chair. We hadn't used the chair most of the winter, for it had been too cold to sit that low.

"Well, I always imagined that I would put a false culvert under a road someplace, entering and leaving only by night. I guess I never thought there could be a place with no people. My schemes were about how to live among them without being seen."

"I built a bomb shelter when I was six," I broke in. "Well, first it was going to be an ocean. I'd seen the ocean once and when I got home I started digging. I spent my savings (about half a dollar) on salt. I really intended to dig that ocean, then it changed to a swimming pool, and finally a bomb shelter."

"My brothers and I once built a neat fort in the middle of a great big bush," he told me. "It was a dandy fort, but the bush turned out to be poison ivy." He was scraping hair from wet moose hide, rhythmically fleshing it with the back of the drawknife. The hide was intended for the bottom of a sled. Its birch frame was drying over the stove, steamed runners curling around the purlin.

I laughed. "I wanted to live in a forest. I would have secret tunnels under giant trees with stairways cut inside the trunks up to the branches. I didn't believe I would ever grow up. Growing up was a myth."

We were silent for a spell, each with his task. It was a comfortable, companionable silence. "My mother encouraged our dreams," I told him. "She was never what she called a 'cookie baking' mother. She didn't nurture as much as inspire us. I remember her bringing lunch to us up into the chinaberry trees. She used to let us build campfires in the front yard. One time a neighbor called the fire department. I suppose many people thought we were neglected or uncontrolled. I can hear her saying, 'Poor city kids.' She believed in freedom for children. For every living thing—each his own person."

I continued crumbling jerky, nibbling as I worked. "She grew up wild," I continued. "She was sickly so her mother took her and my Aunt Janet to live on a remote lake in upstate New York. Her father, a brilliant and unstable doctor who didn't like her, stayed in town. My mother used to slip out of the cottage and spend the night sleeping in her canoe adrift on the lake. She had no fear of the woods or of being alone."

I was quiet, thinking about my mother as a wild girl, roaming the woods alone, like a forest spirit or a fairy child. No wonder she used to say, "Poor city kids."

Phil interrupted my thoughts. "I miss apples," he told me sadly.

"Well, maybe we'll find some at the mine," I said. Then, as an afterthought, "I miss Chinese food and salads and sunbathing."

"Yeah, and apples . . ."

"I miss chocolate and music and talking with friends."

"And apples . . ."

"I miss swimming and pretty clothes and hot showers and coffee and movies . . ."

"And..."

"Yes, I know. Apples."

❖

The omens were promising as our planned departure date neared. Daily the sunshine grew in duration and power, and the calm air seemed full of springtime. We now saw many signs of animals on the move. Moose tracks crisscrossed the river, restless for green shoots that would not appear for another two months. We saw no more caribou tracks, but lean carnivores traveled hard in search of the increasingly rare snowshoe hare. This was the hungry season for them, when snow lay deep and last year's little folk had been well depleted. It was also the mating season for many, and they covered great distances to renew their species.

Bull moose had performed this vital function in the fall and dropped their antlers before Christmas. Thin from the rut and a winter of slow starvation, they conserved energy and waited in the thickets, innocent of calves swelling in the dark bellies of their autumn loves. There, safe from cold, tender life waited its first spring in secret comfort. The cows, heavy with the future, still traveled with last year's calf, seeking unbrowsed buds in the deep snow. Like the juvenile wolves, these young moose had yet to survive their first winter. If they did, a surprise awaited them in late May when their faithful mothers would drive them away in preparation for the new life, and they would begin their solitary wandering—heritage of moose.

Our troupe of chickadees added musical twitters to their hushed winter calls, and birds that had been silent since autumn were speaking out once more, warming up for spring. Much squabbling ensued as real estate took on some of its old value and new birds filtered into our area disturbing the established order. Oblivious of us, they blew into the yard like a swirl of dried leaves, bringing the exciting news of the coming spring.

On the first of March a snowstorm hit. We listened quietly as gray winds pounded into the cabin, rattling the stovepipe. Our thoughts turned to the journey before us. I remembered that my own parents had almost died in a March snowstorm when they underestimated the Arctic. They had been out of food and forced to travel in search of game, but we were well-fed and could afford to sit home. However, you tend to get cocky when life is good.

We would remember March as the fickle month—the month of winds.

The cabin becomes our obsession in a race with arctic winter.

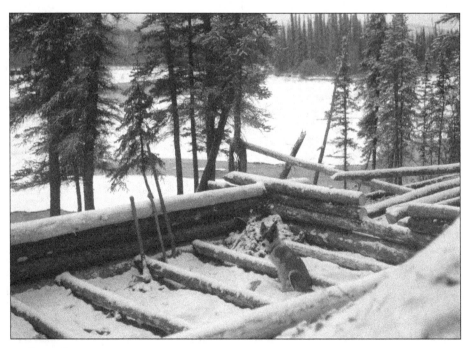

Snowfall catches us unprepared.

188

Finally, a roof shelters us from the sky.

Phil places his door and we are safe from winter.

Phil and Net-Chet set out for firewood.

Phil tans caribou for mukluks by the light of the window.

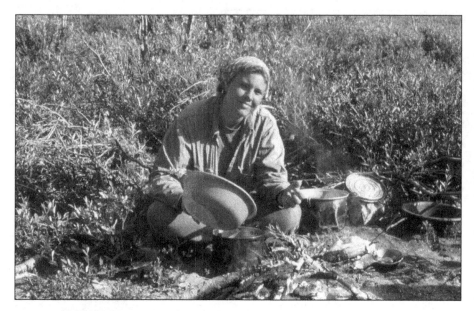

Jeanie cooks on our summer trek to the Divide.

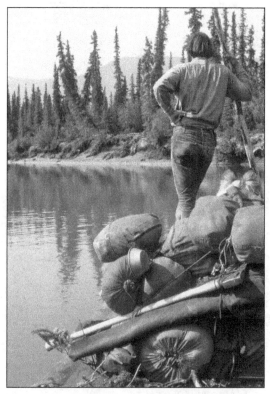

We hit a calm section on our raft trip home.

CHAPTER 9

Perfect smoke rings puffed from little holes in the stove, and a flickering light filled the dawn-gray cabin. A familiar rushing sound grew as the shavings caught in the stove. Shivering in my bare feet and dirty long johns, I blew upon the frosted window for a look at the outside thermometer. Rose-edged peaks appeared against a satin sky as the pane cleared.

"Eight below," I called cheerfully to Phil as he ducked outside in his long underwear and bare feet.

"And calm," he called back. "It looks like a good day."

March days were already long, the sun returning in spring as rapidly as it had departed the autumn before. We intended to hike up Olson Creek and scale the mountains. From there, we would drop into a large drainage that paralleled our river and follow it high into the Brooks Range to the dot on the map, which we called "the mine." We had originally planned a circular route up the river and along a series of lakes before climbing to the mine, but after our experience with overflow, it seemed safer to go directly over the precipitous peaks. We hoped to find people and be able to mail the letters we had written on bits of notebook paper.

We were going well prepared. We had the tent and down clothing as well as pemmican for more than twenty days, an ax, rifle, and camera equipment. I had even baked a treat of oatmeal cookies. We didn't plan to hunt, but the rifle was insurance. It all weighed a good deal.

Hurriedly, we dressed and set about last minute packing, finishing breakfast as morning light filtered into the cabin. Phil loaded bulky items onto the little sled that Chet was to pull and lashed a gusseted tarp over the load. He lugged the heavy backpacks outside while I wrote a note and tacked it to the bed. It seemed unlikely anyone would be here in our absence, but I outlined our plans—just in case. The darker side that neither of us mentioned was that if we failed to return, perhaps someone would piece together our story. I thought a moment and laid my journals beside the note.

Phil was lowering the frozen quarters from the snow-shrouded racks, complaining under the tumbling deluge when I appeared. We had already eaten two and a half moose, the caribou, and half the bear. I wrapped a cord around my hand and dragged a side of ribs over our high sill log and through the little door. At last we had all the meat safely inside. I double-checked the cabin and he wired the door bolt shut.

Getting all of us saddled up took time. While we adjusted our snow-shoes, Chet danced gaily around and around, fouling her traces. Finally we heaved on the packs and set off for the cache. We planned to ascend Olson Creek to its terminal amphitheater before confronting the peaks.

We didn't get far. It was soon apparent that Net-Chet could not handle the sled alone. It caught on bushes and was too heavy for her. I stopped to adjust a snowshoe while Phil retraced his steps and stooped to untangle the dog. Delighted at this attention, she knocked him sideways, and his heavy pack pulled him backwards into deep snow where he struggled feebly. Sensing his playful mood, Chet pounced happily upon the sprawled body, sled and all, while he beat at her helplessly.

We returned home to repack. When again we started up the trail, sun-light showered the high country, lighting the broad sky where clouds wreathed a gauzy mist along the ridges. Chet now carried heavy packs that Phil had sewn from nylon and webbing. Phil wore his backpack and trailed the ungainly sled. He hated to leave it behind after all the hours he had invested in it. I thought it a bad arrangement, but said nothing as he tied the traces to the back of his pack.

Net-Chet bounded happily ahead, delighted with a romp. She burrowed along the old packed trail, snow to her shoulders. The path was difficult to see, hidden under new snow, but led by some sense of her own, she never wavered.

When we reached Chris's cache we left the packed trail and my real work began. I searched out his old trail, wading slowly through soft snow to my waist. We had not been up this way since autumn, when we had taken a day to explore the drainage. I remembered that the trail ran straight up Olson Creek, sticking always to the best ground and maintaining a uniform grade. It had once been almost a road—four feet wide and dug evenly into the hillside. Now it was overgrown with willow and alder thickets, buried under snowdrifts.

The canyon bottom was brushy, and we fought off snow-laden alders as gradually we ascended into alpine country. Small stands of spruce trees fol-lowed the creek bottom or clung in protected hollows. The little valley was larger than it looked in the clear air, and at times major drainages merged with it, our trail taking one fork or the other.

Our progress was slow as I labored through deep snow with Phil behind me hauling the sled, and it was late afternoon when, tired and hungry, we entered the great, snowy bowl of the amphitheater. There at the last fringe of trees stood the remains of a small structure. It was a trapline cabin of Chris's and had his distinctive hinges and gable work. The roof had caved in long ago.

High above loomed the towering walls of the amphitheater. I felt chilled and sweaty as I gazed at this grand scene of snowy desolation. An evening breeze spilled off the mountains where the feeble sun rested on the rim of the bowl. Even in summer there would be shadows here someplace. How grand and wild it looked across the clear distance. Remembering it in autumn garb with snowbanks splashed among the crags, I squinted into the last rays of the sun, choosing a route for our ascent tomorrow.

"We should camp where there are still trees," I said, indicating the barren slopes ahead. Already the sparkle was fading from the land and a vast silence hovered over us, blue with evening. There is a certain comfort in a world so bounded, I decided. It was awe-inspiring and yet we could see all of it. We turned from the lonely cabin, leaving it to guard memories of another era.

The fringe of scrawny trees ended abruptly a few hundred yards ahead. I studied them, choosing a place to camp. Phil looked very tired. By the time he chopped enough firewood, I had pitched the tent, laid out our sleeping bags, and started supper. Chet circled us, disgruntled at the prospect of spending the night out. I felt strangely at home. Weary and contented, we sat before the hot blaze, encircled by a scattering of twisted, black spruce. Above us, the silver bowl contrasted sharply with the darkening, smoky-blue sky. Thin clouds smeared the evening and soon an occasional big flake floated down as we shared dinner of boiled pemmican with plenty of hot water. We were thirsty after a day of panting in the cold, dry air, though drinking now meant getting up later. It was a necessary price.

Phil's mukluks were becoming rimed with ice as he sat before the fire. When he got stiffly up and went to his pack to dig out dry footgear, I noticed that he was limping.

"What's wrong with your leg?" I asked as he settled again on the log beside me. Reaching for the boiling teapot, I singed the fuzz on my mittens. Carefully I poured steaming water into two enamel cups balanced on a strip of dead bark.

"I twisted my knee awhile back, and it's getting stiff sitting here." He untied one mukluk and pulled it off, hanging it over a twig.

"Phil, I know how much time you put into that sled, but it isn't working out."

He took a sip of the tea and spit out a spruce needle. "What do you suggest?" We had dreamed of hauling home a few goodies, perhaps donated by some kindly person.

"We've been on a trail so far, and on fairly level ground. Tomorrow we go over the mountains." I gazed up at the pass. It was only slightly lower than the brooding peaks. "I think we should tie the excess baggage onto our packs and leave the sled here."

To my surprise, he agreed.

Chet started uneasily from her snow nest as a deep wolf voice came trailing through the twilight. We were in new country now, and she stayed close, sniffing with apprehension. This was probably one of our wolves, I thought, but that will change when we cross the range tomorrow.

Most animals are territorial. It ensures adequate hunting grounds for some and a detailed knowledge of exits for others. We were no different; the familiar contours of our valley had come to mean security.

Net-Chet dropped back into the snow, ears twitching. She had experienced her first estrus at Christmas, and although we had worried that she might stray, she was in no danger of motherhood unless a very sporting rabbit gave it a try. Chet had a healthy respect for wolves.

She flicked her ears half listening to us, searching the silence.

"Well, let's turn in," Phil said, and stretched. "We've got a long day tomorrow."

Early the next morning, I led off through the deep, crusted snow. It wasn't easy, and I was soon panting from the exertion. Where summer walking was a matter of finding a way from place to place, winter was a tedious process of breaking trail. Above us the ridges were swept nearly bare in spots, but snow was piled deep in the bowl. I wallowed slowly out of the ravine and began to switchback up the steep slope onto a ridge.

Phil's knee was quite stiff and he allowed me to break trail, content to be carrying the heavier pack. He could normally handle perhaps thirty pounds more than I, his top limit around one hundred pounds while mine was closer to seventy. He insisted that he was okay, but I stole a few items from his pack anyway.

I was sweating profusely as we mounted the knees of the mountain and stopped to remove our snowshoes. I could see why caribou traveled the high country, avoiding the deep drifts. The ridge was packed hard and smooth as glass. I stomped steps for Phil as slowly we wended our way ever higher, mounting onto a steep ridge. The slick moose-hide soles of his mukluks turned the granular snow to ball bearings, and he had a difficult time keeping his footing.

Away to the east, the sun was wreathed in a beige glow. As we rested a moment, looking down on the headwaters of the newborn Olson Creek, the first gust of wind struck. We shouldered our packs and, shoving mittened hands deep into our wool trouser pockets, angled up the endless ridge. Distances are deceptive above timberline, and we climbed slowly into a shifting dream of cold, blowing snow and thickening mist.

Despite the exertion, the constant wind sucked body heat away, and I stopped to dig out my parka with shaking hands. The ridge was a jumble of jagged slabs turned edgeways. Below me, Phil appeared as a blurred, dark figure, struggling over the slippery, sharp rocks or plunging into hidden, snow-swept holes. He was falling repeatedly, unable to manage the footing with his injured knee.

"Come on, let's get out your parka!" I yelled at him over the rush of the wind. We could no longer see the canyon below. I helped him drag off his pack and slide the fastening toggle with nerveless fingers. Misery welled up within me. The precipice rose endlessly above us with sheer drops into gray nothing on either side.

"Are you okay?" I shouted. He nodded wretchedly. "You just watch your feet and I'll choose a course." The stinging blast tore the words from me and flung them into space. Granular snow streamed by, making the ground dance. It was hard to see my feet. Net-Chet scurried uneasily ahead and snow drifted about the twinkle of her legs. She would stop and tramp a nest into the snow as she waited impatiently for us to catch up.

Soon we were forced to use our hands, clinging to the sharp, bare rocks as we mounted always higher along the knife-edge of the ridge. We should have reached the pass by now, I thought, anxiously peering into the tawny, drifting haze. Looking up I could make out the sky, pallid and distant. I suddenly realized how huge the land up here was and how easy it would be to become disoriented. At last the ridge began to flatten and finally stretched into a broad pass.

"Where are we? Can you reach the map?" Phil yelled above the wind. His beard was matted with snow.

"Oh, let's just get down from here!" I shouted back. I had never seen a more godforsaken spot. Only hard exercise was keeping me from freezing to death.

Chet moaned loudly.

"We have to study the map!" he insisted.

With numb hands we drew it out, sheltering the precious paper with our bodies. For a moment the clouds pulled back, displaying the land beyond. It was unbearably dismal—not a tree in sight. Across from us lay our chosen route, a deep valley between great, frosted crags that marched awesomely into still higher mountains until they were lost in the blowing snow. It was the kind of scenery, vast and grand, that belongs on calendars, and my heart withered at the sight of it. I had known that the mine was above tree line, but was unprepared for this fierce desolation.

Phil tucked the map inside his shirt and then extracted a small cloth bag. He began working the strings free with his teeth. "I figured we could use a little cheering up," he told me. He grubbed out cookie crumbs with his mouth, for his hands were dead cold, and offered them to me in his bare palm.

We scrambled and slid over the broken ground, falling often in our steep descent as we followed another exposed ridge that cut above a series of cliffs. These continued out of sight into the blowing snow. I was afraid we might become trapped, unable to get down. There was no place to stop or even pitch a tent up here. No way to build a fire. Perhaps we had overextended ourselves, I worried. What would I do if Phil's leg gave out? I couldn't carry him. We would both soon die on this high, exposed ledge.

The ridge continued to drop sharply until it dumped us into a narrow, twisting ravine. There we donned snowshoes and floundered slowly down toward the valley through reassuring thickets of little willows. Here at least was a bit of shelter and something to burn should we be forced to camp. The air was now thick with falling snow. Walls of stone closed about us, funneling us down the tortuous gully.

Phil was slower now, obviously pained by his knee. I looked about, wondering what I would do if he were to badly injure himself in one of his frequent tumbles. I was acutely aware of our complete isolation. No one would even find the bones. Let's face it, I thought grimly, no one would even look for them. I glanced at the frowning peaks that overhung us with a feeling akin to loathing.

"Hey!" I yelled, startling Phil and the dog out of their respective suffering. I shook my fist at the icy crags. "I'm glad you're up there and I'm not!" My thin voice puffed into the wind and disappeared unnoticed. I felt smaller than ever.

Phil looked up, face gray in the filtered light.

"I refuse to kill myself for the chance to tell people I'm doing fine. The mail can wait until spring," I declared. I waved at the shifting canyon below and the mountains beyond. "All I want is to get out of this wind. Where will we even camp?"

"We can go downstream if you want to call it off."

"Yes. This is senseless."

"There will be trees down around that bend," he said, pointing south.

We had rounded a corner and could now see the valley floor dimly below. It looked grim.

I stared doubtfully. "Maybe by the time it hits the river, twenty miles downstream."

Chet was moaning loudly at the delay. I was shivering.

"No, there are old cabins on the map. Where there are cabins, there'll be trees."

I shrugged. What did we have to lose? Our planned course lay upstream, but that was just too depressing.

The steep gully emptied us into a valley formed by a large creek, now frozen in winter sleep. This too seemed endless as we trudged slowly downstream in the gray of a snowy evening. The valley was bigger than I thought, perhaps three hundred yards across with mountains rising abruptly from the floor on both sides. Hummocks obscured the route ahead as wearily I broke trail, plodding numbly through dips and over hillocks.

Ahead rose a gentle hill, the jutting toe of a mountain mass where two streams joined. As I made the bend, this slope was suddenly fringed with spruce trees, dark and pointed against the drifting white. We labored forward, drawing gradually near. Already dusk was pressing into the margins of the day, blanketing the light. The canyon swung southward and we found ourselves at last in the merry company of great old trees—larger than any we had seen. A narrow ribbon of forest wound along the frozen, white streambed, cut off abruptly by the mountains. It was like coming home for the cold and weary, this natural haven, this gift of the wilderness. Soon we came upon old cabins spaced along the stream—a little community of days gone by. We felt suddenly revived.

"How did they pack in all this stuff?" I wondered aloud, dropping my burden inside a stoutly built cabin with an intact roof. The floor had been carefully removed by someone, exposing the joists. I lowered my body onto an old straw-filled bed frame where a porcupine had spent a previous winter. Chet curled up on the ice between the joists. It was cold and dark inside, and my sweaty skin contracted uncomfortably over sore muscles.

Phil shook his head. He was busy examining the woodwork, chuckling inanely to himself whenever he discovered something of interest.

I felt annoyed. "Do you want to stay here?" It was getting late and we hadn't stopped walking since breakfast—ten or twelve hours before.

"We can do better I think," he said. "Whoever removed the floor probably built a new cabin nearby. Anyway we can't have a fire in here because the stovepipe is missing."

"At least it's out of the wind," I answered, beginning to shiver. I was irritated at him for his patient interest in antiques.

Net-Chet looked doleful as I buckled her pack saddles back on, my fingers stiff and gray. Back into the twilight we went, pushing our tired bodies along to restore circulation. Soon we lost the trail. The promised "better cabin" began to fade from my vision, and pain descended again. What was wrong with the other one? I thought irritably, upset with Phil for his pickiness.

We struggled on through alternate forest, muskeg, and stands of large, tough willows in gathering dusk. I wanted to go back. I felt like crying in my exhaustion, forcing one aching step after another. My shoulders hurt, my feet were numb with cold.

I looked back at Phil, stumbling and limping along. This is stupid, I thought suddenly. Have we lost all sense in our weariness? We were in the midst of a beautiful grove of ancient trees, a secluded dell encircled by living wood. From high above came the gray rumble of wind, but very little penetrated their vigilance. Why had I forgotten? We needed no dank old cabins.

"This is home," I declared, taking charge with my remaining strength. I let my pack fall against a spreading patriarch and unsaddled Net-Chet.

It was reassuring to build our nest and make a home in this great, wild land. Soon a fire drove back the darkness and golden shadows danced over the snow between the friendly tree trunks enclosing us. I extended my fingers to the warmth as wood released the sunlight gathered in seasons long past. We found ourselves laughing together over boiled pemmican, enjoying the cheerful blaze and the big trees. Here, at the limit of its existence, this sliver of forest had crept—hardy giants sheltering one another, and now us, from the storm.

"Who would destroy so thoughtlessly this hard-won gift of Nature?" I wondered aloud. These trees were safety and protection for the men who had dwelt here. Yet they had cut down living trees to thaw the ground, often chopping into old giants only to abandon them. Many lived still and will perhaps when I am forgotten, bearing the scars of thoughtlessness.

I leaned back against the wide trunk of a white spruce and sipped my scalding tea. Phil forked a rabbit pellet out of his cup, one of the hazards of snowmelt.

"I'm glad we're turning around," I said, passing him the spoon and cooking pot. "You could make it with a broken arm or rib, but if a leg gives out, you've had it. A person who can't walk is helpless. What would we do? I doubt if I could carry you far."

Phil ate in silence, staring into the coals.

"We could have died up there today," I continued. "It wouldn't have taken much—a small accident or finding those cliffs at the wrong place. Any of a dozen things. We can't afford to take such chances with no backup. Lord, I dread going back over that pass. Do you realize that by walking downstream, we have backtracked in a circle? A fork of Olson Creek ought to be right over the mountains to our east."

"I was thinking of that," he answered. "The shortest route home is that way." He pointed across the canyon. We were hidden in the strip of forest, but somewhere off in the night would be another bleak pass dropping back into Olson Creek. "What do you think?"

I was thinking that I'd rather travel ten extra miles than break a new trail. But then there was Phil's knee. "May as well have a look at the new country," I said. "We're about ten miles from home, I'd guess. If we push, we could make it tomorrow."

"No reason to push," he replied. He was stuffing more snow into the charred little teapot. Carefully he balanced it over the fire. "In fact, we should take a noon break when we can. We didn't eat all day. It's not smart to get so overextended."

I agreed, thinking how stupefied we had been this evening, unable to even stop walking and choose a campsite. "Accidents happen when you're least prepared. We really have no reason to rush, as you say. Except on the pass."

"This wind makes me uneasy," Phil said. We both listened. "It feels like a big storm blowing in."

Although the trees protected us from most of it, we could hear the steady throb of black air seething through the darkness above. Enfolding us in strong arms, the spruce trees whispered nameless tunes of comfort, eternal in the wisdom of their ancient kind. I listened contentedly, filled with affection for these, my fellow lifeforms. I was lifted on their nighttime song of wind and living branches. We arrogant, mobile creatures must never forget that it is the gentle, silent plants that nurture us and give us life.

"What about your sled?" I asked suddenly.

"Well, it's not really litter, being only moose hide and birch. The skin will be gone before long. The frame in a few years."

"All your work, my L'ammal!"

"It wasn't wasted," he said slowly. "The next one will be better. My only regret is not sending the mail. And apples."

I woke sometime in the night, feeling rather than hearing, the sound of snow ticking soft and thick onto the tent, blanketing the black and seething canyon. How beautiful life is, I thought, tears coming to my eyes. How miraculous each breath of my body, never to be repeated. I hung there, cradled in the lullaby of that wild spot, rocked in the arms of the night, joyful at my living breath and in love with the sound of my own heart.

We were late breaking camp, reluctant to desert the sheltering forest. The wind seemed stronger than ever, but realizing that it might well last for weeks, we trudged slowly out of our sheltered hollow and into another small drainage. We were pleasantly surprised to find the deep gully sparsely timbered as it climbed steadily before us, twisting into the mountain. When at length the ragged spruce trees gave out, dissolving into the sheer, white sides of a canyon, we traveled up a narrow stream choked with stunted willows, still sheltered from the stinging wind and snow.

Finally, this canyon abutted into the peak. Above us loomed the last bare ridge to the pass. It began abruptly and we packed away our snowshoes for the final ascent. Again we entered a dreamland of mist and snow as we crept up the windswept ridge. It was very steep and we could look down on either side and behind as our little battle carried us upward. How inadequate legs appear with a mountain under them! One step at a time we toiled toward the shifting horizon.

This pass seemed somehow friendlier to me as we lumbered up the final broad curve of skyline—white mountain against white clouds. Perhaps that was because it was my land that I now looked down upon, Olson Creek and far away the familiar loops of our river. Still, we did not tarry. Descending another steep shoulder, we found ourselves in a large tributary of Olson Creek. This too was a gentle canyon, cutting far into the mountains, and a better route than the final amphitheater. When we hit good stands of timber we stopped for tea, and because it was growing late and cold, decided to camp. Within a mile or two we would find our broken trail and be safely home by noon the following day.

We broke camp early the next morning, eager to be home. Phil fell steadily behind as the day progressed and I waited for him. After we rejoined the broken trail, I waddled slowly before him, singing little songs and telling him stories to shorten the trip. Net-Chet scurried ahead, satisfied to be going home. Gamely she helped out, carrying packs that were too heavy for her without complaint. For practical, humane packing, one-third of an animal's weight is a healthy load.

We arrived home stiff and tired in the late afternoon. Our floor, however, was littered with frozen quarters, which would need to be rehung before we could move back into the cabin. The sky was clearing, although the wind still blasted and snow rippled into twinkling dunes on the exposed river. The peaks were pluming rooster-tails of blowing snow, and I shuddered to think what the high passes were like. I was grateful to be home.

Suddenly, a small plane shot into view a few hundred feet above the river—the first one we had seen all year! Almost before we heard it, the Cessna was gone, flashing red and white through the trees. Still excited by this brush with the other world, Phil and I resumed dragging moose quarters from the cabin and piling them outside the doorway.

And then it was back! The plane circled once, banking over the river, and then dropped from the sky in a noisy rush across the snow. With splayed legs extended and skis slamming into the packed dunes, it came to rest before our very door.

We looked at one another in wonder. I scrambled down the hill and was plunging awkwardly through the crusted snow even before the magical bird had drifted to a stop. A door swung open and I grinned stupidly up at a tall, pink-faced man in sunglasses and a clean, blue uniform. He looked so well scrubbed that I didn't know if it were proper to offer my own chapped and grubby paw.

"You're the first person we've seen in most of a year!" I blurted inanely.

The man peered over his sunglasses then pulled a black, leather notepad from within the white fleece of his jacket. "Are you the folks who have a mother in Canada?" he asked.

I stared up at him in confusion. "Why no," I answered weakly. "You must be looking for someone else."

To my great disappointment, he turned back toward the plane and I resisted an impulse to grab him. He was going to hop in and fly away! Instead, two other men climbed from the Cessna: a large one in a pressed, khaki uniform followed by a familiar little Indian dressed in dark, friendly looking clothes and a wool cap.

"Now let's see," said the one in blue, starting over from his notes. "Your mother's name is Helm . . . ?"

"Yes, yes!" I replied, delighted to have something we could agree upon. He would stay a moment! "Do come up to the cabin and get out of this wind."

He seemed to agree to that also, for the group migrated toward the cabin, the big men plodding solemnly through the drifts while Net-Chet and I herded them wildly on. Phil was still limping out to greet us.

"I got a letter here from your mother in Vancouver," he began again as he mounted our familiar hill.

I nodded vigorously this time, for I did indeed have a mother.

Reassured, he went on. "She was worried about you and asked if we might try to locate you. She sent a money order to a . . ." here he paused and consulted the black notebook . . . "Jessie Williams and asked her to buy groceries for you. Mrs. Williams is also keeping your mail. Quite a lot, I understand."

The khaki man didn't look very friendly, so I addressed myself to the smiling blue one. The familiar Indian man kept smiling too, and I grinned back—too overwhelmed to recall where I had seen him before.

We stepped around the frozen carcasses adorning our yard and I flung open the door. Phil was skipping about on his stiff knee, shaking hands with anyone who would shake back, oblivious to his long, icy beard and hair ladened with twigs. His hoary eyebrows looked more formidable than ever and his big eyes gleamed eagerly from a dirty face. Self-consciously, I ran grimy fingers over my own tangled hair and flicked a bit of breakfast from my stained parka.

I darted inside and turned to see Blue crack his skull on the doorframe. Khaki stooped awkwardly and fared better, rising into a face full of frozen meat. Our doorways seemed unusually small; the dark cabin was cold and unlovely with meat and snow scattered over the floor. For the first time, seeing it through the eyes of these laundered men from the sky, our home appeared dingy and mean.

"How's it going, Robert?" Phil boomed, vigorously pumping the Indian's hand. At last I recognized Robert Frank, the man who had hauled us upstream so long ago. He and Phil were soon in a conversation about trapping and weather.

"We just got back from trying to hike over to the mine on the other side of the mountains," I told Blue, offering our only chair. "We wanted to mail some letters. Could you do it for us?" The cabin seemed bursting with loud people.

"I'll be glad to. You're lucky you turned back. There's no one up there," he told me, deep voice jolly after hours of searching. Alaska State Troopers try to keep an eye on people in the bush, but it is a vast country. His name, he said, was Gene Kallus. I tried to remember it.

I carefully extracted the wrinkled scraps of paper from my backpack and handed them to the trooper. "We don't have any envelopes or stamps," I apologized.

"Don't worry about it," he answered. "I'll send Maurice Christie in with your mail and groceries next time he's up this way. I stopped in Venetie on the way up and the entire village came down for news of you."

On the other side of the cabin Robert Frank was saying to Phil, "You got mighty fine trapline cabin here. Maybe you let me trap up here next winter?"

I frowned. I didn't want to open this area up for exploitation. Normally the Indians didn't come up this far, for their boats couldn't make it, but with a cabin here, it might be worth flying in. I felt dizzy with so much happening at once.

"Oh, I think we're planning to stay awhile," Phil answered him.

"I bet you got lotta furs," Robert said. "What kinda furs you got this winter?"

Phil told him that we hadn't trapped and Robert laughed and looked like he didn't believe it. A whole winter out and no furs?

"Well, gotta go," Trooper Kallus said, cautiously ducking through the tiny door. "Glad to see you folks are okay."

Before we knew it, they were gone. Net-Chet chased wildly down the frozen river, as trailing a spume of white crystals, the Cessna again took to the sky. We watched it circle overhead gaining elevation, and then slip southward and dwindle into nothing. All that remained were penciled tracks on our familiar river. Somehow everything had changed, and yet we were as alone as ever. We could still starve or freeze to death. We still had only ourselves to depend upon.

Their visit jolted me back into an awareness of the twentieth century. Looking after the vanished plane, I realized that they would never know how big the country is or what it was like to live as we did. No matter how they studied the land beneath them, they were only an hour or two from hot rolls, coffee, and the morning paper.

It seemed more than coincidental that they should have arrived at this very moment, and I was inclined to laugh at the vagaries of fate. God has a sense of humor, I thought. I turned to catch Phil staring at the strange tracks.

"They were really here?" he asked in a dazed tone.

"Sure," I replied grinning. "Come on, let's unpack. Hey, Phil! Who do you suppose is president?"

Suddenly aware of appearances, I started cleaning. I swept the cabin with a little patch of caribou fur and carefully combed the moose-hide carpet free of shavings. I washed clothes, cut our hair, and trimmed Phil's beard. With a bit of our remaining flour, I even baked cookies, saving them for our expected guest. Phil had never put much stock in tidiness, and my two companions tiptoed nervously about the cabin.

One snowy evening, the ghostly form of a small plane roared suddenly from the clouds. He came in low between the islands and landed upstream, trailing snow. We rushed down to greet the laughing young man that crawled forth. It was Maurice Christie, flying a two-seater red and orange Super Cub. Born and raised in my hometown of Tucson, he had come to Alaska with his wife to live in the bush, but had settled for Fairbanks.

"This must be the right address," Maurice grinned as he emerged. Snowshoes were strapped to the struts. "You folks expecting some mail?" Out of the cramped plane he began dragging boxes of groceries and parcels.

He seemed very much at home in our little cabin, sitting comfortably in the chair while I fed him cookies and Phil looked hungrily on.

"I brought you some books of my own," he told us. "Figured you would probably enjoy some new literature. And there's a stack of back news magazines. I hardly ever get the time to read them."

"We were just starting *Hawaii* for the third time," I burbled, pushing more cookies at him. "Would you like it? By the way, who's president?" I pulled out a list of questions.

"Old Tricky Dick is in for another term, so you may as well stay here. Oh, you probably haven't even heard of Watergate. Well, you ought to enjoy the magazines."

I laughed and clapped my hands with glee and then timidly withdrew. I wasn't used to talking with strangers. My voice seemed too loud and fast. I watched Phil and Maurice conversing happily, and wondered if Phil had the same sense of confusion and awkwardness. I thought so, for he seemed excessively hearty.

Maurice had eyes of light Nordic blue that missed nothing: cop's eyes. He wore a khaki shirt of remarkable cleanliness with soft cream-colored long johns showing at the wrist and throat. Over his uniform was a heavy fleece jacket that he didn't remove. I caught the momentary flash of a shoulder holster. Like the other men, his hair was shorn in a military crew cut. I studied him furtively, wondering if his head got cold.

"I have three little ones now," he was saying, "so I doubt if we'll ever do it, but I do envy you folks the experience."

Net-Chet had been her least-mannered in the excitement. After getting up the courage to sniff Maurice, she had forced herself into his tailored lap and, despite frequent removals, was rubbing a bit of the valley off on his immaculate trousers. We evicted her outside where she wailed her laments—willing to be anything but excluded.

"She's normally very well behaved," I found myself repeating to our skeptical guest.

Too soon the visit was over. Maurice glanced at his gold watch, exposing clean, even fingernails, and said, "I've got to be off before dark. I don't have radio contact until I climb above the peaks." He set his full cup of tea and half-finished cookie down and rose.

We followed him to the plane, still jabbering our excitement. Net-Chet remained locked in the cabin because of her wild desire to chase planes. Her sharp voice trailed after us and I could see her teetering in the window, balanced on a five-gallon can, face plastered to the pane.

With a rush of wind, Maurice was gone. At the last possible moment, the little plane shook itself free of the snow, and raking the treetops, popped into the featureless sky. He circled once and then slid south to vanish in the falling snow. I stood a moment, sending my thoughts after him. Every second carried him days from us as I watched. People are small up there too, I thought. The plane serves them well, but if it fails they are as much in the country as we. I hoped he was prepared.

"Hey!" Phil laughed, swinging me in a circle. "It's Christmas!"

Chet was silent as we ascended the hill, arousing my suspicions. We opened the door to see her glaring. The cookies were gone.

Jessie had used the money order well despite high prices in the village. Dusk found us sorting happily through our bounty by candlelight. There were staples such as oatmeal, flour, powdered milk, and sugar as well as special treats like pilot biscuits, canned butter, and jam.

"No apples," Phil said sadly when the last bundle had been opened.

"They wouldn't keep well in these temperatures," I reminded him. "I think she did a very good job of shopping."

He had to agree. "Do you know we have 8,160 matches?" Phil asked, looking up from his calculations. "At our present rate, that should last another twenty-three years." He was drinking Maurice's cold tea and mopping up the crumbs that Chet had missed.

The cabin was a shambles of containers and paper. Phil patiently folded away every scrap as we transferred supplies to permanent containers. I was reading letters aloud. One large cardboard box was crammed with mail, letters, and packages sent from our families and friends.

Phil's parents had sent a shoe box full of prepared spices. A box from my sister, Annie, was stuffed with chocolate chips, coconut, and nuts. My mother was our most faithful correspondent, with a dozen thick letters telling in hilarious detail of her adventures in Vancouver. She really did live in Canada now, having remained there after a raft trip down the Fraser River.

"Your brother is getting married!" I said, scanning a letter from Phil's folks.

"Just read it," he intoned.

"Okay . . . 'We're going out to their wedding in June. Jeanie, your sister made a beautiful bride . . .' Beautiful bride!" I zipped down the lines. "It doesn't say who she married!"

Phil laughed, slapping his thighs. "Go on! Go on!"

" '. . . we are now in the new apartment and your dad is doing very well after heart surgery. We had a hard time with selling the house. You know your dad. After all the years he put into it, no one could keep the place like he did.

We finally took old Junior to the vet and had her put to sleep. . . . She was so old and crippled up, it seemed the only kind thing to do. Your dad, with all his gruff talk, you can guess who had to take her. . . .'"

"L'ammal, I'm sorry. . . ."

Phil said nothing, indicating that I should finish reading, but his eyes were swimming. I finally put aside the letter and slipped my arms around him, remembering the gray-muzzled, female dog named Junior that had been his childhood friend.

While our past reclaimed us, the Arctic was coming awake. Without our help, and for the most part without our knowledge, every twig and crystal followed its own path in its own time. Each bud, perfect to its kind, awaited the signal; each snowflake, scattered by the restless air, mirrored the advancing days.

The winds of change thundered endlessly down our river, exposing at last the ice below. As March progressed, more pale-blue ice stood naked under the glaring sun. Our raven, Holly, had deserted us, but Net-Chet spent much time playing Wild Dog of the North—chasing dried leaves that were wrenched free and tumbled for her delight. Phil, active as always with new projects, was building a full-length counter under the windows, planing logs while I read aloud to him through the storms of March. From my perch upon the bed I could see snow streaking down the river and hear the constant bluster of the wind. I was glad we were home and not on our way to the mine.

One evening the wind stopped. For three weeks it had blasted, carrying tons of snow southward. We stood in the eerie stillness of dusk and listened. A pink glow suffused the land, blushing the motionless dunes and frozen peaks. Every few seconds a CRACK! ZZZzzinnnnngggg! rocketed over the silent river, zipping swiftly past the cabin and into the distance. Not since the uneasy rumbles of autumn had we heard such ice-talk. I studied the river, half expecting to see a rift appear. But it remained impassive.

With the onset of still days we went outside to play. Under the spring glare, our hill had started to thaw. The snow became like sugar, coarse and granular. Down on the dazzling river we spent three days constructing an igloo for fun. We cut blocks of snow from the hard-packed dunes with a handsaw and built a structure we could almost stand up in. We intended to camp out there some night, but never did.

Net-Chet lay panting in the nearby shade as we worked, her thick pelt beginning to shed. The sun was warm on my bare shoulders, and about us birds flitted to a feeder we had erected in the front yard. It was made of moose antlers—fitting enough, for moose cracklings was the dish served. From the hill came the intermittent racket of squirrels, and on the bank a troupe of chickadees whooped it up as they refilled their crops with sand from a patch of brown earth, compliments of Chet's overgrown nails.

Before the end of March we began to dry our remaining meat. In many ways, summer is the off-season in the Arctic. It is a time when travel is complicated with rivers, swamps, and lakes. Game is thin and meat spoils. It is a time of bugs. We soon had more bones than Net-Chet could handle and so hauled them over to the Snack Bar to share with the wolves. These bones were our only garbage. We had nothing to spare. Any can or piece of paper was carefully saved and reused. Wishing to minimize our effect upon this wild land, we even burned toilet paper.

We kept the camera ready, but with the sun's return, our neighbors had become shy, active mostly during the dwindling twilight that partitioned one day from the next.

One morning Phil burst into the cabin and grabbed the twenty-two. "There's something peculiar up on the hill!" he told me. "A sick wolf, I think. Hold on to Chet."

He had been gathering firewood behind the cabin. I restrained Net-Chet while he hurried back up the hill. I slipped a rope leash onto her collar, finding it with difficulty beneath heavy fur. Following cautiously, I spotted Phil through the trees. He was bending over something, and as I came closer, I realized it was a gray wolf.

"He's dead," Phil told me, looking up from where he squatted over the animal.

I glanced around. No snow covered the carcass. "He must have died recently," I said. The body was curled against the bole of a spruce tree and the ground about was littered with half-digested bones and his final tracks. The animal had survived its last weeks here, eating the barren moose bones that Net-Chet scattered. White droppings contained pulverized bones and nothing more.

I lifted a paw, raising the stiff body from the snow. The sunken eyes stared lifelessly. "He hardly weighs a thing, poor beast," I said. "She," I corrected. I gazed down over our friendly hill, seeing it through the hunger of a wolf. It wouldn't look quite so homey to a starving animal.

"Looks like one of last year's pups," Phil said. "Probably a sister of the one we ate. Doesn't make our little murder seem so awful, does it? . . . Better get Chet away," he said suddenly. She was intrigued by this spectacle, drinking it in with eager nose. "She may have died of starvation alone or been helped along by disease."

I pulled the dog off and started with her back down the hill.

"I'll drag the body over to the Snack Bar," Phil called. "Otherwise Chet'll just sneak back up here."

April. Even the name sounds magical—an end and a beginning. I had been born one Easter Sunday, twenty-three years before, so I thought of April as my month.

The sun made daily headway and darkness departed for another season, stealing off with the full moons, stars, and aurora borealis. Snow crystallized into coarse, wet grains and our paths became muddy. Twigs and leaves sank into the river ice, forming delicate patterns. Furry willow buds, looking like hungry caterpillars, climbed the awakening shoots. I brought in several and soon had a living bouquet sending forth leaves and roots on our counter under the windows. Still our white front yard, which ran to the far horizon, seemed changeless under an expansive dome of baby blue. It takes a long time to thaw the North.

We spent much of each day outside now, happy to be alive and alone in this yawning, wild land. There was an almost perceptible stretching in the ground, an impatience to throw off winter. Riverside boulders and drifted logs began to sun themselves on bright days, icicles growing from them like so many diamonds. We could sense the tide turning as spring warmth flooded up the southern exposure of hills by day only to be beat back with the sinking sun. We were swept up in a land awakening as it swelled against the grip of winter. How gentle it seemed, and yet here was a restless power nothing could withstand. The ice groaned and cracked, blisters piling in uneasy mounds as waves of tension swept the river. Although the ice was no thinner, I could feel the mounting strength of the water beneath. Drip by drip, the sun was winning.

We wore snow goggles now and became sunburned as we snowshoed shirtless in the still, crisp air. One day I looked up and saw that the ridges were no longer white. Up where the wind had ruled all winter, the sun shown without relief and great slabs of brown greeted my eyes.

Travel became steadily more difficult in the saturated snow. I spent much time on photography. The drip and scallop of frozen water formed a moving canvas of intricate ice-art for my lens. I devoted whole days to tracking down bird calls, in particular one that sounded like a sheet of metal being wobbled. I came up with owls, jays, shrikes, squirrels, and a dozen assorted tweeters, but never a wobble bird. At last I found this most elusive bird, only to discover my old friend the hawk owl. The great gray owls sang too now, filling the blue dusk with their deep booming "Hoooooos."

One day a turquoise stain appeared, spreading over the ice. We walked upriver to take a look. It was good to hear the laugh of running water again, and we stood beside the expanding color watching the insatiable snow turn milky blue as the water gushed forward. It would be even with the cabin by nightfall, cutting us off from the islands. A resonant gurgling came from deep within the ice and great belches of air escaped as pressure ridges sagged under the added weight. Three-inch fissures opened into the bowels of black ice.

As we plodded homeward along the familiar shoreline, we could see our little cabin golden in the low sunlight—so small and friendly against the backdrop of mountains. I felt a sudden pang in my chest at the thought of leaving it. Had a year almost passed? So soon? We still hadn't decided where the next year would find us.

By sunset the overflow was merrily babbling by on its way to the Olson Creek junction, eating the snow before it and buckling the old, scarred ice. However, a few cold nights later I was again creeping hesitantly over the new ice. It was beautiful, layers of green, gray, and brown in a mosaic. A dark runoff from our hill had joined the seep and lay stratified beneath me as I stole over the slippery surface, following Net-Chet. With her bare feet and keen ears, she had an excellent sense of the ice and seemed to know where it was weakest even when I had no visual clues.

This new ice was by no means solid. In many places open water rippled the surface. Where I walked an inch of glass covered the saturated snow, which extended a foot or more to a solid floor of old ice. Here and there delicate feathers of frost decorated the slick surface and a collage of leaves or bubbles were fixed stark and clear below.

I had long desired to find the source of overflow, when suddenly ahead of me loomed a black depression, frozen in mid-gush. I tiptoed close, drawn by the spooky, dark hole. Fractured blocks angled away from the collapsed pressure ridge in a still life of violence. I crept as close as I dared, fascinated by the inky danger. There were rocks down there, I noticed. It really was a hole in the solid reality of my world, a place one might fall into and disappear. The fact that the water was scarcely four feet deep didn't lessen my thrill.

It was almost May when winter rallied one last time. One day summer had been upon us; the next, it was twenty below zero. Our open seep froze in nameless blues that reflected the cold, crescent moon. Frost flowers curled again on the windowpanes, and the honeycombed igloo stiffened in its decay.

Snow followed, retouching the landscape, dangerously hiding the painted ice, and freshening the woods in purest white. On this virgin snow, Net-Chet and I set out for the island the next morning to cut firewood. I crept over the blank surface of the river—so changed from the day before—and stopped to look at the cabin through the drifting white. A stampede of big flakes blurred the outline of our hill, but upstream I could detect the dark stain of creeping water. A wet nose thrust into my bare palm and I knelt and put my arms around Chet's soft neck. We stayed that way for some moments, two dots in eternity, before continuing on to the island.

I thought about the haunting news Maurice had brought us with the mail. Another pair of kids had spent this winter in the bush, and Maurice had been sent to search for them. A boy and girl they were, like us, out adventuring in the Arctic. A pilot had dropped them in the wilderness last fall with back-packs, two dogs, a bag of beans and, no doubt, a how-to-live-off-arctic-roots-and-herbs handbook. They were vegetarians.

They had hiked until winter caught them and then built a tiny shelter in what Maurice described as a "god-awful place." In December, the dark month, their beans ran out. They had but one lightweight mummy bag between them, and into this they crawled, head to toe, cradling one another's feet to keep from freezing and pulling their dogs over them.

In the icy dark of December the boy went to bed, saying that if he must die, let it be there. The girl refused to surrender, and continued cutting wood for their fire and dragging it home on frostbitten feet. She laid branches on the roof, spelling S.O.S. in the snow, and no doubt learned to pray, but the Arctic is big and the chance of an unmarked shelter being noticed from the air is very small indeed.

January, the month of cold came, and February, the month when the sun returns. Through March, month of deep snows and strong winds, she kept the little fire going beyond all hope. Then one day a plane spotted them. She ran joyfully out, throwing herself facedown in the snow, arms outstretched in supplication as the plane circled. But the pilot, seeing smoke from the cabin, disregarded the signals and flew away, convinced that all was in order. He had only circled so that his passenger, a tourist, could photograph the scene.

How heartbreaking! How bitterly disappointing it would have been to see that straw of safety snatched away! What frozen tears of anguish she must have cried, lying there in the snow as her life vanished with that plane, leaving a greater desolation. Yet the pilot couldn't forget that strange little shelter and the figure cast upon the snow, and some days later mentioned it to a friend who spoke to a state trooper. A short while later, their arctic winter over, the young couple were tucked into hospital sheets.

They had come foolishly unprepared, poor city kids, and suffered unspeakably for their lack of judgment with misery and starvation. They had wanted to live in Nature and now may never wish to see a mountain again. People can laugh at their naiveté, but it takes courage to commit to one's dreams. Even being prepared is no guarantee. An old-timer had frozen to death that winter when his cabin burned down, and another couple almost died of tularemia (a disease normally caught from uncooked rabbit) that was in the water. Again, a chance plane had made the difference. Even Maurice had almost died once of appendicitis.

My ax bit deeply into a dead snag, the sound echoing back from our hill as chips sprayed into the snow. One must approach this country with humility, I thought. Nevertheless, there is magic in committing to a dream which attracts the most unlikely of allies. I recalled how our winter had been changed by Chris Olson. Serendipity often comes to those who dare. Life, I decided, is never safe no matter how carefully you plan it. Grace is that dynamic balance between wisdom and courage. To live your dream, you must commit to the river.

I finished cutting the snag. Gathering up my load and hitching Net-Chet to hers, we started slowly for home, dragging the logs. The land still drifted, fuzzy and gray in the swirling snow, but the clouds were lifting. The sky was beginning to clear and the snow had almost stopped by the time we reached the cabin. Peaks appeared above the mist in fresh relief, clean against a falling twilight. Soon the overflow bubbled darkly past on its way downstream, cutting us off again from the islands.

Late that night we were awakened as if by a distant memory. Soft and steady, a drenching spring rain beat upon the cabin, bringing with it smells from long ago.

Winter was over.

CHAPTER 10

The snow had melted considerably by morning. Large patches of bare ground splotched the hillside as I slowly picked my way up the familiar trail. Sniffing deeply of the rich smell of dead leaves and cold rain, I penetrated the Cathedral of Trees and stood looking back over the valley. Low, gray clouds obscured the mountaintops and wisps of fog trailed over the ice below, swirling oddly in the sluggish air. From the earth, a mist began to grow. Swelling silently into the dawn, the ragged vapors crept up draws, snagged in dripping trees, and caught in the crevices of hills. The call of a single bird echoed through the space, clear and sweetly monotonous. I watched the wilderness disappear until only a few ghostly spruce trees remained and that lilting solitary trill that seemed to come from everywhere at once.

The next day the flies arrived. Up from the snow they came, thawed by the gentle rains of spring. I opened the door to a sunny morning and was swept up in the happy drone of big, green-backed buzzers warming themselves in front of the cabin. Squatting comfortably by the woodpile, I watched their resurrection. They had lain frozen, unresisting and dead these long months, awaiting the call. Now they were everywhere, mating in the dappled light, redistributing their genes for the new season. They swarmed happily about me trying various couplings until arriving at the correct combination. Their iridescence seemed as much a part of spring as the few stiff butterflies who were also about. Flies were the garbage collectors come to remove the accidents of winter. They would clean the earth and with their millions feed the new birds and fish.

I shook myself, reminded of the souring meat I had come out to fetch. Barefooted, I stepped toward the meat rack and the tedious job of drying the last of our provisions. Net-Chet lay panting beside the path in a mud hole of her own design. Tufts of her faded winter fur were scattered about her. She raised her head in greeting at my approach.

On the island below, six ravens screamed at one another over our scrap pile. A familiar cry from above announced a gull, dazzling white against the blue. Eyeing the bone pile, he slipped upwind into a soft landing a few feet from the ravens.

The river ice had a blue, granular quality, darkly saturated in places where water seeped up through its rotted matrix of long crystals. Tea-colored streams trickled off the land, flooding the ice and eating the surface into a living sculpture of white, blue, and brown. Water and twigs percolated through the layers, forming a vertical crystal lattice that permeated the ice from top to bottom. One could feel it now, four feet of ice giving slightly underfoot, weak and dangerous. Currents undercut it, gnawing up from below or sucked down into cracks from above—molding and carving it.

For months the Arctic had waited as the sun gathered strength. Now all at once, spring swept over us, routing winter and pursuing it northward in a babbling flood. A score of new bird calls erupted overnight as migrants arrived in droves, carrying the future through trackless miles within their small bodies. Soon the twilight of summer night rang with song.

There was a humming in the air, and my ears long accustomed to silence, tingled with the merry voices of water. In countless places, drop by drop, it chuckled with new liberty as the rigid crystals dissolved. Boughs sprang up and leaves unfurled. Moss stretched as the blankets of snow became fluid and trickled down its stems, slithering between root hairs to arouse the plants from slumber. Water gushed off the hills, its impatient roar sounding even from under our floor. At first these rivulets rested with the sinking sun, but before long a constant drone joined the birds in proclaiming an endless day.

One afternoon six caribou trotted over the rotting ice along the far shore. Soft crunching sounds came to us clearly, and spokes of sunlight slanted through their legs, casting long shadows before them as they traveled north along the river. Whenever open water blocked their progress they would drop into it in single file, scarcely slowing their pace. They seemed to sense our presence for they stopped a moment, listening toward us, before continuing their journey. As they rounded the upstream island, we grabbed the camera and raced along the bank.

The beach lay naked in many places, and a broad stream gurgled over the ice near shore. Every rock and bush stirred memories for me. Even our old footprints were as we had left them, souvenirs of fall. Now thawed and free of snow, they were oddly familiar, like dinosaur tracks in sandstone—footprints from another world of long ago.

The caribou trotted into view. They spotted us, and with a clatter of small stones bolted up the embankment and into the trees before we could photograph them. Phil eyed me dolefully and recapped the camera.

"Look there!" I said, pointing to a gray shadow tracing the far shore. A big wolf was traveling the route of the haggard deer, only slower. Where water glinted blue, he changed course, edging along the crack until he could leap it. He looked lean and footsore.

Wolves keep the caribou strong, I recalled the old Eskimo saying. I can dissect an animal down to the last molecule and still be no closer to the Great Mystery. Perhaps the Universe is holographic rather than additive: the smallest bit, a microcosm, the tiniest part containing all the secrets. I looked down at my familiar hands, wishing I could comprehend the majesty in a single cell of my own skin.

"I'm going on up to the bend," I told Phil. He handed me the camera and lenses and turned for home.

I picked my way over boulders and through the soggy, yellow sedges where runoff flowed in a hundred rills into the weathered ice. Already, green shoots were climbing from the mud, forcing through last year's faded garments. Scales were popping from willow buds along the bank, and a bright flurry of leaves pushed against my bare legs. *Behold, I make all things new.*

With staff in hand, I dawdled beside the river, shepherding blocks of ice into the brown current that tumbled between the ice and shore. Many were as clear as glass and furrowed with complex holes. On my elbows and knees I chased them with my camera, trying to capture spring and make it be still. Again I squatted to turn over a rock and watch the ants hurry their lumpy charges underground. They had brought the larvae up to warm.

At the river bend I cut inland, hopping over muskeg where snow still obscured deep potholes. A moose had been there, coming around twice in a loop as they often do, walking, walking. Her big, heart-shaped prints bit into the moss and the saturated snowbanks, heedless of water or bushes. Each animal leaves a stream of history—a dotted line that trails him until death overtakes, sometimes by following those tracks.

I returned to the beach and scrambled up a game trail above the cliffs. Cautiously, I moved onto an outcropping and settled over the river to observe the restless ice. The rapids were open now, and occasional slabs from upstream would twist and ride onto the stationary ice below them. The sun was warm despite a breeze and I planted myself in the fragrant earth, nestling my spine into the overhanging rock. Lulled by sun and river song, I was soon drawn into a miniature world of waxy, cream-colored flowers that sprouted from the bare slate a few inches from my head. Down, down into the satin petals I looked. There, in a marble hall, a tiny cream-colored spider stared back.

My attention was drawn abruptly to the rumble and grate of ice. A ponderous block had broken loose and careened into the shore-fast ice below me, sending spray far up the cliff. Momentarily, the balance was lost and water piled wildly up, driving into the barricade and flooding the downstream ice with new frozen jewels.

Ground squirrels were out. Their sassy voices carried clearly above the grumble of ice and current, shrieking an alert. From my perch, I scanned for the intruder. Then I spotted him on the beach upriver: a grizzly, glinting like a copper penny in the sun!

I hurried for the river and then wallowed slowly through deep slush, sinking clear to the ground with each step. I worked my way into the willows that fringed the exposed bar, knowing that I could not retreat with any speed through the drifts, yet drawn by this rare opportunity to photograph the bear. A few yards away, he was intently turning over stones. He was far larger than the one we had eaten, and for a moment I considered a quiet exit. Grizzlies can kill a bull moose. Taking a good photograph of a wild animal requires more skill than shooting it. Still, the wind was in my favor, wafting power noises off the ice, and I continued to advance.

I froze to steady my telephoto lens against a spindly spruce tree. The bear filled the frame. I clicked off a shot and his head jerked up. I was standing in the open, fringed by stunted trees. The grizzly was perhaps twenty-five yards away, but I didn't think he could see me. Bears are said to have poor vision, although their hearing and sense of smell are remarkable. They are intelligent and, as my mother had drummed into me, dangerously unpredictable.

At my next picture, the grizzly came up on his hind legs—a towering intensity, swaying slightly as he searched the wind for me. Slowly he rolled forward, smooth as a cat despite his size, big head scanning from side to side as he tasted the air and focused his small, furry ears. The sun glinted like polished bronze from his coat as he rose again, blunt nose questing. Scarcely breathing, I readjusted my focus and continued to shoot, the rough bark beneath my fingers adding little reassurance.

On he came, head swiveling. The muscles rippled under his fine coat as he swayed toward me with that peculiar waltzing gait of a bear that allows him to move in almost any direction. I could clearly see his power and grace. Twenty yards, fifteen, ten. My heart was thumping hard enough for him to hear, but I kept taking pictures. I had decided to charge and yell at the last moment, a move that had once saved my life while photographing a wild buffalo. Running from a hunting animal is never wise, and bears have been clocked at thirty miles an hour for short sprints.

Suddenly, the bear caught my scent. A few molecules of me had drifted to him, eddied back on the gusting breeze, and with a speed hard to follow, he pivoted and ran. Splashing through the slough he vanished uphill, leaving tracks the size of dinner plates filling with muddied water. As I squatted over the prints, my heart still racing from my encounter with this remarkable animal, I heard the distant bark of geese. Warmth flooded my heart as I saw the wild *V* written across the sky. They spotted me, wise old honkers peeling from formation, also shunning human presence in fear well earned.

All wildlife runs from man. I felt a sadness that this should be so. Natural predators like wolves travel almost unnoticed with the herds of caribou, each knowing the limitations of the other, but humans can reach out and kill as no other creature. Even animals who have never seen a person flee in panic at our approach.

❧

Two days later the ice went out.

Phil had just stepped from the cabin door when I heard him yell, "Come quick! It's moving!" By the time I joined him in our yard, the ice was again still. "Right there," he said, pointing to a fifty-foot crack that marred the old terrain.

We stood watching as minutes ticked by and nothing seemed to happen, but far upstream the tension was building—a wall of ice piling up at the bend and damming the flood. Then it all started to go! I remember only frames of it, like the pictures I was taking, and of shouting with Phil above the din. Great seams rippled as cakes the size of houses split free. Slowly, the whole vista began to move, gathering momentum. For nearly eight months our yard had remained a dependable and solid highway, carved with trails. Now suddenly it was under way! I saw the old igloo sail past, a sight as disconcerting as if the land were moving.

Ponderous slabs hit our reef and slivered into blocks—hundreds of tons shoved into the air. With massive force they piled skyward until the mounting pressure behind pushed them over the barricade. Great blocks bobbed and tossed, gathering speed like a runaway train. Soon they spun past at a dizzying rate—irresistible, flushed in a mad stampede. The river couldn't handle them and the packed flood shot up banks and mowed down trees. They rammed together, fifteen feet high, in a grinding, jostling roar. How useless was the faint struggle of lower spruces that whipped a moment and then were plowed under.

I glanced down to see the water climbing toward me. The choked river rose eight feet in the first three minutes and we scrambled higher, fleeing the seething current. Although a small outcropping deflected the major assault, our yard was invaded by playful bergs. For the first time I was truly grateful for Phil's patient cabin site selection. The island was no place for us now.

The big rush was over in about half an hour. When the water began to drop, tons of ice remained stranded at our doorstep. The blocks were between four and five feet thick, their bellies heavy with stones where the ice had frozen to the river bottom. Within an hour, the flow had thinned, leaving the islands buried under slabs of ice. Only the forested areas remained inviolate, guarded by dying trees.

Remnants of winter rapidly departed. The enormous blocks of candled ice slivered into long crystals that quickly dissolved into the river. Snow disappeared from the low country and the hills turned green overnight.

With the change of season, the urge to wander came over us. We postponed deciding about our future and chose instead to spend much of the summer exploring higher into the mountains. With only the weight of our backpacks, we might walk as far as the Arctic Continental Divide. It would be a six-week journey of about two hundred miles. That would still give us time to canoe down to the Yukon before freeze-up. We had gained confidence, experience, and skills over the past year. This wilderness had become home, and now that the time to leave was approaching, we were reluctant to set out.

It took only a few days to cache our belongings beyond the reach of bears and load our backpacks. Our diet was mainly dried moose, tallow, and a few staples. We planned to carry the .22 rifle and a collapsible fishing rod to augment our diet. We would take the .30-06 rifle as well, as insurance against starvation. An active person eats about sixty to eighty pounds of dried food each month. In addition, we packed the little tent, sleeping bags, jackets, wool caps, a change of socks and underwear, the cook kit, camera and lenses, and the ax.

We started out up Olson Creek. Walking over the mountains seemed preferable to following the wide loops of river around lakes and through swamps. The day was hot; blue sky hung with fleets of thunderheads—the clouds of summer. Olson Creek still raged with a torrent of amber water encased in a sluice of ice. It was hard to recognize the friendly little stream as it cut under ledges and pounded through thickets with incredible power.

Along the creek bed grew stands of birch, their tender leaves opening before our eyes. As we climbed, the valley stretched below, turning greener by the moment. Tiny, red flowers speckled the blueberry bushes where already summer's work was underway. Black storms licked the ridges ahead, washing them in vivid colors as cloud banks crept northward.

I stopped thrashing through the tough willows and looked about. The roar of mosquitoes could be heard even above the creek. They had arrived the day before—June 9. There had been a few out since early spring, parents of this sudden population. When we woke that morning, there seemed more, and by evening the air was choked with tiny, flying bodies.

Shifting the heavy pack on my shoulders, I studied the bushes, lost in thought. On the nearby hill, slender willows stretched their few buds to the open sky while many lay crushed by winter snows. But here in the stream bottom where the moose had been browsing, a forest of sturdy shrubs was bursting with vigorous life.

Absently I fingered the buds. "Why, it's turnabout!" I said aloud. Just as caribou need wolves, so too do plants depend upon those that eat them. The hedge about me showed years of pruning by moose, who need forty to sixty pounds of buds each day. On the neglected hillside the plants were overgrown and had been broken by the weather. Somehow I had always imagined plants as the silent, martyred base of life. The relationship is far deeper and more beautiful.

In my excitement, I lumbered through those steel willows, looking for Phil. I found him examining a half-eaten moose antler.

"Probably porcupine," he said, pointing out the tooth marks.

I disclosed my new discovery to the back of his head as we picked our way through the high bushes. Between one breath and the next, the gardeners bolted—a cow moose and her yearling calf, still far from grown. They were thin, their long winter coats faded and tacky. Ballet dancers, they melted through the thickets and vanished like smoke. There is grace in even the largest of wild creatures, a poetry of movement that is lost with domestication. Perhaps it is danger that keeps them so.

We reached the amphitheater and plodded across the hummocks of moss that separated us from the rock ribs of the mountain. Here a wide slope of boulders was pitted with deep, wet holes and overgrown in a tangle of bushes. The final obstacle was a ring of "slide alders," guarding the ridge beyond. They are named this because the branches grow downhill so that they won't be broken in avalanches. They are almost impenetrable for someone climbing.

Net-Chet gamboled by me, red packs bobbing, as I paused to enjoy the cool touch of wind on my sweaty face. The center of her own hairy world, she stopped to grin up at me, jaws gaping. Directly ahead, Phil waited in the bushes, sitting by his backpack, rifle, and ax. I swung my backpack onto one knee and dropped it to the ground. Propping our packs together, we drew a tarp over them and crouched beneath it while a brief storm chased over. The three of us huddled there (with a host of mosquitoes) reading aloud while hail pounded into the thicket.

As the storm passed on, we could look down upon the river. The muddy water appeared blue-green, reflecting the sky and trees in late sunlight. We saw ducks dropping like petals from the deep, blue sky onto ponds below. The sweet smell of growth seeped from the ground, and birds called, flutelike in the stillness.

Although it was late, we decided to climb further. There was no level place to camp and we probably would not find one until we reached the valley on the other side of the mountain. The bushes ended abruptly leaving a soggy carpet of moss and rocks trailing into the clouds. Clear pools of melt-water remained among the stones giving a fairyland appearance to the miniature plants. Lichens of white, red, brown, and yellow grew like coral, curling daintily in the green- and rose-colored moss. Dwarf berry bushes pushed up through this sponge, adding to the undersea appearance of a magic world. God is very good at detail.

The ground fell sharply away below as we climbed into the evening. Many had trodden these heights before, and we found traces of porcupine, caribou, moose, ptarmigan, bear, and wolf. Distant mountains came slowly into view, their naked sides protruding from snow. Near midnight we topped a small peak that straddled a ridge only to see the mountain stretching ever up beyond. In the shelter of rocks we rested, eating drymeat and discussing our course. Little birds glided shrilly over cliffs, flinging themselves recklessly into the abyss. Across the amphitheater some areas of the boulder-pocked walls were beginning to blush green.

"Look at the difference in growth," I said, pointing. Each change in terrain was distinctively marked in vegetation. Plants flourished on southern exposures but were absent from the brown northern slopes, and gullies were matted in tiny bushes. From a distance one could see that the steep terrain was scalloped in slippage bands, like soft icing on a cake. In lower elevations we had come upon trees ripped apart at the base by this glacial migration of permafrost flowing downslope.

Phil squatted beside me, his back pressed into a rock overhang to escape the cool wind. Net-Chet levered his arm up with her nose and wedged herself between us. She watched me intently as I gnawed drymeat and passed the fibers to her. A low moan of wind whistled through the crags. I listened to the wind and gazed out over the mountains. A little white flower caught my attention, poking bravely between the gray rocks at my feet. It consisted of a single stem, perhaps an inch long with one wraparound leaf, crowned by a tiny, white star. It grew alone among the stones, a whisper of defiance to the harsh winds.

What could you build that would last millennia? I thought. Where would you put such a legacy? Mountains dissolve and are lifted again; deserts become oceans. Yet the genetic code—that intricate blueprint of life—has been passed in an unbroken chain for more than two billion years. The fragile individual is the link between yesterday and tomorrow.

"I suppose we are just putting off leaving," I said suddenly.

Phil glanced at me and shrugged.

"But then," I continued, "we leave when we do." Not very profound perhaps, but true. The ice goes out when it's ready.

Another squall swept the ridge and we shrank into our outcropping as hail danced on the old rocks—decaying ribs of the mountain. Mist rolled down the peak, disintegrating before it reached us, but advancing. Swirling tendrils spilled into the canyons on either side like water. Stiffly we roused ourselves and climbed through trailing clouds onto the gentle swell of a pass. Here lay a meadow of big yellow flowers adrift in the sky. The pass dwindled into the distance or faded in banks of clinging fog. On this hilltop of the world, the song of nesting birds surrounded us and patches of old snow glinted among scattered pools in growing morning light.

By the time we reached timberline on the far side, a snowy day had dawned and I was very tired. The ground was slippery with new flakes. Wearily we dropped into the valley and trudged south to make our camp in the friendly old trees. I was practically asleep on my feet, having walked for twenty-two hours. Phil entertained the slow miles away with descriptions of foods he had known.

Row upon row of mountains marched before us, becoming steadily more serious. They did not seem to be arranged in any order, but were splattered randomly across our path. Sometimes we would follow a clear brook, fishing grayling from pools and cooking them over tiny fires made of twigs the size of my fingers. At other times we slogged through jumbled muskeg and thickets caused by melting subsurface ice. There were high mountain lakes, hung like jewels between cliffs where streams cascaded white from snowfields, and black peat bogs guarded by mosquitoes so thick we choked on them. We forded rivers, carrying our packs overhead—preferring mountainous terrain to following their overgrown bends.

Occasionally we crossed a pass where snow lay plastered in gullies like mashed potatoes or hung in blue cornices, carved by the wind. We were wary of these bleak crags and the unforgiving sky. Summer never conquered these forbidding heights. From their dismal slopes we could look down over the grand desolation of gray shale, tinted in green and gold, to the sparkle of countless rivulets and ponds snaking through the upland tundra. Sunlight and cloud patterns would chase over the land below, spilling colors from a leaden sky and dusting the peaks with lacy new snow.

The play never repeated itself. We think of seasons as repetitive, but this is because our attention span is short, I decided. Could it be that cycles are only an illusion of our limited perspective? True, the snows come yearly, followed by mosquitoes and then snow again, but every year is different, every hour. The driving force of Nature is creative abundance. It is another name for God. The river flows by me, different water every moment. Is it the same river or not? Always different, forever the same.

I felt small and frightened by the mountains and their casual drapes of ice. Yet even here, wildflowers hugged the rock. It was in such a place that we found the mine. A mile below was a bleak ramble of trailers and sheds, all but lost in a steep, treeless valley. The twisted airstrip angled dangerously into the mountain where a plane's remnants attested to the perils of landing. Erosion is very fast at this raw edge of the world, and tons of stones were embedded in twenty-foot snowdrifts that still covered many of the shabby buildings—rocks peeled from the mountains during winter storms and flung down at the deserted settlement.

Shored up with timbers dragged from friendlier lands, the mine had been worked by a few determined men off and on for half a century. The drift tunneled into a ridge, its walls penetrating the mountain between glacial deposits of old snow. We entered its low vault and were amazed at fragile designs of great beauty. Shimmering by the light of our match were feathers of ice and flowing crystal palaces. I gently brushed some away to reveal the gray, frozen mud for which men suffered. They yearned for gold, yet it was the ice that held me. You couldn't transport ice-butterflies into the sunlight or place one on your dresser. They grew only here, where no one would ever buy them. Unnoticed, they remained a transitory elegance as remarkable as wildflowers: growing, dripping, changing. Exquisite. Ephemeral. Delicate things of unsung power: water, ice, life, the seedling that splits and devours rock, love.

❀

We made camp one night in waist-high willows of a rocky gulch with snow-capped peaks rising about us. Three weeks had passed since we left home. For several days we had traveled above tree line, climbing beside a milky-blue stream through a green and rolling upland. On either side had marched the slate peaks, gleaming silver in sun or black and forbidding in storm. Slate beaches of flakes the size of dimes crunched like crackers underfoot, their silver-blackness offset with pink and yellow flowers. When again the dark heights had blocked our way, we spent a hazardous day traversing a pass and were still uncomfortably exposed high on the other side. Tomorrow we would descend to a large creek and follow it up the final ascent to the Arctic Continental Divide.

"I don't think the fire is hot enough," Phil said, poking a biscuit for the tenth time. "Maybe we'd better just eat it?" I had made a special treat and spread the dough on a flat rock balanced over the fire to bake.

I grinned at him across the smoke.

"They're warm," he told me, extending a tentative finger.

"We could start with the fish," I suggested. "They really will be better if they cook."

A fine drizzle fell from the steel-gray sky and whipped up the canyon on a gusty wind. I sat cross-legged on the rocks holding chapped hands over the fire. The fist-sized blaze was tucked between two stones and into it I fed a continuous selection of dead twigs.

Willows are remarkable plants—heroes of high latitude and elevation. Their roots send out vigorous stems to replace dead tops. In some places a visual gray zone separates winter-killed tops from this year's growth. Even in defeat, willows are victorious. When a raging stream gouges out a plant, tumbling it in a matted wreck, it will lodge upon some rock and soon take root. I have seen bleached driftwood putting out new leaves. Would that I could be as the willow, I thought, humble and tenacious.

I finished eating my boiled fish and dumped the bones, feeling unsatisfied. Turning the dough again, I sat back on the cold stones. Above the crackle of fire came the thunder of water falling into a chasm a few feet below camp—a torrent squeezed from snowfields above. Here limestone cliffs abruptly closed on the canyon, forming a cataract that was jammed with great blocks of ice, striated and blue. Down this twisted slot bounded the young creek, gray as a dove.

"So much for naming it 'Slick Crick,'" I said, nodding toward the canyon that had stopped our descent. "Friendly Crick" and "Graystone" had also been proposed earlier that day. We had a custom of naming landmarks so that we could communicate, for the map was generally devoid of names. "More like the Grand Canyon. What now?"

Phil was studying the map, shielding it with his wool shirt. Like me, he was cold. When it rained, we got wet, and there was not much use in fighting it. His face was dirty and weathered, blistered by the constant sun and wind. His soggy moose-hide boots were coming apart in the continual wet. Even in the rain, clouds of mosquitoes hovered about us. I glanced at my hands. The great outdoors isn't very romantic.

"Well, it looks pretty grim," he admitted at length. In this giant landscape, a wrong choice might entail days of backtracking. He leaned forward to show me the map in its plastic sack, tracing a possible route with a moist finger.

The map had become a maze, with contour lines squeezed together and curled back on themselves in ingenious ways. It was difficult to determine which way was up, and I would have shrugged it off, had not the terrain been similarly arranged. Each little squiggle represented a two-hundred-foot drop in real life. I studied it carefully, glancing from the mountains to the map.

"Looks like we're going to have to cut high here and go around the gorge," I said at last. "I wouldn't trust it, even if we could get through this first part. It looks like a trap to me."

Phil nodded agreement.

"This creek over here should be no problem," I continued, running my finger along the stained and tattered map. "It's that final ascent to the Divide that will make or break us."

We bent low, following the intricacies.

"I think they're done enough, don't you?" Phil asked, poking at a biscuit again. The drizzle had almost stopped and a somber evening was settling in.

I nodded. "Go ahead. Dig in."

He lifted a slab of warm dough from the rock and crouched there, chewing contentedly. I reached down and ran my hand over Net-Chet's damp coat. Her pads were worn, and I examined them carefully.

"You know, I've been thinking. . . ." I began.

"As usual." He licked his fingers and reached for more, offering some to me.

"I know I'm different from you." I took the offered bread.

"I'm sorry. I didn't mean to make fun of you. It's just that you're always so full of deep thoughts. Don't you think about anything else?"

"What else is there?"

We sat together in silence. The ominous roar of the canyon filled my thoughts. I could almost hear the tempo of my mind slow and feel the breeze off the glaciers above. My consciousness pressed into the icy cliffs, exploring the textured surface, knowing them intimately. Physical reality.

"Danger is our animal heritage," I finally said.

"And death?"

I shrugged. "It's the other side of life. One could not exist without the other. Creativity is all we have. Creativity is motion. There are no endings, only beginnings."

"You suppose."

"I suppose. But it doesn't matter anyway. Death is death, and I shall know when I get there. Or I won't. Meanwhile, I may as well live my dreams."

Phil nodded slowly and then shrugged. "You're right. It doesn't matter."

"Phil, the power in life comes from celebrating what comes and not holding on," I said suddenly. He retreated a bit and lowered his head into the biscuits. "Security is a myth. We are not containers to collect things. Instead, think of yourself as a tube—a glass pipe perhaps." I stretched my cold arms out, extending my fingers. "Power lies in our ability to direct the flow in our lives and then to *let go of it*. The minute you grab life, you flip into a vessel and become finite."

Phil did not care for the direction of my thoughts. I sat there feeling sad and alone.

"It doesn't mean anything," he said at last.

"Of course not. It's only the truth. The truth never MEANS anything," I snapped. I was immediately sorry for my impatience. "What I'm struggling with is letting go. To love and live and let things be as they are instead of always trying to control life. It's my fretting, don't you see, that causes my pain. Whatever choice we make will be right. Just different."

I stopped and gazed about. Unseen, the sun was traversing below the peaks; the clouds about us had turned a luminous tangerine, their margins woolly and red. Below us the canyon fell away into darkness; above, the silver glint of slate peaks were striped with snow. I gestured out over the fading land. "How beautiful it all is. Is Life."

I sat there a long time, feeding twigs into the tiny fire and thinking. Our camp was littered with mossy bones. Generations of wolves had run caribou down this very draw. Here the frightened deer had seen the gorge and known their ambush. The ebb and flow of life giving to life.

That night I wandered through dreams searching for Phil. From room to room I traveled throughout the bowels of some cavernous, deserted building, finding only traces of him—a mitten or pocketknife. Then I saw him in a tunnel a few paces away. I hurried to catch up, but he seemed always a turn ahead and he could not hear me. I rounded a corner in time to see him step through a kind of window. Through the glass, I could see him gradually vanish into the falling snow outside.

I awoke sobbing, "Don't leave me! Please don't leave me, Phil!"

He shushed and held me until finally I drifted back to sleep.

Four days later we began the final ascent to the Arctic Continental Divide. Above the great, terminal amphitheater, a hogback of rock wavered and doubled back through the sky, spilling water north to the Arctic Ocean or south to the Yukon River by a hundred nameless canyons. We would not drop down to the North Slope, but instead angle right, entering the headwaters of our river. Because of sudden and dangerous weather at these heights, we decided to push on through the night until we were again low enough to camp, for we were five thousand feet above tree line.

As we left the little willows behind, the going became steadily worse. Raw alluvial fans and naked moraines dumped into our twisted canyon and the steep ground became jumbled with rocks. Above us "Red Horn Pass," as we named it, blocked the colorless sky, dwarfing our feeble progress. Not wanting to be caught on those treacherous slopes, we climbed on into a cloudy evening. No bit of green relieved the tortuous gully as we wound higher over snowfields and steep slopes of red shale. Here and there, trails of mountain sheep transected our way, and I wondered what they ate. A constant, frigid wind spilled from snowfields above as slowly we clambered upward, reaching at last the knife-edge of reality.

Standing on that lip of the world, we looked down on the birth of our river. To the left, the route lay open to the Arctic Ocean. Below us, red and gray, stark peaks pushed edgeways into the sky, their bare bones rising in wall after wall of lifeless rock and snow. Deep-cut ravines zigzagged downward in a precipitous maze of canyons. Far below, banks along the glinting ribbon of our young river were stained green, and toward this haven we descended, sliding downward into the dawn.

We seemed caught in the evolution of a mountain range, ants traversing a stretching monster. The slanting snowfields were littered with rock, often several feet thick, blasted from the peaks during the gales of winter. A torrent of meltwater plunged for the valley, tearing away its bed as it rushed dangerously under the ice—a hollow rumble beneath us. Where the snow was gone, a fluffy layer of flat stones littered the frozen slope. We moved to a constant tinkle and rustle of tumbling shale, which I thought of as the music of sheep hooves. Net-Chet enjoyed the snowfields, often tobogganing down slopes on her belly.

I was dizzy from fatigue and twenty straight hours of hard work when we finally reached a small meadow where our flood joined another. There we set up camp among the brief bouquet of summer: Iceland poppies, tiny pink and black orchids, daisies smaller than snowflakes, miniature dandelions, and hairy, gray-green herbs that smelled of mint.

For a week we dallied along the growing river as it wound west and then south, gaining strength. We entered a broad, U-shaped drainage, a glacial remnant where the stream braided into dozens of clear channels. We splashed along, often in the creek to avoid brush, talking and laughing while showers and rainbows chased up and down the valley. Caught in a rush of nesting birds, clouds of knee-high flowers, and the clear arctic air, we smiled at the grim peaks that hung above us still but no longer threatened our homeward journey.

Often we rested upon a sandbar at noon, fishing the tumbling pools and enjoying the sun. Our clothes were worn and filthy, the cuffs frayed to ribbons by waist-high bushes. Our boots were falling apart, and Phil spent the evenings stitching them. Despite the fish—which seemed of little substance—and an occasional ground squirrel, we were running seriously low on food. It would take weeks to walk home, but we spoke of making it in a few days once we reached tree line and could build a raft using the ax Phil had carried so far and our hank of parachute cord. We were overextended with no one to come to our aid, but unlike the summer before, our world now had a center: home.

When at last spruce trees began to fringe south-facing slopes, the river had pulled its wandering channels into a single purpose. Ahead it appeared to enter between the mountain shoulders. We camped here for two days, gathering dead logs and constructing our raft. Then lashing our backpacks atop cut spruce boughs to keep the load dry, we set out.

At first all went well. For half a day we sailed downstream at a healthy clip, working hard with long poles to keep our craft straight in the swift current and set it around the numerous boulders. Chet cowered on top of the packs, obviously displeased with this turn of events. When the river rallied and shot into a gorge, I began to have second thoughts. By then, it was too late to change our minds, for three-hundred-foot cliffs dropped straight into the water, funneling us through narrows.

The raft was a ponderous affair and our only means of steering it were the poles. As the river snaked between the cliffs, piling up at each abrupt turn, we were frequently rammed against the walls, out of control. Still we managed a wild ride, shooting through in a sort of dynamic disaster and recovering from each near-catastrophe. Down over the frothing rapids we flew, zipping between boulders while the river raged about us and our yelled commands bounced off the overhanging cliffs where peregrines nested.

I saw it coming, but there was nothing I could do. We had just swept over a seething mass of bedrock and the raft swung about, putting me in front. Ahead, a gray wall of jagged shale leaned far out over the water. I caught a glimpse of tangled trees where the current sucked away into blackness beneath it. Frantically, I shoved for the bottom with my pole, but the water was too deep. At the last instant, I rammed the stick into the cliff, hoping to deflect our course, but there was not a chance in hell.

The impact of the raft drove us under the ledge where the brunt of the river thundered relentlessly down upon us. I was smashed against the black rock and forced to my knees beneath the overhang—pounding water to my chest. Phil was thrown from the raft and swept under. I screamed and grabbed for him, catching his hair with my fingers as he vanished. His hand clutched my wrist as the current dragged him under the raft, pulling him toward that black oblivion beneath the mountain.

Sobbing hysterically, I pulled with all my strength against the torrent. Another feeble hand caught my arm, almost unfelt under the weight of water. Madly, I groped downward into the blackness. The raft was disintegrating under the force of the current, twisting into a wad of sticks. Any moment the frail parachute-cord lashing would rupture, dropping us all into the churning abyss.

"Phil! Phil!" I kept screaming, my voice drowned in the roar of water. My free hand found his shirt somehow, and bracing my body into the crush of the wall, I strained with all my might.

His face broke the surface a moment, wild and frightened, and one hand caught hold of the raft. Again I pulled with every bit of my remaining strength, inching him onto the submerged pile of twisted logs.

"We can't stop!" I yelled. The river belted down on us, mercilessly smashing us further under the ledge. A precious two feet of air separated the water from the rock.

Phil was shaking with exhaustion, his eyes bulging. My body had turned to jelly against the tireless flood. "Brace your back against the wall and push!" I shouted above the roar.

My legs felt like water. My head swam as I strained.

"Shove!"

Suddenly something gave. The raft contorted under the forces and then swung out from the wall a moment, collided with the torrent and was rammed back.

"Chet!" I screamed. Phil lunged for her and snatched her aboard just as the raft drove into the rock, nearly crushing her.

Again we pushed, drowned rats, plastered under a ledge. Again the raft surfaced.

"Keep it out! Keep it out!"

We fought off the cliff, throwing everything we had into that one effort, that one chance at life.

"Keep going! Keep going!" We nosed into an eddy and swung around the horrible trap.

And still we could not stop. There was no place to get out of the river. Down through more rapids we were dragged, exhausted almost beyond endurance, clinging like kittens to this bit of safety. My knees were shaking so badly I could scarcely stand. I had lost my pole—my only means of steering. At last we hit an open stretch where the current was brisk but the water was only a few feet deep. Falling overboard, we kicked along the sliding stones, finally towing our sodden outfit to the bank, and tying it securely in a rocky shoal with numb fingers.

As I pulled myself ashore, I started to cry. Shaking and sobbing, I fell into Phil's arms.

"I almost lost you!" I said, over and over, clutching his chilled frame. "What would I have done? I never would have even found the body! How could I have looked in this gorge? What would I have done?!"

The horror of it hit me in waves. What if I had escaped alone into this wilderness! To walk the weeks home without him! Never even knowing! Repeatedly I saw Phil's beloved head slide under the water, saw his terrified, outstretched hand. Like wet and frightened children we stood trembling and crying together on the rocky shore of that uncaring river.

It was evening by the time we had camp set up and our belongings strung like some collection of junk from every bush and tree. Luckily we always carried matches in waterproof containers, for little except the camera had escaped the general soaking. Miraculously, the only thing lost was the map, which Phil always carried inside his shirt to plot our course. Considering the circumstances, it was no small loss. As incredible as it sounds, we were to find it—still in its plastic bag—lodged on a rock in midriver two days later.

We sat beside the fire, drying clothing and wondering if it was worth going to bed in soaked sleeping bags. We also asked ourselves if we dared return to the river or had best tighten our belts for a very long walk home.

The mosquitoes weren't bad by the fire, and here at least was real firewood again. I shifted on my sitting log, turning a pair of socks on my knee. Phil handed me the cooking pot and spoon. I smiled tenderly across at him, acutely aware of how precious each moment is, how totally irreplaceable. I reached through the drifting smoke and stroked his weathered cheek, feeling afresh the fear.

About us, scraggly spruce trees were backlit by the evening sun—yellow light streaking gently through the still air. A few feet away, the emerald river sailed steadily past, strangely quiet and benign. Here and there a grayling popped the surface, disturbing the ragged reflection of far shore, cliffs and peaks beyond. Fireweed was in bloom, I noted, summer maturing.

Looking up, I suddenly saw a moose. Phil's jaw stopped chewing and he turned slowly to follow my gaze.

Like a painting she poised, knee-deep in orange, gliding water. It was a moment before I made out the small creature at her flank. The mama peered anxiously ahead, big ears working, hooked nose probing the future. The calf nuzzled her side, uncertain and questing. He looked small for July, I thought. He must have been born late. The cow dropped her head to sniff him.

In long, easy strides she flowed into the water, the calf pumping doggedly at her side. Together they crossed to an upstream bar, drifting silently before us like shadows. At one point, I thought the cow uttered a low call of encouragement. Chet awoke from some dog dream with a start, and the cow's head shot up. She could not smell us, yet her ears twitched uneasily and the young moose froze at her side.

They stood for perhaps a minute thus before melting into the wilderness, the great dark cow and her calf.

Life giving to life.

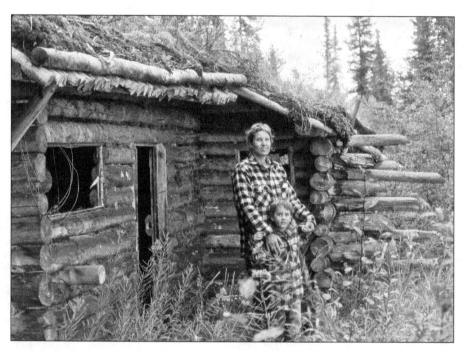

Jeanie shows her first cabin to four-year-old son, Luke, when our family paddles the river in 1990, seeding a new dream.

EPILOGUE

The log raft served us well. When we arrived at our cabin four days later, we had decided to leave the wilderness—at least for a while—but were already planning our return. Perhaps next time, Phil said, we'd fly to the cabin instead of walking.

"We wouldn't have the canoe," I cautioned. "How would we get out?"

"I can build one of canvas and willow," he assured me. "Next time we'll spend two years. And bring more food."

So we loaded *Lady Grayling* with our few belongings and paddled downstream on a flooding river, erasing in two weeks what had taken all the previous summer to accomplish. We found our cached outboard and gasoline unharmed, and when we reached the Yukon River were able to motor slowly up the brown current. In Fort Yukon, Jim and Charlotte Peters, a generous Athabascan family, took us in. Phil went to work at the power plant, earning money for our trip back to Tucson. We were married in the log cabin church with Jim and Charlotte as witnesses.

Phil and I spent only five months "outside" (as Alaskans refer to the lower forty-eight), working with my sister and her new husband on his family's ranch in southern Arizona. The following March, a small ski plane set us down on the river ice in front of our cabin. Net-Chet was pregnant with two puppies—our future dog team. That summer I built a meat house while Phil added another room to the cabin. We grew a marginal garden, corned moose meat, and explored the mountains as far as our feet would take us. We became experts at building rafts to carry us home.

It was a time of great change for Alaska. The pipeline was under construction and outsiders flooded the North as the first road linked the Arctic Ocean with civilization. It was also a time of political turmoil with federal, state, and Native corporations divvying up this last great wilderness. None of this changed the cycle of our seasons much, but we started to see people—helicopter crews working for mining companies engaged in a huge land grab.

To them, wilderness meant "natural resources" to be "developed." They landed at old cabins and hauled off artifacts for their living rooms back home. It was the end of an era.

With the growing comfort of our cabin through the years, I began to feel oddly restless. I didn't want to leave the mountains and yet something drew me, as it has all of my life. I realize now that it is the *process* of living that inspires me—that shining moment of becoming. Although Phil would happily have remained there forever, I needed to move on. When we departed for the last time, we spoke of burning the cabin to protect the country from exploitation, but in the end we wired the door shut and left a note telling our story. We hoped others might learn to cherish this great land as we had.

We returned to Tucson where I would finish my degree in biology and apply for medical school. Our marriage, however, like my mother's, did not survive civilization. Although we were kind to one another—an improvement on history—Phil was soon drawn north without me. For years I believed I had failed when he chose another mate, but I now see it as a divergence in pathways: Phil needed defined answers, while I sought always the Quest. Though he built a home near Fairbanks for his new wife and their three sons, Phil never got back to the bush. He died in 2008 at the age of fifty-nine.

Net-Chet and her two daughters returned to Alaska with Phil, and all three dogs lived into advanced old age. True to form, Chet preferred the comforts of town life to the wilds. The cabin is still standing—though hunters have stripped it and littered the area with their trash. The frozen hill beneath it has gradually flowed toward the river, twisting the joists and log walls in glacial progression; the roof now sags beneath a healthy forest of young trees.

I met my husband, Tom Irons, in 1981 and we have traveled more than three decades together—a journey of discovery that grows sweeter over the miles. Also a seeker, Tom is willing to explore those deeper passages of the soul, as well as wild landscapes, with me. Our son, Luke, learned to toddle in the Brooks Range. He was four, trailing fingers in the bright river, the first summer we canoed past the old cabin. Seeing it there on a sunny afternoon—golden as a hobbit hole against the overgrown bank—our family began to dream of returning to this river and building a cabin of our own. This we did two years later.

The Brooks Range would draw us back repeatedly over the decades where we spent many wild summers and two fourteen-month sojourns as Lucas grew to manhood. I invite you to share our lives through my books

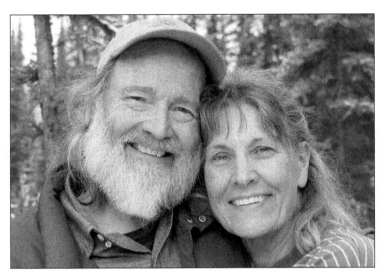

Jeanie Aspen and husband, Tom Irons, Brooks Range, 2013.

Arctic Son: Fulfilling the Dream and *Trusting the River.* We also filmed and produced a documentary, *Arctic Son: Fulfilling the Dream*, which currently shows on PBS stations across the country. You can find links at www.jeanaspen.com as well as updates on our continuing odyssey.

Life beyond a map is not easy, and yet conformity is no protection against pain. To relinquish your dreams for the illusion of safety is to lose your one moment upon the planet. Listen to your heart and sing your song. You are a unique gift for the world. While it is wise to prepare before setting out, the act of stepping from the path opens magical possibilities.

Now in our late sixties, Tom and I dwell in a small Alaskan town and continue to spend a third of each year at our cabin—roaming the Brooks Range with backpacks and canoe. I am grateful that I lived in an age when there were still vast tracks of wilderness, that no one knew my whereabouts for years at a time, and that I didn't wait for permission to embark. I am also deeply indebted to the generosity of people along my way. In retrospect, even the hardships were a blessing. How else can one discover courage?

Life is the great Mystery. All attempts to orchestrate and control it do not change this essential fact. Despite human technology, the world remains our mother. In the *Tao Te Ching* it was written twenty-five hundred years ago that our Earth is sacred. Our molecules are a gift from sun, rains, sweet air, and soil. We are birthed of a living, evolving Universe—beloved children, fifteen billion years in process. We may imagine ourselves separate from the community of Life, adrift on a dead rock, yet we are inextricably woven into this miraculous fabric. We can dance a wild love affair with the Creative, or battle a nightmare of our own construction. The choice is ours. What do we value? How will we bless the next generation?

The human Journey has been redefined during my short span. We have been misled by those who treat the Earth as a commodity. We are taught that our purpose here is to make and consume things. It is time to remember Who we are and to reclaim our personal visions. It is my prayer that we mature in wisdom—choosing restraint over arrogance, and grace over domination. May there always be wild lands to wander.

Wishing you Beauty, Joy and Wonder,
Jeanie Aspen, October 2014

Still wild, Jeanie, 2014.

BOOKS BY JEAN ASPEN

Arctic Son: Fulfilling the Dream
With companion documentary: Arctic Son: Fulfilling the Dream,
Filmed and produced by Jean Aspen and Tom Irons
Trusting the River
A Child of Air (a novel)

BOOKS BY CONSTANCE HELMERICKS
(Jean's mother)

We Live in Alaska, 1944
We Live in the Arctic, 1947
Our Summer with the Eskimos, 1949
Our Alaskan Winter, 1950
Flight of the Arctic Tern, 1952
Down the Wild River North, 1968
Australian Adventure, 1972

Visit us at www.jeanaspen.com